Accidental Ethnography

WRITING LIVES
Ethnographic Narratives
Series Editors: Arthur P. Bochner & Carolyn Ellis
University of South Florida

Writing Lives: Ethnographic Narratives publishes narrative representations of qualitative research projects. The series editors seek manuscripts that blur the boundaries between humanities and social sciences. We encourage novel and evocative forms of expressing concrete lived experience, including autoethnographic, literary, poetic, artistic, visual, performative, critical, multi-voiced, conversational, and co-constructed representations. We are interested in ethnographic narratives that depict local stories; employ literary modes of scene setting, dialogue, character development, and unfolding action; and include the author's critical reflections on the research and writing process, such as research ethics, alternative modes of inquiry and representation, reflexivity, and evocative storytelling. Proposals and manuscripts should be directed to abochner@cas.usf.edu

Volumes in this series:

Erotic Mentoring: Women's Transformations in the University, Janice Hocker Rushing
Intimate Colonialism: Head, Heart, and Body in West African Development Work, Laurie L. Charlés
Last Writes: A Daybook for a Dying Friend, Laurel Richardson
A Trickster in Tweed: The Quest for Quality in a Faculty Life, Thomas F. Frentz
Guyana Diaries: Women's Lives Across Difference, Kimberly D. Nettles
Writing Qualitative Inquiry: Self, Stories and Academic Life, H. L. Goodall, Jr.
Accidental Ethnography: An Inquiry into Family Secrecy, Christopher N. Poulos
Revision: Autoethnographic Reflections on Life and Work, Carolyn Ellis

Accidental Ethnography
An Inquiry into Family Secrecy

Christopher N. Poulos

Walnut Creek, California

LEFT COAST PRESS, INC.
1630 North Main Street, #400
Walnut Creek, CA 94596
http://www.LCoastPress.com

Hardback ISBN 978-1-59874-145-2
Paperback ISBN 978-1-59874-146-9

Library of Congress Cataloging-in-Publication Data:

Poulos, Christopher N.
    Accidental ethnography : an inquiry into family secrecy / Christopher N.
    Poulos.
    p. cm. -- (Writing lives : ethnographic narratives)
    Includes bibliographical references and index.
    ISBN 978-1-59874-145-2 (hardback : alk. paper) -- ISBN 978-1-59874-146-9
    (pbk. : alk. paper)
    1. Ethnology--Authorship. 2. Ethnology--Biographical methods. 3. Problem
families. 4. Secrecy. I. Title.
    GN307.7.P68 2009
    305.8--dc22
    2008043119

08 09 10 11 12 5 4 3 2 1

Printed in the United States of America

∞™ The paper used in this publication meets the minimum requirements of American
National Standard for Information Sciences—Permanence of Paper for Printed Library
Materials, ANSI/NISO Z39.48—1992.

Contents

Dedication

This book is dedicated to my nuclear family: my wife, Susan, and my sons, Eli and Noah. We are beautiful together! And it is a tribute to my family of origin: my grandparents, James and Ethelyn and James and Fair Jewel; my parents, Bill and Nancy; my brother, Mike; and my sisters, Mary and Sarah. Other important characters in my life include members of my extended family: my aunts Nicky and Lana; my uncles Jim and Bud; my cousins Lynn, Norman, Wordie, Jimmy, and Terry; my in-laws Jackie and Ray and Amy and Ann and Katie; and my nieces, Abby, Ieva, Natalia, and Namaste. Thank you all for your part in making me who I am. Some of you are still here with us; some have passed to other worlds; you are each magnificent in your own unique way, and I love you all. Finally, I dedicate this work to the power of story to stretch, to heal, to transform.

Foreword

I thought writing this foreword would be an easy assignment to complete. After all, I've known Chris Poulos since I hired him out of his PhD program to be an assistant professor in a department I then chaired. Too, I knew a thing or two about family secrets, having spent the better part of five years researching and writing about my own. And I've read and admired his previous ethnographic work. So, when Chris invited me to contribute a few words to his book, I agreed.

Like I said, I thought it would be easy. Knock it out in a weekend easy.

It has *not* been easy. And the work has added up to a lot more than a weekend. Why? Describing why that is the case, in fact, is the nature of this particular narrative problem. It is the problem—albeit a happy one—of explaining what hasn't been easy.

For one thing, I have found myself delighted and yet confounded by the rare intelligence and true innovation that ranges throughout this book, which is, I warn you in advance, an intriguing story and totally absorbing read. I knew Chris had great talent, just not *this* particular great talent. What he does so well is to engage the concept of family secrets by interrogating his own family's secrets, at once seemingly as ordinary as yours or mine—from the spoiled innocence of utterances such as "Let's not tell them" or "Let's keep this between us"—through a steady and increasingly telling accumulation of the long-term effects of keeping those sources of lost innocence lost. So, instead those family secrets and conspiracies of silence seek, and find, alternative forms of expression: unspoken and therefore unresolved alcoholism, failed and problematic relationships, explosions of violent anger, nightmarish fears of being found out, and yet—through it all—moments of genuine humane surprise and sudden, almost noetic sensemaking, which sometimes occurs, as he shows us, through the alternative symbolic forms of expression we simply call "dreams."

I couldn't put it down. I couldn't stop identifying with it. Not that my stories are the same stories, of course, but they are close enough. Too narratively close, in fact, for personal, much less scholarly, comfort. Chris's family secrets are not my family secrets, nor will they be yours, but my bet is you will find in them a certain symmetry of secrecy, silence, and its aftermath, which is the until now untold story

7

of what it costs all of us to live this way, with our old secrets, with our uncomfortable silences, and with our troubled if occasionally revelatory dreams.

Yes. Exactly. *That's* what Dr. Christopher Poulos is really talking about. What he titles *Accidental Ethnography* is all about finding ourselves suddenly and irreversibly in unknown situations—"accidents"—that cannot, and should not, be ignored. We find ourselves in the most everyday of family experiences—finding an old photo album, listening to a story told reluctantly by a relative, anxiety about an encounter with someone close to us, a heart-pounding waking in the night, a peaceful, reflective walk in the day or even in the midst of a daydream itself—and at the heart of it is a poignant ethnographic moment, layers of cultural coding inscribed on the very soul of the everyday. If only we take the time, and have the tools to examine it.

Chris teaches us to examine it. He provides the tools.

Here's the other thing. This is an immanently teachable book. The writing exercises that populate the ends of the chapters are entirely useful ways to think about and apply the lessons contained in the text. These lessons are no surprise to me. Chris has always been a gifted teacher who works very hard to show students how to engage ideas through examinations of their own personal experiences and taken-for-granted or at least unquestioned narratives. What makes this book's applications unique are their ability to make students, including those of us who think of ourselves as lifelong learners, think on a higher level of reflective engagement.

Which brings me to my final point. One of the consistent joys of reading Chris Poulos's work is that it so thoroughly integrates his intellectual background in religion, philosophy, and communication studies. Because he draws on these diverse and seemingly disparate sources of understanding, what we have is an inspiring record of a cultivated habit of mind—a way of disciplined thinking through life experiences that makes productive and creative uses of intellectual engagement. Many times reading through these chapters I found myself stopped in my tracks, saying "Hmmmm." Some time later, I would once again return to the narrative after having made a sympathetic mental and emotional journey of my own based on his encouragement to do so and his own musings.

All of which is only to say, "Oh my!"

"Oh my," because what you have in your hands is a truly remarkable story that will engage, I have no doubt, your most creative and intellectual energies. If it were a new novel or work of creative nonfiction, and if this were a perfect world, it would win some important awards for its narrative quality. If it were a textbook on how to do "accidental ethnography," it would become a standard reference work, which, anyway, I think it will. From the other side of this story, let me say only this: I envy you the reading experience you are about to have.

&Your secrets will never be the same.

H. L. Goodall, Jr.

Preface

On a recent morning, I happened to stop by my parents' house for a brief visit. My parents, Bill and Nancy Poulos, are in their mid-seventies and semi-retired. It turned out that only my father was home, but he was apparently in the shower; my mother was out running errands. I decided to wait, to at least visit with my dad for a few minutes. As I strolled into the kitchen, something caught my eye. On the little built-in phone desk by the kitchen door sat what looked like a very old photo album. Perhaps these were photos of our family? My curiosity was aroused.

As I flipped the oversized book open, my hunch was confirmed. What greeted me were very old photographs—ranging in age from some time in the early twentieth century to the mid-1950s—mostly of my dad's Greek side of the family. Some of the people in the photos were easily recognizable to me: my Greek grandfather and his oldest child, my Aunt Nicky; my uncle Jim; my grandmother; my dad as a teenager. The family photos were arranged in no particular order and interspersed with photos of people I had never seen or heard of, most of whom appeared to be Greek like my grandfather. As my dad entered the room, he said:

"Yeah, that was Pop's old photo album. Mary found it when she cleaned out the basement."

"Cool," I replied. "Who are these people?" I point to a photo.

"Ah, those are some of Pop's Greek buddies. I think that guy's name was Nikkos or something," Dad replies with a slight smile flickering across his lips.

"And that would be one of Pop's stores?"

"Yeah, I think that's the one on Broad Street."

"This one of Uncle Jim is funny. He looks tough. Very much the James Dean type." My uncle Jim, who died in his early forties of cancer, is standing, in this photograph, next to a friend. His hair is thick and swept back, a little greased. His short sleeves are rolled up a notch. He has a cigarette in his hand, a pack rolled up into one sleeve.

"Yeah. Jimmy was cool." My dad looks pensive, which is not his usual mood.

"Too bad about him, Dad. I'm sorry you lost him so early."

"I know. He lived a rough life. I think it *all* killed him."

"What do you mean?"

"I mean his *whole* life—everything about it—broken marriage, no real prospects. He was smart, but he just couldn't find a line that suited him. Sure, he died of cancer. He smoked way too much, and he worked in the dry cleaning biz for too long. All those chemicals. But worse, he never seemed to be able to get it together. He just sort of drifted. And he kept drifting back home."

My father is opening up here. I decide to go with the energy of the moment: "Tell me more about Jimmy. What was he like?"

"Well, like I said, he was smart, and funny. But I think he drank too much. All those strange moments, like the time he came home with only part of the car. I think it was the drinking. And, well, that sort of ruined his marriage. But worst of all, it seemed he could never really leave home," Dad says.

"Why?"

"Well, I remember one time he asked me, 'How'd you do it?' I didn't know what he was talking about, so I said, 'Do what?' 'Leave home,' he replied. 'Leave *her*.' He was talking about Mom, of course, who was pretty possessive. So I just told him I had to, I got married, got a job, had a family. He looked at me funny, and said, 'Yeah, I tried that. I just can't seem to escape, to get away, to *leave*.' He just looked at me funny and walked away."

"Wow. That's tough," I respond. "I guess he found a way out eventually, eh?" My dad looks sad, very sad. It seems like he's had enough of this story, so I move on to another photograph: "Who's this?"

"Oh, that's your great-grandfather, George."

It's an old-fashioned photograph of a man with dark eyes, staring intently at the camera. He's wearing a suit, an old-fashioned hat perched jauntily on his head. He does not look happy.

"Seriously? In America? I thought he lived in Greece. Actually, I've never heard anything about him, never even knew his name until just now."

"Well, that's because we don't talk about him."

"Really? Why not?"

"Uh, I guess the story goes that he sort of abandoned his family in Greece."

"Really? What happened?"

"Well, I think he left his wife, my grandmother, when she was sick, and left her in the care of Pop's sister. Apparently, he came to America and never contacted them again."

"Wow. That's harsh."

"Yeah, Pop was furious at him. I think George followed Pop here. I mean, Pop came first and then his dad came. They were in contact at first, but when Pop found out what had happened, he refused to speak to his father again. He never talked *about* him, either. As far as I know, my grandfather moved to California. Then, when he died, Pop got a call, asking what should be done with the body. Pop told them, 'Bury him.' That was it."

"Seriously? I have never heard any of this story until now. I didn't know he came to America, didn't know his name, nothing. How do you know all this?"

"Oh, I sort of pieced it together."

"And why have I never heard any of this until now?"

"Like I said, we don't talk about this kind of thing." We fall into thoughtful silence for a long moment.

"Hey, Dad. I like this. We should get together and talk more often. You know, you could tell me stories about your family."

"Well, if you put me on the spot, I may not be able to think of any."

"That's fine. Maybe we should just talk and see where it goes."

"Sure."

A brief, simple interlude in an ordinary day. But inside an aging book of photographs, we somehow found an opening to a story. What's more, at least one of the stories was a family secret, which seemed to just "slip out" in the spirit of the moment. A story that might otherwise never have been told, and certainly a rare moment for my otherwise taciturn father. I find hope in this moment: Secrets slipping into stories, stories building relationships, family history becoming *present*—all because of the opportunity presented, and seized, in the act of opening an old photo album.

There's a lesson here somewhere.

Indeed, perhaps this is a significant moment in my family's history—a turning point, an opportunity to engage our "narrative inheritance" (Goodall, 2005) in a new way. An accidental discovery—the photo album, hidden all these years in a dusty basement storeroom—led to an accidental revelation of a family secret, long held in silence—or at least relegated to the dusty basement of memory. Later, I asked my father if he had ever told that story about his grandfather to anyone else. "I think your mother knows," he replied.

And I found myself thinking, as I stared at this old book of photographs, "I wonder how many stories are buried here?

How much of what's suggested by these photographs has never been spoken?" I thought immediately of Annette Kuhn's contention, in *Family Secrets: Acts of Memory and Imagination* (1995), that a family photograph is most interesting because of what is *suggested* by it. It's not what's *in* the photograph—though that content may be our first clue—but what's *around* it that is most fascinating. The space outside the frame of the photograph—and the people who inhabit that world and interpret both the photograph and the world it shows up in—have rich, varied, and sometimes startling stories to tell. Funny how something as simple as a photograph can trigger a revelation; funny how much is missing from every photograph, and how much each photograph might suggest.

And I was immediately struck by the contrast between this moment and most of the rest of my life in this family. This is a family that has long locked away "secret" knowledge behind a veil of silence. *We just don't talk about that sort of thing*—about the "skeletons" in the family closet, about abandonment, and alcoholism, and abuse, and suffering. We don't talk about our hurt, our loss, our grief, or the wrongdoings of others, especially of family members.

When we do talk, it is usually either "small talk," or a kind of verbal sparring match that seems to function as a way to skirt around the secrets, to keep people in their proper places in the family pecking order, and to keep the deeper emotional connections that may be available in genuine dialogue at arm's length.

We are separated, rather than united, by both our silence and our talk. We rarely fall into story. My family's "narrative inheritance" is an interrupted, truncated, cleansed narrative, mostly filled with long spaces of silence, the gaps only occasionally filled by words.

I have always wondered why.

Why don't we talk more?

Why *don't* we talk about *that* sort of thing?

What purposes are served by holding our secrets close?

Is the pain of our collective grief just too much to bear?

Are we afraid to "bare our souls" through deeper engagement?

And what might be gained by moving from secrecy to story?

Why do families—which, presumably, could be the most intimate relationships we share in this world—so often have so much difficulty engaging at a deeper level?

Finally, what hope may be found in the possibilities presented when secrets do slip into stories?

Well, this is exactly what this book is about. As an inquiry into family secrecy, I hope that it will be read in the spirit of finding hope in the thin places we may fall into—by accident or by intention—that allow for openings to new possibilities, that allow families to move out of the shadows of secret misgivings into the reassuring light of story.

Hope

As I inquire into the depths and contours and possibilities of the secret worlds of families, I necessarily encounter some of the "darker" moments of the human spirit. But, along the way, I discover—in the eruption of a story, in the soft reminiscent light of accidental talk, in a burst of memory overstepping forgetting—a world of hope.

Of course, as we spin about on this blue planet we call Earth, we all suffer from moments that seem to be driven by whims of fate—moments of loss and pain and grief. Try as we might, even those of us who spend time preparing ourselves spiritually are almost never ready for the shock—the trauma, pain, grief, and suffering that come with significant loss.

Even when we expect it.

Disruption and tragedy, trauma and loss, death and destruction: Events in our world often strike us mute, leave us breathless, speechless, shaken, stunned. We find ourselves shrouded in the mists of confusion, lost in the shadows of dislocation, covered by the veil of sorrow that seems to engulf us at these moments.

At these times, we are acutely aware of the finite nature of this life we lead.

At these moments of interruption, anxiety may seize us. And anxiety can be a formidable force in this world.

In this post-postmodern moment, in these years after 9/11, in this Age of Anxiety, in this world of wars on terror and global warming and nuclear threats and grinding axes and explosive violence and disappearing resources and stiffening ideologies, we may well feel lost, bewildered, anxious, afraid. Despair, as Kierkegaard (1980) tells us, may, at these times, lurk about, just waiting for the opportune time to pounce and take hold. And despair, says that mad philosophical genius, is a sickness—a "sickness unto death."

When trauma strikes a family—especially a family not trained or prepared or talented in the arts of fending off despair—the wound may quickly grow so deep that it cannot heal of its own accord. What happens at this point is crucial. We are at a moment of the most profound choosing. We can lapse into silence, the kind of dead/dread silence that morphs into secrecy—and thus spin a life of pain and sadness and mistrust and defensiveness and continuing, growing, living, darkening despair.

Or we can open ourselves to possibility. Here we find hope: in the soft conversation, in the thin wisp of a dream, in a flash of insight, in the in-breaking of memory, in the warm embrace of a friend, in a moment of laughter, in the light that finds its way in through a crack, in a story well told, in the joy of a child at play, in the music of the spheres, in the accident of discovery, in the drama that proceeds around us and through us and with us—proceeds inexorably, continues whether we want it to or not—here we find hope!

And hope may be our last best weapon against the darkness that threatens us.

I locate the nexus of possibility in this hope.

And then: We are called to *action*.

The action we are called to from this space of hope is, it turns out, *communicative* action. And in communication, as flawed and messy and misguided as it can be, I find a shimmering thread of hope. If, as my friend and colleague Buddy Goodall (2006b) puts it, "communication is—like our lives—best understood as a spirit in transit made manifest through *voice*—in talk, through stories, through what we say and what we choose not to say, as well as the other bodily architecture of sensing, feeling, knowing and being" (p. 37), then I, to achieve my full humanness, must find my voice to penetrate the dark shroud of secrecy.

So, in seeking to penetrate the dark veil of secrecy that can shroud family life, I hope that this project will help us all move toward transformation. To put it simply, I want to show a way to transfigure silence into talk that counts. If we can, somehow, carve out a space for stories that matter, perhaps we can heal our deeper wounds. Perhaps we can live in a new, brighter world of empathic, therapeutic, healing dialogue—a world where we need not fear the pain, the grief, or the icy grip of secrecy. This is the gift I can offer to my family and to the world: I write secrecy into story. It is a gift born of light and shadow, of dreaming and waking, of stories and silences. It is a gift issuing from a dream—the thin but powerful dream that, in shining a little light on the dark contours of secrecy, we may yet be released from anxiety, despair, pain, and grief.

It is a gift of the heart.

It is a gift born of hope.

It is a gift driven by faith in communication.

And communication—that "spirit in transit"—is, if anything, an adventure.

Come, join me on this adventure.

Overview of the Book

At the end of *Writing the New Ethnography*, Goodall (2000) calls on ethnographers to engage "a *dialogic* ethic and a *transformational* vision" aimed at "evolving to a higher state of scholarly consciousness" (p. 198, emphases in the original). I believe that this evolution to a higher level of scholarly consciousness through the practice and implementation of a dialogic and transformative ethic of writing is best served, in this moment of anxiety in our broader culture, by carefully probing the shadows that sometimes hover at the edge of daily life.

Then, in the *Ethnographic I*, Carolyn Ellis (2004) calls us out, and urges us to push the boundaries of what we can do with this kind of writing. There, she defines autoethnography as "research, writing, story, and method that connect the autobiographical and personal to the cultural, social, and political" (p. xix). And she does that by writing an ethnographic *novel* about teaching ethnography, thus truly engaging her transformational vision, and helping all of us evolve.

So, in this book, following these pioneers, I focus on blending writing about potential and actual revelations with musings on the methodology of writing in this way. The stories are drawn from the shadowy, liminal spaces of human life—between dreams and daylight, between memory and action, between secret and story—and then placed within a framework of the communicative dynamics of contemporary everyday life among friends, in the family, and in the broader community.

My aim is to illuminate, develop, and open up to readers and writers of "new ethnography" the often-unexplored thresholds that lie between the conscious and unconscious realms of human life. I explore the anxieties, dreams, secrets, memories, musings, dialogues, silences, stories, visions, shadows, imaginings, relations, and flashes of insight that push their way into everyday consciousness—and, sometimes, into communication.

In Chapter One, Family Secrets, I explore the openings and the eruptions and slips that can lead the researcher into a family's "heart of darkness"—that place in the closet, under the floorboards, down in the basement, behind the photographs—where secrets may reside. Here we are drawn into exploring some of the most difficult, painful, dysfunctional, and powerful material that a family scholar may ever encounter. But on the far side of the "dark night of the soul" is the light of hope. Hope is drawn out of despair as the courage to create a new vision and a new life for the story that may transform the family's trajectory. Renewal is found in the soft conversation, in the story, that moves the secret out of its place of captivity into the communicative repertoire of the family.

In Chapter Two, Accidental Ethnography, I offer a story about weaving the shadows and shreds of memories, intuitions, dreams, fantasies, insights, and reflections into everyday story writing practice as I struggle to engage spirit as fully embodied, courageous consciousness. A methodology of the heart pumps life into the project, as I face questions of spiritual knowing as a primary pathway to health and well-being (Pelias, 2004). In the end, I tilt toward a call for embracing rising spirit as an opening to "accidental ethnography."

In Chapter Three, Dreaming Autoethnography, I move from the world of story to the world of dreams and back again, making a case for the inclusion of dreaming into the methodological repertoire of the autoethnographer. I dream my way into writing and find, along the way, all sorts of signs, clues, and pathways to follow. I offer suggestions for the integration of the dream/story into the larger storied life of the (accidental) (auto)ethnographer. And, following the suggestions of my own dreams, I begin to center the praxis of autoethnography within the context of an unfolding family story of pain and loss, of secrecy and silence, and of the potential for the dream/story to bring light to this project.

In Chapter Four, Out of the Shadows, I explore the common practice in families of keeping secrets close, thus allowing them to develop a life of their own. The problem with this practice is that the secrets often won't stay put, and begin emerging into everyday life as (sometimes unwelcome) interruptions in the flow of healthy living. Indeed, secrets and memories—if they remain untold stories—may, at times, be crippling. As I write the secrets into stories, I discuss the process of storying family secrets as a way

to engage personal and family healing and as a way to develop a
deep, evocative, and healing autoethnographic practice in difficult
contexts.

In Chapter Five, Evoking Archetypal Themes in an Ethnographic
Life, I work toward the possibilities inherent in drawing on the
mythical and spiritual traditions and archetypes available within
our broader cultural and historical context by invoking symbols
and story-lines from our mythological heritage. I see the evocation
and invocation of *mythos* as a way to explore the deep, unconscious,
shared patterns of understanding that illuminate the meanings of
our lives, our relationships, our writing, our stories. At the mythical
center of human life lies the bonds of family, and the threats that
those bonds endure in times of grief; here, I invoke the option of
re-engaging and re-creating a shared *mythos* for the wounded family.
In this way, I offer new avenues of hope for the family mired in
secrecy.

In Chapter Six, The Storied Life and the Courage to Connect,
I explore the meanings and the ramifications of living the
ethnographic mystery in the face of trauma. I suggest the possibility
of rising to engage in a courageous dance with the storied,
autoethnographic life, thus carrying our core life stories into the
center-space of our most significant relationships. Employing an
imaginative personal extension of the pattern of a storied text that has
appeared in popular culture—the novel and film *Big Fish*—as a way
to probe the centrality of story as a connective "glue" for our human
social world, I move toward development of an *ethos* of storied
family life as a primary means of healing and redemption. Accidental
ethnography, coupled with the courage to connect, then, becomes a
primary means of dialogic living that can illuminate relational life in
ways that other methodologies, practices, and actions cannot.

In the end, I focus on the organic process of writing
autoethnography as a way of living. Beginning with the story of
how I came to write autoethnography, I fold together the embodied
writing of life's dreams, memories, shadows, secrets, and stories as
they emerge and offer some practical help for the new ethnographer
hoping to open a new way of life by writing life.

For students and others interested in engaging accidental
ethnography as a *practice*, I must acknowledge off the bat that it is a
little strange (and maybe even paradoxical) trying to teach people
how to stumble into accidental life moments and seize them as

writing opportunities. After all, what I am advocating is a *way of being* constituted in an imaginative openness to the possibilities inherent in the strange eruptions of memory, dream, and secret that may occur in one's life. As such, it is hardly a step-by-step process. Nevertheless, I offer, at the end of each chapter, a section entitled Reflection, in which I attempt to offer some advice on how one might go about engaging the accidental ethnographer within. These sections, which include my personal reflections on the process of writing accidental ethnography, followed by some exercises and queries the reader might engage with, are meant to be suggestive only. I do not argue for a methodology for practicing accidental ethnography; rather, I seek to help you become attuned to the possibilities for story available to you in your life world.

In the end, you may find the beginning of a new story. You will have arrived at a crossroads, an intersection that offers great promise for living a storied life in a new context of illuminated memories, dreams, secrets, and imaginings that reach toward the unveiling of mystery and toward imagined possibilities for meanings engaged in the writing life. I propose engaging narrative conscience and accidental ethnography as a primary pathway toward reaching beyond our current consciousness into Goodall's "higher state of scholarly consciousness" (Goodall, 2000, p. 198).

In short, I offer two primary suggestions: (1) that the writing of lives is a deeply meaningful and significant ethical process arising from a *call of conscience* that cannot be ignored (Hyde, 2001, 2006); and (2) that the storying of our secrets via the practices of accidental ethnography may be our best hope for the ongoing survival of our families, communities, cultures, and world. As we find secrets swirling about us, darkness encroaching, we must find a way to light the path to the future; the light that ethnographers can offer is the light of compelling, engaging, imaginative, heartful story-making.

As you go about the business of living, learning, and relating—as you seek to connect with the other humans in your home, in your workplace, in your classrooms, in your churches, your synagogues, and your civic groups, with your families and your neighbors and your friends and your colleagues—I hope you will find, somewhere in the pages of this book, hope for a storied, meaningful, well-written life. And I hope you will find inspiration for crafting your own autoethnographic story.

Acknowledgments

My maternal grandfather, James N. Leckie, was the beacon light of hope for me as I was growing up. He was a strong, bold, and forthright man. And though he has been gone now for nearly ten years, he still shines brightly in my memory. He taught me much about being a human, about taking action, and about courageously facing my challenges and my demons. Without him, this book would not be possible. And without my grandmother, Ethelyn, who stood by him through the many turns of his life, always steadfast and strong, my grandfather would not have been able to walk this world for so many years with a twinkle in his eye. Besides, she made the best damn green beans I have ever tasted.

My paternal grandfather, a Greek immigrant who changed his name to Jim Poulos and became an American—a *Southern Baptist* American!—was always a bit of a mystery to me. He spoke in a thick accent, and we didn't talk much. Pop was taken from this world early in my life, and so I only have a few memories—and the shards of stories I have been able to piece together. His wife, Fair Jewel Poss Poulos—though *everyone* called her Grandmommy—was, first and foremost, a cook. Everyone I know who ever tasted her fried chicken, or her biscuits, or her macaroni knows that they have tasted a bit of heaven and longs for just one more bite. But, alas, she has gone on to cook for God.

My parents, Nancy and Bill, and my siblings, Mike, Mary, and Sarah gave me the gifts that allowed me to survive—and eventually to thrive—in this world. They are the foundation on which my life stands. I owe them my very existence and I love them more than they will ever know.

Like most little boys growing up in the 1960s, when I was ten years old, I had a best friend. His name was Eddie Hampton, and we had many adventures together. He is still the source of many great memories and stories.

Today, my wife Susan makes all things possible in my life. She carries the light that my grandfather has now left behind. Her spirit infuses our home and our lives as a family in ways that I can only be inadequately grateful for. And my kids, Eli and Noah, who are a source of daily inspiration and very real magic, will, of course, carry the torch long after we are gone. What a gift!

My many teachers come next. Mrs. Eaton, my seventh-grade English teacher, was the first who believed in me as a writer. She taught me the tough lessons about using language, but she also encouraged me, once I knew the rules, to go out on a limb. Many great teachers would follow. My world and my life were challenged and changed by you all, but I owe a special thanks to Bob Gilgulin, Evelyn Boggs, Gary Cummings, Jim Campbell, Nancy Hill, Hazel Barnes, Jim Palmer, Mike Preston, Wallace Clift, Greg Robbins, Will Gravely, Alton Barbour, Al Goldberg, Darrin Hicks, and Carl Larson. I owe the deepest debt of gratitude to my teacher and advisor, Roy Wood, who encouraged me from the beginning as I embarked on this ethnographic journey, and who remains my teacher, mentor, and friend.

And then there are the great writers—oh, the writers! A large part of the intellectual exigency, the inspiration, and the energy that drive the writing of this book arises from close reading of the work of many friends and colleagues who operate in the vibrant, emerging, and experimental realm of autoethnographic and performative writing about human social life. I am inspired by the spirited, heart-pumping, life-filled, and passionate writing that constitutes what Bud Goodall (2000) has called the "new ethnography."[1] I owe much to the many novelists, playwrights, poets, and philosophers in the existential-phenomenological traditions of evocative writing about the human condition. The great writers, philosophers, and poets of the Western tradition have taught me much about the beauties and rhythms and calls of the written word. I also owe a debt of gratitude to the many scholars of family and relational communication, who seek in their work to shed light on the most fascinating aspects of human life. There are too many to name, but each, in his or her own way, has influenced this work.

My story-loving colleagues Jennifer Baker, Sharon Bracci, David Carlone, Kim Cuny, Dan DeGooyer, Jessica Delk McCall, Pat Fairfield-Artman, Joyce Ferguson, Spoma Jovanovic, Pete Kellett, Etsuko Kinefuchi, Killian Manning, Jody Natalle, Donata Nelson, Roy Schwartzman, Carol Steger, and Sarah Wilde have helped and supported me more than they will ever know. And my many friends and colleagues around the country have had deep and lasting influence on my scholarship, my writing, and my life. There are too many to name, and I am afraid I will forget someone, but at the very least I must acknowledge Melissa Aleman, Ron Arnett, Will Ashton,

Ken Chase, Devika Chawla, Chris Davis, Diana Denton, Norman Denzin, Deanna Fassett, Elissa Foster, Amira de la Garza, Pat Gehrke, Michael Hyde, Bob Krizek, Lenore Langsdorf, Lisbeth Lipari, Denise Menchaca, Melanie Mills, Jeff Murray, Carol Rambo, Ron Pelias, Larry Russell, Lisa Tillmann-Healy, Nick Trujillo, and John Warren. You have all influenced my thinking and my writing in ways that I can only begin to imagine.

My students, especially my graduate students, many of whom are now out there seeking to become full members of the academy, have often been my greatest teachers, pushing and challenging me to reach new heights, and, of course, reading and commenting on my work. Here's to you all, but I must thank especially Jennifer Aglio, Scot Aitcheson, Korrie Bauman, Kris Bell, Robin Boylorn, Lori Britt, Debbie Cardamone, Dwight Davis, Cindy Dew, Becky Diverniero, Rich Jones, Susanne Jordan, Erika Lytle, Heather Murdock, Emily Quinn, Jason Quinn, Victoria Richard, Meg Miano Robinson, Amy Smith, Kristin Southworth, Armond Towns, Katie Hicks Williams, and Sherri Williams, all of whom have tried their hand at accidental ethnography. I could not do this work without you. More recently, I have had the great pleasure of working closely with the students of colleagues around the country, especially Tony Adams, Bert Ballard, Andrew Herrmann, Michelle Leavitt, and Jillian Tullis-Owen.

Very special thanks must go to Bud Goodall, who first hired me to do this work, who has believed in me and supported me since the beginning, and whose writing, after all, is what inspired me to become an ethnographer. And to Art Bochner and Carolyn Ellis, who have supported, inspired, and stood with me through this book and other projects, I can only say this: The world is a much better place because of your presence, your writing, and your teaching. Ethnographers around the world are writing great stories these days, and you are the true pioneers. Thank you.

Note

1. Some of the new ethnographers are: Alexander, Ashton, Bochner, Boylorn, Chawla, Chester, Clair, Conquergood, Davis, de la Garza, Denton, Denzin, Drew, Ellis, Fassett, Foster, Frentz, Geist-Martin, Goodall, Hocker Rushing, Holman Jones, Jovanovic, Krizek, Lincoln, Lockford, Pelias, Pineau, Rambo, Richardson, Rushing, Russell, Scott-Hoy, Tilmann-Healy, Trujillo, Warren, Weems, and

others. I also owe much to the participations and observations of Bateson, Garfinkel, Geertz, Giddens, Goffman, McLaren, Philipsen, Turner, and Van Maanen. I have grown intellectually with (difficult but rewarding) help from the philosophical words of Arnett, Bakhtin, Baxter, Baxter and Montgomery, Buber, Camus, Cissna and Anderson, Deetz, Fisher, Gergen, Hyde, Jung, Kierkegaard, Levinas, Marcel, May, Merleau-Ponty, Rawlins, Rogers, Sartre, Schrag, Shotter, Stewart, and Tillich. I have been inspired, since childhood, by great writers from Annie Dillard to C.S. Lewis, from J.R.R.Tolkien to William Faulkner, from John Steinbeck to Walker Percy, from Thomas King to David James Duncan, from Michael Parker to Anne D. LeClaire, and so many, many others whose work you simply *must* read.

Chapter One

Family Secrets

Language brings us together; it pulls us apart; it makes possible our fictions of the past, and our imaginings of the future.
—Annette Kuhn, *Family Secrets: Acts of Memory and Imagination*

You're only as sick as your secrets.

—Anonymous

An (Accidental) Introduction

This project is born out of an uprising—an eruption if you will—an in-breaking of a story that won't stay put, won't die, won't be kept down, won't fall away, won't bow to the forces of darkness, won't be beaten into submission by the demands of secrecy. The book consists of memories, dreams, reflections, secrets, whispers, and imaginings shaped into stories aimed at developing our understanding of human communication and extending the sensibilities and practices of the autoethnographer as she or he sets about the process of "writing lives." It is also a story about family, about those most intimate connections we experience in our human world. And it is an inquiry—specifically, into the commonplace practices of family secrecy. It is a challenge to the shock patterns that people fall into in the face of trauma.

I have set out, in these pages, to shed light on the dark folds, to open the doors to the closets of secrecy, to engage the power of story as a way to penetrate—and perhaps lift ourselves out of—the darkness of despair. Most of all this is a story, a story about the healing power of story itself. It is a story about the primary counterforce working against secrecy, about the practice of spontaneously and vigorously developing a dynamic and centered family storytelling practice—a practice that, when fully engaged, breaks down the barriers of secrecy. Along the way, I offer a narrative exploration of the questions, dilemmas, obstacles, pitfalls, and contours of the journey of autoethnographic/narrative research into the communicative lives of self, friends, and family members.

I embarked on this project because I firmly believe that we need, in these troubled times—need perhaps more than anything—stories of mythic proportions, stories charged with the power of love, stories that evoke change in longstanding destructive patterns, stories that urge us to shift the energy of pain and loss and secrecy toward the light of joy and integration and communication.

I also believe that one powerful way to get to that release from anxiety and despair—and thus turn toward wholeness and healing— can be found in the active practice of autoethnographic writing. So this book is an autoethnographic meditation on the craft of the family autoethnographer, on the spiritual and ethical and methodological and practical concerns and practices of the autoethnographer who writes about family lives. The book is thus framed within a series of stories about the complexities, anxieties, and eruptions that occur in everyday family communicative life and about how these matters affect the writing of autoethnography.

I ask as a central question: By what alchemy might a reflexive, conscientious storyteller evoke, emit, and open the secret lives of families into stories of powerful, transformative healing?

And, from that question, many more pour forth . . .

How might we represent the memories, dreams, reflections, secrets, silences, stories, dialogues, and deceptions of those we come to know?

What are the consequences of particular choices of representation?

What is the role of memory, and the status of "truth," in the writing of narrative accounts of these matters?

How might we who aspire to write lives become open to stumbling, sometimes accidentally, into a story?

How might the autoethnographer mindfully follow the urgings of the heart, the flood of dreams, the breath of a secret, the wisp of a memory, to find that great treasure, the evocative tale of human life?

How might we expand the practice of autoethnography to include the incremental, the accidental, the spontaneous, the random spark?

How do mythic consciousness, archetypal and personal shadow energies, dreamwork and synchronicities, memory and narrative conscience inform the choices and the work of the autoethnographer?

What are the ethical contours of the relationships between the writer, the reader, and the characters in an autoethnography?

These and other vital questions will be raised, opened, played with, wrestled with, cared for, responded to, and storied.

So, in the end, the book is a study of the deeper contours of memories, dreams, reflections, silences, secrets, and stories as they play out in family relationships. At the same time, through positioning engaged/accidental autoethnographic practice at the center of a conscience-driven research life, I offer direct reflection on the process of writing autoethnography, with a particular focus on the troubled, sometimes agonizing, often contradictory needs to evoke and stimulate actual life, while at the same time being careful not to harm others.

The study is deeply grounded in the idea of dealing with anxiety and secrecy via the invocation and practice of *narrative conscience*—a way of approaching the writing of (auto)ethnography that emerges from the synergy of the ethical and the mythical impulses that reside deep within each of us. It deals directly with the "shadow" worlds of secrecy, deception, dissembling, silence, and silencing that emerge so often when traumatic events interrupt our lives. The study rests on—and demonstrates—the claim that writing autoethnography is a fundamentally *ethical*—if sometimes *accidental*—performance that can, in the end, lead to healing, wholeness, even redemption. Invocation of the ethical impulse as a guide for evocative writing is woven into the stories.

So, I focus explicitly on developing the autoethnographic project as a way to heal wounds and transcend silence. By extending our imaginative expansion of our storied repertoires through the incorporation of memories, dreams, and secrets as a vital space within the nexus of our story-making practices, we can surely begin to story some sense into our lives, which may otherwise be agonized by the dark, lurking shadows of anxiety, silence, secrecy, hopelessness, and despair.

The inspiration for this book comes from the thin shards of memory, from the foggy wisps of dreams, from the shaky silences, and from the dark underbelly of secrecy in my own life and the lives of people I've come to know along this journey. In my quest to develop and, at the same time, unravel, the mysteries that abound in this quest, I have stumbled on an idea that I think shows promise: accidental ethnography. More on that in the next chapter. But I begin at the beginning: with the idea of attending to the signs, which, if read properly, may open up the possibility of exploring what to do with family secrets.

Signs and Mysteries

"I pay attention to signs," Opal says, "Don't you?"

"No," Rose says. She knows better now than to trust in such foolishness.

My Aunt May says signs are the Lord's way of letting you know He's always making plans for you way down the road, plans you can't even imagine. I'm not so sure about the Lord part of it, but I do believe there are signs giving us information. There's meaning to things. We've just got to have patience to find them.
                                    —Anne D. LeClaire, *Entering Normal*

These are mysteries, questions without answers that speak to imagined possibilities for meanings.
                                    —H. L. Goodall, Jr., *Divine Signs*

There are moments in every life when it is unclear what will come next, but during which, somehow, we know we are caught up in something significant. There is a feeling that something powerful is at work, though often what exactly is going on—or what will come of it, if anything, is a mystery.

I have found that these moments just come on me at times, catching me unaware. They can come as little wisps of memory, as an experience of falling back in time, triggered by some seemingly random event in my current world—a sight, a smell, a texture, a sound. Or I might just rise from my chair spontaneously, pushed upward by an intuitive sense that something is not quite right. Or perhaps I sense a dream hovering at the edge of my consciousness, the kind of dream that recedes before me as I try to catch its meaning. Sometimes a fantasy surges up and grabs me, and plays itself out, tugging at my heart. Or, as I move through my day, I might find myself caught up in a moment of reflection, where something nudges my consciousness, or my conscience, pulling my attention to a new place. Or, as happens once in a while, I feel a surge of joy—or of sadness—rising up through my heart.

Sometimes events in our lives seem meaningfully connected, linked not just by chance, but by some larger organizing principle.

At others, it all seems so random.

Have you ever been in a conversation (or elsewhere) and found yourself in a moment of breakthrough, an "Aha!" or epiphany?

Have you ever been minding your own business, going about your day, and found the tattered shreds of a dream, or a memory, or a secret, seeping into your consciousness?

Have you ever woken up in a cold sweat, your heart shattered by a dark dream?

Have you ever felt the thin wisp of a partial memory hovering at the edge of consciousness, just out of reach?

Or, have you ever had a full memory come flooding back, unannounced, suddenly overwhelming you?

Have you ever felt something being triggered, something inside you that is, perhaps, unpleasant, and only marginally linked to the current situation?

Have you ever been in a conversation, and found yourself or someone else, saying or doing something that seems inappropriate, or out of turn?

Have you ever had or witnessed an outburst?

Have you ever felt a shadow creeping up into your mind, over your heart, through your consciousness?

Have you ever wondered at the darkness within your—or someone else's—soul?

Have you ever pondered how thin the line might be between sanity and madness, or between dream and reality, or between memory and truth, or between secret and story?

These and other questions hover at the edge of my mind sometimes. And I look around the world for signs, for something to make sense of these experiences. I seek clues. As a detective of everyday life, an ethnographer, I observe and participate in this world, and I seek to bring a storied sense to my experience (Goodall, 1996).

My neighbor, a woman in her late seventies, has an adult son, middle-aged, probably around fifty or so, who is a diagnosed schizophrenic. He sometimes comes to stay with her, as he finds it hard to maintain a household or to live among other humans. He is prone to outbursts of shouting, though this is not usually directed at another person. Rather, he shouts aloud to unseen people, in words and sounds most of us cannot understand.

One day recently, as I was walking down my driveway toward my garage, something in my neighbor's backyard caught my eye. I couldn't make out what it was, but for some reason I found myself drawn to it. As I got closer, it still took a moment to register what

I was seeing. At first it made no sense. But here it was, lying in the grass: a simple painting of a black background, in the center of which was a large red heart. It looked like the artwork of a child of about age six, with the simple, familiar, valentine-shaped heart we all recognize. But what was striking about this scene was that someone had driven an axe—yes, a full-sized, firewood-chopping axe—through the center of the heart.

As I gazed on it, I found myself wondering how to interpret this particular sign. Was this something that should cause me fear? Or bring me fascination? Was it an obvious sign of madness? A moment of breakthrough? The act of a lunatic? A symbolic gesture? A warning? Performance art? An outburst? The revelation of a secret about this man? About his family? About our world? Was this an opening up of the "heart of darkness"—the secret life of a tortured soul? What, if anything, could a gesture such as this one tell us about the self, about family, about community, about communication?

And this "sign" got me to thinking about the connections between consciousness and communication, between dream and reality, between art and madness, between thinking and connecting with others, between loneliness and community, between secrets and stories—all while I was pondering this idea that sometimes, we are "gripped" by a dream, or by an image, or by a story, or by a secret, or by a burst of insight or creativity or even genius. And I got to thinking about how, sometimes, a moment of darkness or pain or trauma or difficulty from our past may "break in" to our current consciousness and seem to derail us as we go about our business. And this artifact, this savaged painting, also got me to thinking about how thin the lines are between sanity and insanity, between hope and despair, between communication and terrible miscommunication, between love and hate, and, above all, between that part of ourselves that we can call consciousness and that part that is within us that is unconscious but that, from time to time, seems to want—or need—to bubble up into our conscious lives.

If I follow these signs, I begin to learn. Mostly, I learn that I am called to write of or toward or into their meaning, seeking some sense, through the writing of a pathway, of where I should be going and of how I can connect my quest with yours.

You see, I really do hope to meet you some day, to engage you in dialogue. For it is in and through our dialogical movements, through our writing and our reading, our speaking and our listening, that the meanings of our experiences begin to clarify, to resonate, to shimmer with meaning. When we *connect*—heartfully, *courageously*—all sorts of remarkable things may happen. So one of the things I do is to write these moments into life. Then, I bring them before you, and I say, "What do you make of this?"

Sometimes, I sit down to write, knowing only that I must write something, but not quite clear about what may come of the writing. My fingers begin to move, and something turns up.

Occasionally, something meaningful turns up.

I have come to understand and cultivate these moments as moments of spirit rising, of heart. Whether they are shrouded in darkness, or in the dim fog of a memory just returning—or, alternately, dancing in full light before me, shimmering with the magic of creation—these are moments where my body-heart-spirit-mind move into a special fusion. And, though I might feel lost in a fog, or at the least a bit fuzzy, about the potential or the purpose or the meaning or the possibilities that the moment may entail, I have begun to trust that something—perhaps something important or powerful—will come, if only I have the patience, the willingness, the passion, and the creativity to chase the mystery.

At other moments, like when I happened on my grandfather's photo album and asked my father about it, I find myself falling into conversations wherein something important is revealed, whether by intention or by accident. It is in these moments that I locate hope for breaking the bondage of secrecy that can haunt a family, by embracing the ties of story that can bind us together in more liberating, caring, open forms of relating. I have come to take all such moments seriously, as moments of possibility and creation. I have learned to search for and examine signs and other clues that may come to me as I stumble along. I have learned to follow the spirit as it rises.

Making Sense of Family Secrets

Of course, on the other side of this urge to embrace "spirit rising" is the complex mental and emotional calculation that many of us learn at a very early age regarding the question of whether to talk about something that is potentially embarrassing, or painful, or that might otherwise result in sanctions from those in our circle of significant others. When a young child wets the bed, for instance, he or she might well attempt to keep the news a secret. And, from that early formulation of the secret well kept may flow a pattern of silence and deception that can last a lifetime. Sometimes, circumstances in our lives—tragic losses, painful conflicts, shivering anxieties, sharp grief, numbing depression— can seem to surround us, hem us in, strike us mute. Beleaguered, we fall into silence. And silence falls into secret longing, secret pain, secret darkness, secret fear—shrouds of secrecy that take us to a place from which we do not know how to extricate ourselves.

The literature on family secrets is, perhaps understandably, somewhat thin. After all, these are things we just don't talk about! We have stumbled into silence and we don't know how to begin to bring words to this strange, secret world. A quick glance through several leading family communication textbooks and handbooks designed for the college classroom reveals that the concept of "family secret" is often mentioned only briefly or in passing, usually in the context of discussing boundary or role negotiation, privacy, or family rules (Anderson & Sabatelli, 2003; Braithwaite & Baxter, 2006; Floyd & Morman, 2006; Turner & West, 2006a, 2006b; Vangelisti, 2004; Yerby, Buerkel-Rothfuss, & Bochner, 1998).

Annette Kuhn (1995) begins her study of family secrets by closely examining a simple artifact: a photograph of herself as a young child. She seeks to shed light on what is in the photograph, and on what is not in the photograph, what is suggested by the presences and absences that inhabit the photograph, the world and time in which it was constructed, and the world of memory looking back, making sense of a simple family artifact. In her exploration, she seeks to come to grips with the "precarious" and complex connections that constitute a family. Along the way, she presses the issue that I will take on in this book:

> A family without secrets is rare indeed. People who live in families make every effort to keep certain things concealed from the rest of the world, and at times from each other as well. Things will be lied about, or simply never mentioned. Sometimes family secrets are so deeply buried that they elude the conscious awareness even of those most deeply involved. From the involuntary amnesias of repression to the willful forgetting of matters it might be less than convenient to recall, secrets inhabit the borderlands of memory. (pp. 1–2)

It is these "borderlands of memory" that make up the deep layers of archaeology that Kuhn explores in her journey. Along the way, she makes much of the "raw materials" of memory that go into the making of selves through the construction of stories about our lives, about our pasts, about our families. As she writes her story into being, Kuhn cogently offers rich pathways for piecing together fragments and traces of memory, sparked by the presence of objects such as photographs—all of which are aimed, in the end, at drawing a coherent narrative line from the raw materials of a life re-membered.

In the self-help literature growing out of twelve-step programs such as Alcoholics Anonymous, Alanon, Narcotics Anonymous, and Adult Children of Alcoholics, as well as well-known addiction treatment centers such as the Betty Ford Center, Hazelden, and Fellowship Hall, there is a prominent focus on honesty as a cornerstone of recovery and a concomitant call toward openness that will require the revelation (and deconstruction) of family secrets. The idea here is that revelation of the secret life of the addict—or the addict's family, who is also, in some sense, afflicted—will bring to light the dark contours of deception and dysfunction and will engage and enforce the practice of "new" forms of honest, forthright, "functional" communication. Prominently, John Bradshaw (1995) delves into the dark world of intergenerational secrecy, promoting the technology of the genogram (or family map) to come to a richer understanding of the complex, dysfunctional dynamics of afflicted families. In the end, Bradshaw and others (Black, 1985, 2002; Satir, 1967, 1972) call for confrontation, acceptance, understanding, and forgiveness as pathways to healing and laying the patterns of secrecy to rest.

Recently, literature in the field of relational communication has attempted to grapple with the so-called dark side of our communicative worlds, largely by taking a social scientific approach to coming to understand behaviors such as stalking, lying/deception, and abuse (Cupach & Spitzberg, 1994, 2004; Spitzberg & Cupach, 1998). Clearly, an ideology of openness pervades both scholarly writing on communication and our U.S. culture, though recent scholarship—particularly in relational dialectics—has questioned the uncritical acceptance of openness as "good" and secrecy as "bad" (Afifi, Caughlin, & Afifi, 2007; Baxter & Montgomery, 1996). There may well be occasions—perhaps even daily, in many peoples' lives—where it is best to withhold, edit, or avoid revealing so-called secret knowledge, thoughts, or fantasies. But in acute cases—as in denial of dysfunction, addiction, stigma, grief, trauma, or abuse— where communication may be the only hope for recovery, the call for making sense of experience through story has never been more appropriate, or necessary.

This is perhaps a major reason why the new ethnographers, in their turn, have taken up the exploration of the interior depths of the social world autoethnographically. Ellis & Bochner's (1991) pioneering work in "emotional sociology" opened the door for the many layers of memory, story, and emotional evocation that the autoethnographic voice allows, in ways that other modes of research do not. Work by Ellis and Bochner (1991) on the experience of abortion, and later work by Ellis on death and loss (1995) paved the way for emerging autoethnographers to explore their own inner "secret lives" as eating-disordered adults (Tillmann-Healy, 1996), survivors of sexual abuse (Fox, 1996), disoriented children of "mentally retarded" parents (Ronai, 1996), and members of gangs (Towns, 2007), to name but a few. "Confessional tales" and "impressionist tales" (Van Maanen, 1988) have become an important nexus of the literature on the connections between the lived interior experiences of authors and the social worlds they inhabit (Ellis, 2004).

In the growing ethnographic literature on families, two recent books make important contributions to our understanding of the phenomenon of family secrecy. Spurred on by the death of his paternal grandmother, whom he calls Naunny, Nick Trujillo takes an ethnographic odyssey through memory, reflection, history, secret, and story in a quest to locate what he calls "the many meanings of my grandmother" (Trujillo, 2004). Not surprisingly, as he delves deeper into the complex life of his grandmother, Trujillo discovers conditions he had not, at the outset, anticipated. *In Search of Naunny's Grave* offers a rich, textured, and nuanced account of the life of this remarkable woman who was, in many ways, the coordinator and the keeper of the family's central narrative. She was the family historian, the keeper of stories, and a powerful shaper of the family culture. As he interviewed members of his family, and as the talk turned to matters of sexuality—matters, of course, that are central to family life, though not often talked about in most cultures, especially in reference to a *grandmother*—Trujillo began to discover some of the secret life of this woman he had always idealized, including the strong suggestion that she suffered from a lifelong struggle with anorexia.

In the end, Trujillo, through the simple act of asking for stories, through probing and searching, through examination of artifacts, through a tour through the signs left behind by his Naunny, finds the "many meanings" of his grandmother. He tells the rich and evocative tale of a woman, a family, a community, a world—all through the work of writing a life into a storied tribute. This world is surely a better place because of such work.

Similarly, H. L. Goodall, Jr., whose father died a mysterious death in the 1970s, has written *A Need to Know: The Clandestine History of a CIA Family*, in which he painstakingly, imaginatively, and engagingly pieces together the strange cryptic puzzle of his father's life and family legacy (Goodall, 2006a). For Goodall, the investigative process is confounded by large gaps in the archival records he searches; the CIA, of course, is notorious for its sleight of hand when it comes to its field agents. Goodall's father was hired, after World War II, as a "clerk typist" and was later appointed as a "Veterans Affairs" officer for the State Department. But as Goodall traces the thread of his father's thin historical record, it becomes increasingly clear that Harold Lloyd Goodall, Senior was, in fact, a spy. That secret life—of political intrigue masked as diplomacy, of assassination masquerading as "field assignment"—carried with it its own heavy tolls. Unable to reveal his secret work life to even his own family, Goodall turned to drink, and eventually lost his life mysteriously to Legionnaires' Disease in the mid-1970s. The evidence mounts that his father's death was no accident, that his case was "resolved" by someone who wanted, simply, to silence Lloyd Goodall—who perhaps knew too much—once and for all. It's a tragic end to the life of a true patriot, to be sure. Officially, he dies of pneumonia, brought on by Legionnaires' Disease. But, apparently, "a shot of something" at a V.A. hospital is the weapon. But notice: In the end, Lloyd Goodall dies of *secrecy*. The spy (one who sees too much, knows too much) is silenced, once and for all.

But the most intriguing legacy of this cold war story is the price paid by the Goodall family—a life of quiet desperation, with nervous breakdowns and quiet rebellions and plagues of doubt and anxiety. In the end, H. L. Goodall, Jr. concludes that he has no choice but to tell the story of his father's secret life—and to probe and question and expose—the dark contours of a secrecy that ran through the heart of—and, finally, ruptured—the Goodall family. And transcending the shot that ruptured the family is the shot at redemption that emerges through the story of the Goodall family. A need to *know* is transformed into a need to *tell*, that, in the end, offers a new kind of healing, available only through the magic of story.

As they searched the "borderlands of memory," the stories and partial stories, the artifacts and the inheritances available to them, Trujillo and Goodall confronted many obstacles. "Thin" or nearly nonexistent historical records, destroyed documents, muted memories, secret-keeping practices, hints rather than revelations, amnesias and repressions, denials and half-stories, and, quite simply, the winding nature of the path that is the process needed to reconstruct the buried past through the lenses and resources available in the present all seemed to stand in the way of completing their quest. But, with time and perseverance, courage and imagination, they both constructed meaningful stories out of the mysterious wisps of shadow and secrecy that seemed to shroud and block all possibility. Both authors had faith—faith in their ability to come to some sort of coherent story out of the raw materials in the archives, attics, basements, memories, stories, and dreams that live on. And they had faith in their vision, a vision that may be, as Goodall (2006a) claims, irresistible. As he puts it, "I wrote this book because I could no longer not write it" (p. 9).

Why Study Family Secrets?

The emerging literature on family secrets, then, seems to suggest that, at some point in the progression of a family's story, a storyteller must emerge. The storyteller sheds light on the memories that we cannot forever lay to rest. If Annette Kuhn is right in her claim that language brings us together, then the storyteller's function is clear: At the right moment, the story *must* emerge, for it is only through the story that the family can come together. And it is only through coming together that we can heal the rift that tore us asunder.

One way I have discovered to engage the storyteller in me is to follow the (sometimes dark, often edgy) trajectory of my dreams, to see what clues may emerge. And so I begin with the story of a dream—the dream that drove me to write this book.

Memories, Secrets, Roots . . .

There is a thin, reddish light as the mist begins to lift on this new dawn. A leaf blows across my path. A squirrel takes quick refuge in my oak tree. The cold is giving way to the slightest hint of warmth, and the birds have begun to notice. It will be a beautiful day, bringing with it the suggestion of spring, which is, of course, a time of hope. We perch on the edge of the new, breathing with anticipation.

But somehow, I think hope may fade quickly on this day.

Somewhere in the lingering shadows, a dark secret lurks . . .

I awoke this morning with a start, shaken from the darkness by a dream. In my dream, we have to dispose of a body. It is a person, though I do not know who it is. All I know is that we have to hide it, before anyone finds out. We—my family and I—are desperately trying to figure out how to do this quickly, before someone stumbles along and discovers our secret. But we have nowhere to put the body. Eventually, we find a box to stuff it in. But that, of course, just shifts the problem, and only a little.

Now what? Where can we hide the box?

Eventually, we decide that the spare bedroom—a room we never use and that isn't furnished anyway—is a likely place to start. Of course, it won't do to keep a body, even a body in a box, out in the open, even in a spare, unused bedroom. So we get a crowbar and bust a hole in the closet floor, so that we can bury the body underneath the floorboards. As we do this, we discover seeping water under there, but our options are limited so we move ahead with our plan. We dig a hole in the ground under the floor and we bury the box.

But, you know, there is that smell—that terrible smell of death. Even when we put the floor back in place, even when we replace the carpet, even when we lock the door and walk away, that smell will not go away.

So, a few days later, we go back in, and we see that the water is starting to seep up from below and into the carpet. And the water, mixed with gray clay the color of rotting flesh, smells of death.

And the smell begins to permeate everything.

Funny how this smell—long after I buried the memories of early traumas, long after the forgotten secrets seeped out of these experiences—still permeates many of my darkest dreams.

The smell of death.

The whiff of memory.

The stench of a secret.

That insistent, acrid, horrible smell is what tells me the secret won't stay put . . .

The floorboards in the spare room are buckling.

The problem with secret memories is that, no matter how much you try to ignore or bury them, they won't stay put. They show up in the strangest of places, at the oddest of times. Triggered by seemingly random events in our everyday world, the in-breaking of memory can be as faint as a whisper, as nagging as an itch, as blinding as a flash of lightning, as chilling as an Arctic wind, as breathtaking as a plunge into icy water. Or it can just sort of seep into your consciousness, like too much rain seeping through saturated ground into the edges of a basement. When the memory is of trauma, there is often an insistent human urge to bury it. In part, this comes from the difficulty of dealing with pain and grief in a culture that doesn't welcome human discomfort; in part, it simply seems that, to go on in our world, we must work against letting the memory overwhelm. We are, after all, a culture of "doers," locked deeply into the convergent ideologies of Puritanism and the American Dream, and it is hard to "do" when hobbled by pain.

As humans, we often stumble along through life, alternately happy, then sunk in ordinariness, then beset by trauma. In the face of traumatic events in our lives, with pain and grief, anger and fear, loss and loneliness, shame and humiliation visited on us through the death of a loved one, or through the breaking of a relationship, or through the strange and unpredictable and sometimes unkind actions of others, through the twisted dynamics of addiction, through burgeoning dysfunction arising in the wake of compounding problems, and through other harbingers, both ordinary and extraordinary, of "dis-ease," we find ourselves thrown into an ancient human dialectic, which the Greeks represented as the twin goddess Mnemosyne-Lesmosyne. In Greek mythology, this was a two-faced goddess: Mnemosyne, who represented memory, was the mother of the Muses; Lesmosyne, goddess of forgetting, was the creator and tender of the river Lethe, the river of forgetting that the dead cross over on the way to the underworld (Kerényi, 1977). These twin faces of the goddess, memory and forgetting, are dynamic and powerful forces in the play of everyday life. As Alan McGlashan (1986) puts it:

> Perhaps the two most moving chords that can be struck from the human heart are contained in these four words: I remember, I forget. For the unheard anthem of our whole existence is created out of the antiphonal movements of remembering and forgetting . . . perfect balance between this pair of opposites is the mark of maturity. . . . Memory is, in fact, the mortar between all events, a veritable *glutinum*

mundi. . . .But if memory is a vital function, so also is forgetting. To forget is essential to sanity. (p. 6)

And so we find ourselves tacking back and forth between these two vital energies—the memory that holds us in a coherent life narrative and the forgetting that allows us to go on in the face of pain and loss and trauma. Sometimes, with memories surging up from the depths of our (un)consciousness, we find ourselves at a loss as to what to do. We can be frozen in place, or stunned, or even trapped by these memories. On the other hand, sometimes, mercifully, our spirits are protected by the power of forgetting, at least for a time.

Knowing, at least intuitively, that forgetting is essential to sanity, knowledgeable human agents consciously and unconsciously craft strategic means of managing the dialectics of memory and forgetting (McGlashan, 1988). One of these strategies is a strategy of silence, the kind of silence that disrupts the story, a silence that keeps the narrative from being spoken—and thus defusing its power a little—a heavy, silencing silence (Clair, 1998; Glenn, 2004; Poulos, 2004a) that builds into a secret. A story told is a powerful thing that can unleash all sorts of grief; an untold story gives off at least the illusion of control.

We will not talk about this; it will be our little secret.

And thus secret-keeping can become a central form of family communicative practice. Further invigorating secret-keeping as a communicative practice are the concomitant dialectics at play in the presentation of the public and the private "faces" of a family. In *The Presentation of Self in Everyday Life*, Erving Goffman writes: "I assume that when an individual appears before others he will have many motives for trying to control the impression they receive of the situation" (1959, p. 15). A similar rule holds for families: Families work hard to control impressions others have of them. Only the situation is far more complicated than that of individual impression management. The dynamics of family impression management are complicated by the multiple, complex, and sometimes convoluted relationships and communication patterns that exist in any given family. These are matters of increasing complexity as time goes on and alliances are formed, or relationships are strained, or new trauma enters the scene.

In the 1960s and early 1970s, when I was a child coming of age, this impression management often took the form of that ever-looming rhetorical question, suggested by televised families working their charms on our world, continuing the legacy of good old 1950s American conformity, where at least one of the penultimate values was fitting in and looking good: "Now what will the neighbors think?" This question hovered in the background every time I, as a young boy, considered engaging in even the slightest forms of mischief, or when I began to appear *different*, like when I grew my hair long and pulled it back into a ponytail before slipping on my ripped jeans and my black bad-boy rock'n roll T-shirt. It was even more powerful when the family began to edge into conflict—which was, as the years went by, ever more likely and ever more noisy.

In my family's particular case, much of this impression management was instigated, in part at least, because of my father's social position as a rector (head priest) of an Episcopal church. There is simply very little maneuvering room in terms of the impressions such people can be allowed to portray. The definition of the role stipulates that the impressions ought to be positive, perhaps even pious. In such cases, it often comes as a shock to the system if things don't go well; the feeling of loss that comes with the death of a loved one, for example, can topple the precarious "positive" impressions a family works so hard to give off.

Unfortunately, in human social life, we move quickly from the categories of "normal" or even admired or honored, to stigmatized, disavowed, or outcast. A family cast into pain and silence, alternating with grief and rage, can quickly fall into the category of "odd"; it is a short, slippery downhill slope from there into the social hell of stigma. In *Stigma: Notes on the Management of Spoiled Identity*, Goffman (1963) writes of this process of stigmatization, or the reading and application of signs that the person or people under scrutiny are in violation of some social norm or other, and of how difficult it can be, once a person or a group is stigmatized, to extricate oneself or one's group from that unfavorable categorization.

Mediating this stigmatization process is the widespread practice of "passing" for normal; at the center of the dynamics of a developing practice of passing is the active practice of secret-keeping. Sadly, in our culture, if you are *different*—if you are too fat, too sad, too old, too gay, too sexual, too short, too tall, too blind, too deaf, too dark-skinned, too weak, too angry, too poor, too widowed, too hyper, too depressed, too mute, too malformed, too grief-stricken, too thin, too dumb, or even too smart to be considered "normal"—then you are subject to stigmatization. You may well be seen as a *defective* other. And so, we lapse into secret-keeping, because keeping it secret so often seems the neater choice.

"This will be our secret," she whispers.

And you nod before you know what you have done.

But what if the floorboards are buckling in the spare bedroom?

What if the secret won't stay put?

What if, in the damp dark cellar of consciousness, the secret festers and bubbles, breaks down and begins to smell?

What if, despite your best efforts, the damp, dark secret begins to seep into the carpet?

What if the secret comes rushing into your everyday life like an ill wind?

What if memories and dreams and the secrets they birth are like aspen trees, sending out their rhizomes in many directions, disrupting their own earthen burial sites with new sprouts, all of which are connected in some way to the ultimate realities of our shared universe? In the high country of Colorado where I have spent much of my life, the famed aspen trees light up the autumn sky with their golden glory for a brief moment each year. What few people know is that a grove of aspens an acre in size may all be parts, or offshoots, or children, if you will, of one tree standing somewhere in the grove. Indeed, the reproduction of aspens is accomplished through rhizomatic cloning, wherein one tree sends out roots under the ground, and additional trees sprout from the roots of that single tree. Tendrils reaching out through the soil, surging up from time to time to create something new, then sending new shoots downward and outward in ever more complex spirals and configurations . . .

Reflection

The aspen suggests to me a metaphor for the development, production, and reproduction of memories, and secrets, and stories . . . relations between these three genres of experience are complex and deeply rooted—and, often, I think, may be traced back to a single, primal, even archetypal source. At the deepest level of roots merging with soil and water and rock, the aspens draw energy from Earth as a whole—energy to grow, energy to thrive, energy to soar. Similarly, humans, down at the deepest levels of their "roots," may well find access to the unconscious energies that give us conscious, hopeful, growing, soaring possibilities.

What if our memories, our dreams, and our secrets are all part of one story, living just underground, just beneath the surface, waiting to grow, like the aspens, into beautiful forests, gleaming with many golden leaves of story?

What if our secrets push themselves up into the light?

And what if . . . maybe . . . just maybe . . . a secret shouldn't be a secret any more?

Clearly, despite the family rules that guard against stigma, and the scholarly arguments that "facework" can sometimes be positively accomplished via deception or silence or secrecy, a case can be made for embracing the opportunity to transform the secret lives of families into stories that open up new possibilities. That's exactly what this book is about. In the next chapter, I outline the pathway I will take toward achieving that goal.

Exercises

If you find yourself intrigued by the idea of family secrets, and at the possibility of writing those secrets into stories that might transform your path, you might want to begin by considering your memories. The exercises at the end of each chapter are designed to engage you in the process of bringing memory to light. Thus, you might begin to build stories from fragments of your past.

Writing Exercise 1: Early Memories

Spend some time reminiscing about your childhood. Remember as much as you can from as early in your life as you can. Try to remember a compelling story of an important moment in your childhood.

Then, call or meet with a relative (parent, sibling, grandparent, aunt, uncle, etc.). Ask that person to tell you a story of your early childhood, preferably one that involves you as a central character. Write down/record the details.

Make a journal entry every day, focusing on all the details you can remember from your early days on this Earth. Begin to craft your entries in story form, as though you were conveying the essence of your early life experience to people who were not there or who have not heard these stories.

Ponder: How did the events of your early life shape the person you are today? Who are you? Where did you come from? Where were you born? Where did you grow up? What is your earliest memory? What other memories do you have from your early years (ages one–ten or so)? What was life like then, in your family, in your neighborhood, in your home town? Who are the main characters? What did they teach you? What stories do you (and your family) tell of these early years? Focus again on drawing your reader into your world, this time by telling an engaging story. Write evocatively, passionately, performatively.

Write some more. As you write, try following the dictum of the autoethnographer, borrowed from the good novelist, to show, rather than tell, your reader what is going on in your world. Draw the reader into your space, and give her or him a detailed, engaging, and evocative tour of your lifeworld.

Writing Exercise 2: Nowstory

Next, focus your attention and your writing on your daily life in the here and now. Here are some questions to consider as you begin to craft a vivid, engaging story of your everyday life:

1. What is your life like, today? How does your day typically play out?
2. What are your significant spaces (home, school, etc.) like? Can you describe them so that someone who has never been there might see/feel/hear these places?
3. What do you do for excitement, fun, and entertainment?
4. What challenges do you currently face?
5. What are your passions?
6. How do you relate to being a student? A worker?
7. Who are the characters in your life today? Who are your roommates, your friends, your co-workers, and your associates?
8. What are your daily dialogues (conversations) really like?
9. How will you meet the challenge to take your reader with you as you experience an important (or trivial, but interesting) event in your daily life?
10. How do your memories of your earlier days connect with your experience today?

Now, craft your responses to these questions into a story about your life today, here and now—a "nowstory." Remember to use description, action, and dialogue to pull the reader into your story. A good story attempts to show the reader the significant actions of characters across some span of time, in a particular place, with some sort of purpose. Try your hand at writing a conversation from your everyday life in the form of a dialogue, as you might see in a well-written novel. The big challenges here are (1) to render the conversation so that it seems natural ("feels" right); and (2) to write it so that the conversation is vivid, engaging, serious, intriguing, entertaining, or humorous.

Writing Exercise 3: Secretstory

Have you ever heard—and kept—a secret? Write the story. If you feel the need, change the names and places to protect the keepers of the secret. But tell the story—the *whole* story.

Queries

1. What are your earliest childhood memories? How do they connect your past, your present, and your future? How might these memories begin to play a role in the crafting of your ethnographic stories?
2. What role does silence play in the communicative life of your family?
3. How do you and your family relate to one another? Are you close? Distant? Happy? Sad? Functional? Do you fight or argue? Do you laugh or play?
4. Do you carry any secrets? Why do you suppose you do—or don't—engage in secret-keeping?
5. How do you *feel* after writing these stories—of your memories, your present, and your secrets? Has anything changed?

Chapter Two

Accidental Ethnography

Interlude 1: Reflections on Writing Life

Imagine yourself sitting at the keyboard, staring at the blank white screen. You know you have to write, but for the life of you, you cannot call up anything worth writing about. You sit and you stare. And stare. And stare.

Nothing.

You get up, walk into the kitchen, do the dishes. This leads you to look around the rest of the house. You decide it's a mess, so you spend an hour just straightening up the clutter. You still have to write that paper, that article, that book chapter, that book. You know you must write, so you walk back to your computer and sit down with new resolve.

And you stare. And stare. And stare some more. Nothing comes. You decide maybe you do need groceries, after all, since there is really nothing appealing in the fridge or the pantry. So you make a list, but then the phone rings, and as you chat on the phone, you notice that dust motes are floating up from the table across from your sofa. So you decide to finish cleaning the house. You dust, you vacuum, you scrub the shower and the toilet. Then you head out to the grocery store. By the time you unload the groceries, you're late for your meeting. You rush to your car, jump in, and drive too fast, arriving minutes late, apologizing profusely. That night, you fall into bed exhausted. You have not written a single word, despite your looming deadline.

You slip into sleep, but you are fitful. Something . . . nagging at the back . . . you toss and you turn. You fall into dreams but they make no sense. They come in fragments, shards. The pieces don't fit together. You toss some more. You get up, get a glass of water, resolve to fall into a better sleep. You lie down, and slip into a dream.

This time you dream you are a writer. In the dream, the words flow so fast you cannot keep up with them. You are on a roll, but you are worried that the words make no sense. No matter, because you could not stop if you wanted to; there is certainly no time to edit. You decide to surrender to the words, and you are just swept up into the moment, carried along, like you have been dumped in a river . . . the water is made of words and you are in Class Five rapids. You find you can barely come up for air. Suddenly, you go under, gasping, immersed in too many words, drowning, gasping. And then you wake up.

You jump out of bed, rush to your computer, and begin writing. It starts slowly, building one word at a time, like a river begins with a single raindrop. Pretty soon, you start to build momentum and find yourself swept up by a story . . .

For some time I have been contemplating the idea that the process of writing the so-called new ethnography (Goodall, 2000) just comes on me, carries me along, throws me down, pulls me up short, pushes me, cajoles me, and catches me up in a wave of action, passion, and rising spirit. The writing *carries me*, not the other way around. I fall into it, and it takes me where it wants. Sometimes the ride is fast and exciting, sometimes cool and refreshing, sometimes overwhelming and scary, sometimes incredibly invigorating, always fascinating.

In short, for me, the process of composing and crafting an ethnographic tale is, in large part, a leap of faith. It is often a process I do not control. I like to think writing animates me, not the other way around. Indeed, I usually don't know where the journey will lead. But I do know it will be a helluva trip. I also know this: As much as I wish to be in control, that fantasy is belied by the fact that ethnographic writing seems to do more to shape my life than I do to shape it as a "project" or a "product" of some sort.

So, a big part of the impetus for this book lies in that simple insight: My ethnography is, in some sense, *accidental*.

Some academics, who have been trained to justify their so-called research methodologies, might be scratching their heads at this point. Others might be shouting aloud, resisting the idea that we stumble into research praxis, that we don't so much build an agenda as *it builds us*. Fair enough. Let's take a look at that idea.

Interlude 2: Is There a Method(ology) to This Madness?

So . . . the question arises: What, exactly, is "accidental ethnography"? Is it a method, or an attitude, or a process, or . . .? The simple answer is that it is all of these things and more. This idea comes from the insight that, although life is a *performance*, most of it is *improvisational* in nature. That is, we generally go about much of our lives stumbling through its various moments without a script. Many of us like to think we plan things out, but truthfully, much of our daily engagement in various life activities is spontaneous, surprising, unplanned. Knowing that, I see accidental ethnography as a willingness to surrender to the creative, imaginative, spontaneous, apparently accidental signs and impulses that surge up and, from time to time, really grip us, take hold of us, call us out and throw us down, sweep us away, and carry us to places we may not have even imagined if we had tried to lay out a straight line to our eventual discoveries. Here we must embrace the power of imagination, the wandering path of accident and spontaneity and synchronicity, and the flowing, spark-lighting fire of spirited possibility. Thus, we find ourselves in a position to transform our ways of seeing, approaching, conceiving, and developing research "methodologies" in a *performative* direction, a direction that stems from an epistemology that sees knowledge as *imaginative praxis* rather than as an *object* or a *product*. We seek knowing-in-action, rather than knowledge-as-acquisition.

The research methodologies that arise out of this kind of epistemological commitment proceed by a logic different from the methodologies followed by many social and natural scientists. The new narrative approaches do not proceed via a traditional social scientific approach (hypothesis-test-conclusion), a linear-causal predictive view of reality, or a positivist or neopositivist paradigm grounded in prediction and control. Accidental ethnography does not seek to be work that generates data, tests predictions, controls outcomes, or leads to generalizations or explanations. Rather, it seeks to embrace, and possibly make storied sense of—or at least *move through, into, or with*—the mystery that animates human life.

Pioneers in the new narrative ethnographies and other alternative, intuitively driven qualitative research methodologies—including William Braud, Rosemarie Anderson, Norman Denzin, Yvonna Lincoln, Laurel Richardson, Bud Goodall, Art Bochner, Carolyn Ellis, Janice Hocker Rushing, Nick Trujillo, and Ron Pelias, to name but a few—have pushed back the boundaries of human social research. They write texts that are grounded in imagination and mystery rather than certainty, that are unique rather than replicable, that show human social reality in all its complexity, seeking to open pathways to possibility.

This writing seeks to engage a broader audience, including not just the discipline within which it is written, but also other disciplines, our students, and even (maybe especially) communities outside the academy. It seeks to be accessible, engaging, clarifying, and open-ended. The tradition of qualitative inquiry of this sort, of course, has a long history, and its parameters and conventions are broadly accepted (even celebrated) in several fields of study (Bochner, 2001; Braud & Anderson, 1998; Denzin, 1997; Denzin & Lincoln, 2000, 2001; Garfinkel, 1967; Geertz, 2005; Goodall, 1994, 1996, 2000, 2006b; Richardson, 2000; Turner, 1969; Turner & Bruner, 1986; Van Maanen, 1988). The new narrative turn, of which I see accidental ethnography as a natural step, is simply an extension and expansion of this long history—the next moment in its evolution.

Along the way, as I have engaged in the practice of autoethnography, I have discovered that stories are the opening to possibility in moments of trauma, with a storied methodology being a primary textual act that can make real change in our social world. In other words, I have discovered that families and other close, enduring relationships often suffer in silence and thus lapse into secrecy as a result of these traumatic moments, and that, in general, researchers have not found ways to uncover anything more than the dysfunctional dynamics of this secrecy. I have also discovered that the natural storytelling urge, invoked in close relational research praxis, can serve as a counterbalance to that dark, secretive, depressive energy that can overwhelm even the healthiest relationships in the face of loss. In other words, I have discovered that the relationship between the "researcher" and the "researched"—and thus the relationship between the story and the storied life—is critically important in the discovery process.

I have discovered that the world of the unconscious (including the dream world) is a rich source of potential knowledge in the study of family and other close personal relationships and I have proposed that the invocation of dream worlds, dream images, and dream words offers new methodological opportunities for narrative scholarship (Poulos, 2004a, 2004b, 2006a, 2006b). I have theorized that *narrative conscience* is the primary ethical call of the human spirit, that we must invoke narrative conscience in our human dialogue and in our scholarship, and that we must, if we are to thrive as a species, develop new ways of engaging our dialogue, especially in challenging moral conversations (Poulos, 2008b). The primary phenomenological insight is that theory, method, communication practice, and research practice are not separate enterprises; they are formed in process, as a whole, as deeply intertwined networks of lived experience. So, in short, the methodology, if there is one, is a *process-oriented* journey of discovery. But enough about that methodology stuff for now. Let's go back and begin at the beginning.

Interlude 3: Memory-Signs (Spirit Calls)

So, sometimes, I follow the signs I am given. I have just awoken to face another day. I glance outside, and though it is still dark, I can see it will be one of those fine autumn days that settles in in my part of the country in late October—the kind of day where the heart soars briskly, and the world is infused with a new kind of light. The tepid, humid air that hovers beyond the last days of summer has finally given way, just a bit, to light and color and crisp, cooling air. From time to time, a breeze kicks up and triggers a little leaf storm, swirling with reds and oranges and yellows.

Today will be one of those days where the season turns to colors so vivid you'd almost want to cry if it weren't for the pure unbridled joy of it all. In any event, you just want to sit and stare and take it all in, breathing it into your cells, feeling the color begin to *inhabit* you, reveling in the glory of change. Or you want to run through it, leaping for joy, tumbling with ecstasy through time and space and the thin, cool air.

Or maybe you *will* just sit down and cry.

Then: Duty calls.

I have been given a sign.

Knowing this, I sit down at my computer, and begin to write these words. I consider it another sign that the words flow so smoothly, so silkily, so easily onto this page. I will seize the moment, dreaming that they will always flow this way, yet knowing that a dam will build up to stop them, sooner or later. But right now, at this moment, inspiration sparks somewhere deep within me, flows up like a river of fire, surging hotly through my chest, streaming up into my arms and out through my fingers.

I can feel the heat of it.

I can feel the *heart* of it.

My fingers dance with the keyboard, where the last moments of words-in-the-making flow from these strangely facile, flexible endpoints of my hands.

Remarkable tools, hands. I cannot imagine life without them. They are my body's troubadours, singing the work I must do. I am fortunate to have such hands. They seem to know what to do.

I write these words as words-in-motion, words that flow up from a feeling, an intuition, a spark or a breath of fire, welling up from deep within my body—a feeling that I am onto something, though I often do not know what until after the writing is done. From somewhere deep inside me—my gut(?), my heart(?), my soul(?)—first images, then sounds and smells and feelings, then words, begin to form at the edges of my consciousness.

This writing, manifested as embodied energy in motion, is something I have learned to trust. I see it as spirit rising, surging into the world of (meaning) making. And, as with the turning of autumn in the hardwood forest I inhabit, I find myself struck by the wonder of it all. Like Binx Bolling, Walker Percy's famous "moviegoer," I will not let the wonder slip away. Indeed, I find myself, like Binx, driven to "poke around" and seek meaning in apparently random events, embracing mystery and wonder, even while I try to make sense of it all.

So, today, I must write. I have been given a sign, and, as often happens these days, I am called to attend to it, to see if I can, as Goodall (1996, 2000) urges, seek to develop an "ethnographic imagination" to cope with the mysteries that surround me. I am called to read the signs I am given as speaking to the possibilities entailed in the divine presence of spirit in this world.

The sign was a simple one. It was a small up-surge of memory. It was just a thin little wisp of a memory, but I can't help thinking it is significant.

It happened as I was walking out to get my paper in the early morning light. Something familiar was in the air, but I could not put my finger on it. A smell? Something alive. And I stepped on a small stick of oak, shed by the towering tree that stands just a few feet from my front door—CRACK!

And, suddenly, I am striding through a thick forest. I am young, and strong, and . . . lost. But I feel a sense of exhilaration as my muscles work to carry me along on my quest. I am looking for the way . . . searching . . . and the land is rising gently, so I know I am generally on track, though there is no trail to follow. And the energy, the spirit, rises in me as I see the woods thinning out, and I know I am on my way.

I will find my way.

Just as quickly as this rush of memory came upon me, it fades, and I am back in the present moment. I bend down to retrieve the paper, and pause to wonder at the possible meanings of this trace of a memory.

Just a little wisp of a memory, of an unremarkable day over thirty years ago. But I have come to take the in-breaking of memories—no matter how small, no matter how apparently insignificant or disconnected from my current experience these memories may seem—seriously. I probe the possibilities they present, actively. And so I find myself, like Binx Bolling, undertaking a search:

> As I watched, there awoke in me an immense curiosity. I was onto something. I vowed that if I ever got out of this fix, I would pursue the search. . . .What is the nature of the search, you ask? Really, it is very simple, at least for a fellow like me; so simple that it is easily overlooked. The search is what anyone would undertake if he were not sunk in the everydayness of his own life. (Percy, 1960, p. 13)

For Binx, it turns out, the search is a search for meaning, for connection, for transcendence in a world of ordinariness. It is a search for truth, for love, for a life of the heart. Like Binx, I am now in a state of immense curiosity. The search is on. What is the meaning of this memory trace? Why remember that little moment? Why *now*? What might be going on? Where might my unconscious self be leading me at this moment (Jung, 1989)?

And I find myself walking back into the house to write.

The trail of my memory carries me back to my childhood. I begin writing, and the story that comes is one from those early years of my life, when I often wandered in forests . . .

Interlude 4: The Wanderer

Sometimes I think people are born to certain things. Me? I was born to wander. My brother, Mike, was born to make things. When he was very young, he became fascinated with Indians. He started to order kits and to make various "authentic" Indian costumes. He once spent a whole year diligently sewing hundreds of feathers onto a long piece of red felt, creating a genuine Sioux headdress.

My friends and I, who were a couple of years younger than him, thought he was nuts. What was he doing in his room sewing when he could be out here playing baseball or tearing through the woods or blowing things up? What on Earth is the purpose of a ten-year-old boy's existence if it doesn't involve baseball or forests, or explosions, imagined or real?

When Mike was twelve, he spent the summer at our Grandpa's farm building a fiberglass canoe. It took him two months. When the day came to launch the boat, which looked pretty damn good for a boat built by hand by a twelve year old, he begged Grandpa to help him load it in the pickup and take it out to the pond. They carried it to the edge, and he readied the paddle, shoved the boat out into the water, jumped into the back, and promptly sank three feet to the bottom. I don't know how Grandpa managed to stifle his laughter, but they spent the rest of the day hauling the canoe out of the water and taking it back to the shop to see if they could fix it.

But most days, I was out in the forest, alone or with my friends, trying my damnedest to get lost. I had this thing about getting lost.

In the summer of 1963, we moved to Sewanee, Tennessee. I was four years old. The mountain—some might call it a hill—that holds the town of Sewanee rises gently out of the Cumberland Plateau. Atop this ancient knob of southern Appalachia we found the little village of Sewanee, which at the time consisted of a store, a Western Union office, a gas station, a small movie theater, a public school, and the University of the South, where my dad would attend seminary. All of this was surrounded by thick, ancient hardwood forests. We lived in a tiny stone duplex on the edge of campus, tucked back in the woods at the far end of town.

One hot sultry afternoon, I wandered into the cool, dark woods out in back of my house, got off the path, and became hopelessly lost. I spent hours wandering around in circles, trying to find the place where I had begun. I wasn't scared, like a kid that age should be. I just wanted to find the way.

Eventually, I emerged from the woods about a half-mile down the road from where I started and I thought, "Huh. I should try that again." I suppose, even at that early age, I thought I had better try to do better next time. Since that day, I've had this fascination with the idea of being lost, and of finding my way back to where I started—or to a fresh, new place. There is something about getting lost, and then getting "un-lost," that changes you.

The getting un-lost part may actually sound easier than it really is. You see, in the ancient, lush rolling hills of southeastern Tennessee, the forests were so dense that sunlight could barely penetrate in some places. There would be paths, of course, made by the abundant deer and followed by other creatures of the forest, but the paths often wound around and led nowhere in particular—or, at least, nowhere important to a human.

Every once in a while, I would stumble on something special, like a small, dark cave or a secret spring bubbling up from the ground. And I would know I had come to the place where I was supposed to be.

I followed paths like that all through my early life. Pretty much everything I did involved wandering.

And somehow finding special places and moments that I will never forget.

This tendency to wander could be a problem in school, and in structured games like baseball, where the paths are straight and well laid. That's why I preferred the time after school and loved the made-up street and backyard versions of my favorite games, where you had only a few players and had to make new rules to compensate. Out there on the field, or in the yard or in the street, so long as I let my body pay some bit of attention to the game, I was free to strike off into the forests of my imagination. I spent hours staring into space, reacting if a ball came my way, or if it was my turn to act, but in my mind and my heart I was off on a grand adventure, lost in thought and the play of imagination. There I could create my own worlds, my own characters, my own rules. And occasionally I would stumble on some treasure, and my spirit would soar.

One day, when I was about eleven, my friends and I were tearing through the woods on the edge of our neighborhood. By this time, my family had moved to the suburbs of Atlanta, but it was before Atlanta was a mega-city, and the edges of town were still thickly wooded. We lived in the northeast corner of town in a little 'burb called Chamblee. My friends and I spent a lot of time running through the woods, having pinecone and mudball wars. Both of these weapons hurt when they made contact, so there were two special rules: no face hits, and, definitely, no crotch hits. It was the late 1960s, and our Cowboys vs. Indians wars were giving way to Green Berets vs. Viet Cong, but we abided by the civilized rules of warfare.

Summer days, we would bolt out our front doors at eight in the morning, and sometimes we wouldn't return until dark was settling in, somewhere around 9:30. We spent much of our time in the woods, fighting until one side surrendered. In the middle of one such engagement, as the long dusk was fading toward night, my best friend Eddie Hampton and I came upon a clearing in the woods. We had stumbled right into the yard of an abandoned house, set way back from a dirt road at the far edge of town.

"Hey guys! Truce!" yelled Eddie.

Nothing.

"Seriously, man. Truce!" we both yelled.

Gradually, out of the trees, our gang emerged into the clearing. We all stood there, just staring.

The house was a split-level suburban-style popular at the time, not unlike many of the houses in our neighborhood, most of which had been built in the late fifties or early sixties. But what was different about this house was its location—way out in the woods like this, all alone—and the total absence of any human presence. The lawn, if you could still call it that, was just a patch of bare dirt with a few weeds here and there poking through the hardened earth. The house looked disheveled and uncared for, and utterly abandoned. The front door hung at an angle, half off its hinges. The roof was peeling, with big patches of missing shingles. Every single window was shattered, except for one.

"Let's go in," whispered Eddie. And he started walking slowly, as if in a dream or a trance, toward the front steps.

We hesitated.

Eddie ducked through the door, flinching a little as if he were afraid it would fall on him. From inside, he called softly, "Hey, come on, guys. This is cool."

I was next, but I was frozen in fear. This didn't look right to me. Something was wrong. I could feel it.

"Come on, CP," Eddie shouted.

"Yeah, go for it," the others chimed in.

I took a deep breath, and stumbled up the steps.

The shadows inside were long. The living room walls were pocked with holes where vandals had thrown rocks through the drywall. The floor was littered with the glass of windows that had met the same fate. The carpet was old and stained and ripped. In one corner, the ceiling was caving in from what looked like a substantial leak in the roof above.

We wandered toward the back of the house, found ourselves in a little den. Eddie and I just stood there, in the center of another ruined room, taking stock of our new "fort."

"Place needs some work," Eddie quipped.

I stifled a guffaw as something on the stairs caught my attention. A movement? Then, the soft sound of a footstep, above us, where the bedrooms must be. I knew the guys were still out in the yard, and anyway, there was no way they could have gotten past us and up the stairs. The hair on my neck stood up.

Just then, the sound of shattering glass caught my attention.

"Run!" Eddie yelled, and then bolted for the front door.

I turned toward the back door, which was closer, ran toward it, shoved it open, and found myself on a high porch overlooking a steeply sloping backyard. I took the stairs three at a time. Halfway across the yard, I stopped, turned to look at the house for a moment.

"Something's not right," I thought. I turned to run, and slammed into something both hard and forgiving—a person? A big person. Strong arms clamped my arms to my sides. I looked up, directly into the stern eyes of a cop.

Looking up from my computer as I write these words, I find myself laughing softly. It strikes me as very funny today, though at the time I nearly wet my pants. The cops took us down to the station and made us call our parents. By the time our dads came to pick us up, we were all shaking in fear. Our dads just gave us a look, said, "Get in the car." They did not need to punish us; hell, we grounded *ourselves* for a week, sitting inside sorting baseball cards and reading comic books.

For weeks after that, all my dad had to do was give me that look, and I would find myself taking out the garbage. He got a lot of mileage out of that "breaking and entering" experience.

As for me, I have often found myself wondering how I got into situations like that. I seem to have a knack for getting lost, or for being in the wrong place at the wrong time, or for saying the wrong thing to the wrong person. I suppose I should learn something from all these experiences, but sometimes, for the life of me I cannot figure out what.

What I do know is that the memories, dreams, and reflections of my life experiences rise up in me unbidden from time to time and call me, in a deeply *embodied* way, to attend to them. That is, when the CRACK of a memory trigger, or the heavy fog of a dense or difficult or poignant dream, sets upon me, I feel an urging, from somewhere deep within my embodied being, to follow this eruption and to focus my writing on it. I am on a search. It may not lead me anywhere; it may even lead me to be even more lost in the forest for a time, but nonetheless, I must follow. Like a detective chasing the least clue, I know I must continue the search.

The only thing my father ever said to me about this incident came about a week later. It came in the form of one short, cryptic statement: "Son, you need to get your head screwed on straight." I, of course, had no idea what he was talking about.

The next day, I looked out my window and was drawn into the forest once again. I just had this *feeling*. Something out there was waiting for me. I walked down the street toward the woods, uncertain about where I was going, but gripped by that feeling . . .

I wandered off into the woods, walking in a general sort of direction for quite a while, not really paying attention much to where I was going. As I stepped into a little clearing, I came back to awareness of my surroundings. This time there was no abandoned house, but there was a beautiful green patch of grass. I decided to lie down. I looked up through the treetops, staring into the clear blue sky, thinking of nothing. I found myself drifting off . . . and yet . . . something was holding me at the edge of consciousness . . . something . . .

I gradually became aware of a little sound . . . close yet faint, just moving into the edges of my hearing . . . a kind of trickling . . . a familiar sound, but out of place. I shook off the drowsy feeling and sat up, looking around, seeking the source of this sound. Not immediately apparent. . . . I saw no likely spot for a dripping faucet to be placed. But that is the sound I was hearing. There was no place for a stream either. I was seated on a little grassy knoll rising up from the forest, nowhere near the kind of telltale draw or dip in the land that usually signaled the presence of water in this kind of forest.

Yet I was very close to the source of this sound, and it most certainly was the sound of trickling water. I craned my neck a little and spotted a rock that looked a bit dark and a little wet, about ten feet away, near the crest of the little knoll. I stood and walked over to the rock, which was flat and about a foot across. I lifted it up, and there it was—a beautiful, clear little pool—a spring bubbling up from somewhere deep below. The pool was about a foot across and apparently about twice as deep. The water was as clear and beautiful as I have ever seen. I found myself mesmerized by its movements and by the simple miracle that water could find its way to this place, water so clean and cold and crystal clear that I felt a little tear forming at the edge of my eye, from the sheer joy of the sight. I bent down and plunged my face into it. It was surprisingly cold, but I just left my face there for a moment, letting the water wash away all that I might need it to.

Then I stood up, refreshed, invigorated, and looked around. The world seemed to be, somehow, new to me, as though it—or perhaps I—had just been born. I saw the trees and the stones and the creatures of the forest in a new way. They were no longer *ordinary*. I could no longer take them for granted. I felt somehow *connected* to them, to this place, to all of creation. I felt deep joy at this moment.

There was something *special* in that water.

I replaced the rock, and decided not to tell anyone of this little place. This would be my own little place, a place I would visit often over the next few months. And every time I visited, and plunged my face in the water, I felt that incredible sense that the world, and I, had just been born. Again.

Then, one day, as fall turned to winter, and the trees shed their last leaves, I stopped visiting the little spring. By the following summer, I had forgotten all about it. But today, I remember it as though I were standing on that hill, right here, right now.

Reading Memory and Story

So, how to read the sign, the little memory-eruption, that brought me to the telling of this story? Read one way, the memory coming up here and now might be a *specific* message for me to decipher. Perhaps my memory is offering some sort of map for me to follow on my current life path. Perhaps I should learn something from this memory and the story it generated.

Digging deeper, plowing into the *content* of memory morphing into story, I find multiple readings are possible. Read from a mainstream, normative perspective, it might be said that I should never have been wandering in the forest in the first place, certainly not getting lost, certainly not getting lost *on purpose*. I would never have been in danger—after all, being lost in the woods is dangerous, or at least potentially so—and I certainly would never have been arrested for breaking and entering, if my head had been "screwed on straight." I should have been focusing on more important things. Didn't I have homework or something?

Moving further rightward, reading from an even more conservative cultural perspective, there are clear and certain paths to follow in this life. They are pretty straight and narrow paths, and if you keep your head down and your nose to the grindstone, you will find your way. Taken in the context of my life in the academy, for example, I probably ought to have a clear, laid-out, preplanned "research program."

Don't *you* have a program?

Don't you have an *agenda*?

Don't you have a five-year plan?

This linear reading of life's trajectory sets up orderly, predictable ways of engaging in what we call "research" and allows for easy bestowal of institutional seals of approval like grant funding and tenure and so on. After all, I should know where I am going, what I am going to do when I get there, and pretty much what will come of it all. *Before* it happens. In some ways of doing research, after all, I, the researcher, am supposed to pretty much know the conclusions of my research, hypothesizing clearly and cogently what I will find as a result of my inquiry.

Before I even begin.

But that's another story.

Meanwhile, in reading my little memory-story, I cannot resist veering back in the other direction for a moment—see that little trace of a path over there, to the left? Yes, that one. . . . Ah, perhaps we should read the memory-cum-story as a sign that, when I wander, lost in the forest, uncertain but gripped by the joy of the chase, I am *onto* something.

Perhaps being gripped by memory-story is the best thing that can happen to this researcher of the human condition.

Perhaps the memory-story can lead me to places I have never been, to discoveries I would never have made if I hadn't wandered into the forest and gotten lost.

Perhaps the memory-story is telling me to wander, and to hope I can discover anew the kind of spring that gives birth to a fresh perspective . . .

Reflection

"Accidental ethnography" is an idea that gradually began to come to me over a period of several years. The first hints came while I performed my first field ethnography as a graduate student in the winter of 1997. In that project, I observed a ritual practice engaged in by a community of men from a different culture, with whom I had little prior connection (Poulos, 1999). As I sat observing and taking field notes, I began to have moments of reflexive self-doubt. In other words, I became acutely aware of my own internal responses to being the researcher. In fact, the anxiety I felt around the question of whether I would ever be able to capture in words what was going on around me was, at times, overwhelming. Perhaps those of you who have attempted field ethnographies of other cultures have felt this way!

I was, in fact, frozen in my tracks. I did not know what to do. So I did what all good graduate students do, though I did it with trepidation: I went to my professor and told him of my dilemma. His response was simple: "Why don't you write about the anxiety and see where it leads you?"

At that moment, I was released. And though my autoethnographic reflections on that project did not make it into the print version (Poulos, 1999), I was on the road to a new way of thinking about and (eventually) practicing ethnography. I began reading everything I could get my hands on by those who were writing in this newer vein of reflexive personal narrative ethnography. Bochner (1997, 2000, 2001, 2002), Bochner & Ellis (1992, 1996, 1999, 2002, 2003), Ellis (1995, 1999, 2001, 2002a, 2002b, 2004, 2007), Denzin (1997, 2001), and Goodall (1994, 1996, 2000, 2005, 2006a, 2006b) were the prominent pioneers. Others, like Pelias (2000, 2004), soon followed. In recent years, the floodgates have been opened.

Then, one day, it was September 11. And I was thrown into a whirlwind of writing. The writing just *took* me. I could not not write. And, for the life of me, I could not think of any way to write sense into this senseless time other than to surrender to the anxiety that had gripped me, and to *fall into* writing about it. The idea of ethnography being something that directed my attention, seemingly by accident, had begun to take hold. My autoethnographic reflections on that day, and the weeks that followed, really launched the beginning of my career as an "accidental ethnographer" (Poulos, 2002, 2004a, 2004b, 2006a, 2006b). An idea about the practice of accidental ethnography was beginning to take shape. And then I had a dream.

Dream-Signs: Spirit Awakens

I am a seeker. I am on a search, looking for new springs of awareness that will draw me closer to all the vital energies of rising spirit.

So, one of my current methodologies for engaging embodied ethnographic research is to seek to read my dreams, writing them into story, weaving, if you will, a dreamstory (Poulos, 2006b). Each day, on rising, I attempt to recall and read my dreams, with varying success. Sometimes my dreams are vivid, present, direct, and clear. At other times, I find myself searching the foggy edges of my consciousness, only to find my search frustrated, with the thin wisps of dream-consciousness receding before me into oblivion, mocking me, disappearing like a ring of smoke blown into a good wind.

Today, I remember a dream, though I do not know what it means. In my dream, I am walking in a golden forest. My feet spring along the trail, as I breathe in the crisp autumn air. I feel invigorated, the way I feel when I know something good, if challenging, is about to happen. I gradually realize I am climbing a steep hill. It is a long way to the top, but I know I must make it, for beyond that rise in the land there is something—or maybe someone—awaiting me. I walk and walk and walk, and as the land begins to rise more steeply beneath my feet, I begin to breathe harder. But my pace quickens, as I feel my mission drawing me, urging me on. I simply *must* see the other side. There is something there—I just *know* it. Deep in my body. I *know*.

That's it. At that moment, I am jarred awake by a car door slamming outside my house, and the dream fades away.

What was it? What awaited me as the prize for my climb? Was it a far, golden-green country, where beauty and joy spread out beyond the horizon? Was it a dark place, where the shadows of grief and sorrow and despair prevail? Perhaps I will never know, though knowing myself as I do, I know I will try tonight to reenter this dream.

But my dreams do not follow orders. They break into my consciousness, taking me to places I perhaps could not know any other way. Instead of taking cues from my desires, or my will, my dreams carry me along. And so, as I lay down to sleep, my dreams launch me back to a time and a place out of my deepest memory, a time when I was free to follow the urgings of my heart.

I dream of a day when I was four years old. . . . I am walking across a meadow, hands in my pockets, when, out of a short dip in the ground, sprints a little rabbit. And I am off and running, chasing the rabbit at full speed, arms and legs pumping mightily. I am swift, swift, swift as the wind! I ride the wind as it pushes at my back. I know I will never catch this rabbit, but I run and run and run anyway, zigging and zagging through the knee-deep flowered grass, in the end chasing nothing, chasing only a dream. I feel joy surging up through my feet and into my heart, where it is pumped up toward my lips, which spread outward in a great smile. I begin to laugh, because I know I have learned some grand truth about this world, about freedom, about spontaneous joy. I do not know this in words, or in concepts, but I do know it in my body, in my heart.

So I laugh and laugh and laugh as I run. And just as I am about to stop, winded, the wind lifts me up, and I spread out my arms. I can fly! Oh, I can fly! I soar high up above the trees, and now, suddenly, I can look down upon my forest and see it for what it is: a complex configuration of roots and reachings, of the strength of trunks and the possibilities entailed by the meanderings of branches, the floating of leaves, the falling and catching and growing of seeded nuts that open the forest world to new beings, to new inhabitants, to new possibilities.

I wake refreshed, knowing that there is something in this world for me, something that will help me to fly, and to feel, and to learn, and to see.

When night returns, I want to go back there, to fly again, but instead, I dream I live in a new house in a new place. In my dream, I am sleeping in my new bedroom, when I wake to a familiar—but out of place—sound. I hear water flowing, flowing from inside the house, flowing in a way that water should never flow inside a house. I stand up to investigate and notice a door at the far end of the bedroom—a door I have not seen before, a door I would swear was not there when I went to bed. So I stand to investigate, walking steadily but cautiously toward the door. And the sound of flowing water gets louder and louder as I approach, so that by the time I fling open the door, it sounds like a raging torrent.

Sure enough, that is what I find. I am in a room so large that I cannot see its ceiling or its walls. I know it is a room, but it is larger than—and unlike—any room I have ever seen. And through the middle of this room—deep in a canyon that stretches before my eyes into a distance I cannot see—rushes a great river, churning and swirling in rapids and cataracts and high waterfalls. The water is white as the current breaks over large rocks, and I find myself thinking, "I had better not fall over this edge, or I am doomed." At that moment, as if on cue, my foot slips, and I find myself plunging off the cliff and down, down, down into the icy water below. I hit

with a splash, plunging deep. In shock, I battle back to the surface
to catch a breath, and find myself carried along on a current so swift
that there is nothing to do but lay back and let it carry me where it
will. I surrender to the current, and just as I do, I notice that the water
is not water at all but a torrent of words. And it dawns on me: This
is a river of memories ignored or forgotten, of secrets unspoken, of
knowledge unwritten, of stories untold. It is a river of possibility
for communication, but the words have not found their way to their
places in the world. And at that moment, I wake, startled by the
knowledge that I must write some of these words into their places.

That day, I find myself considering the recurring metaphors,
images, and symbols that inhabit my dreams. One recurring image
is, of course, of wandering in the forest, often in the dark. In many of
these dreams, I am lost. I do not know where I am going, or what will
happen, but I know that I must go along. I must chase the mystery.
Another image recurring regularly in my dreams is of the presence of
unexpected or unexplained water—in a pool, or dripping, or seeping,
or pouring, or churning in a torrent—but always water, and always
in an unexpected time or place. Sometimes it is water infiltrating
my home, seeping up through floorboards or walls or ceilings. Or it
might be that I just stumble on water in a place where I did not expect
to see it. A third recurring image in my dreams is of the appearance
of an unexpected or extra, unexplained, room in my home. It is often
an empty room, waiting to be put to use, but in some way presenting
a dilemma or a loss of clarity about how or why or when that might
occur. Similar to the empty-room image is another recurring image—
an image of an unknown place, a destination like the crest of the hill,
where something important or powerful will be revealed on arrival—
a penultimate destination, a place to which to make a pilgrimage.
And then there is the flying—oh! the flying!—and I know that, above
all, I, with my heart pumping, can leap into the air and reach new
heights I may not have even imagined.

According to the tradition of Jungian analytic psychology, dreams
can—and should—be read for their symbolic meaning (Jung, 1989).
Some of these readings are attempts to draw on archetypal imagery or
symbolism rising out of ancient mythological or religious traditions.
In such traditions, forests are often read as places of both danger and
possibility—unknown terrain that is reflective in many ways of our
inner forests—the parts of us that need exploring, that may contain
unknown perils and promises. Further, the presence of water in myth

and dream is often read as a primordial, even prophetic, presence. Water is a source of cleansing and renewal as well as a symbol of the gifts of the unconscious. Meanwhile, flying is a movement toward open possibility, a symbolic action embracing the wider reaches of the world, while at the same time allowing an overview, a holistic seeing/sensing/feeling of the organic connections among parts of the whole. Flying is a holistic symbolic action, a symbol of freedom *and* connection. Finally, the spare room is often also read as a place of possibility, a new and potentially useful space in which to place—or to explore—some part of ourselves (Biedermann, 1992; Jung, 1989).

In each case, I read the presence of these images—forests, water, flying, rooms—as spaces or substances or moments of *possibility* and *transcendence*. They are symbols of spirit rising in and from unexpected places in space and moments in time. These are moments with messages, with mysteries to follow, with clues to be deciphered, with gifts to be unwrapped. In my life, I see them as opportunities to be embraced, or plunged into, or wandered around in . . .

Embracing Spirit, for the Health of It: Living the Life of an Accidental Ethnographer

Eric Eisenberg (2001) and Bud Goodall (1996, 2000) write eloquently about surrendering to the mystery that swirls up around us as we go about this business of living in the world. Eisenberg calls on us to develop a holistic view of communication and identity that might lead us to a life of "interconnectivity," where we all may one day live as though "the whole web of life feels like home" (p. 548). At the least, along the way toward realizing this holistic vision of the interconnectivity of all things, we researchers of the human condition may find ourselves seeking new ways to embrace the mystery, to follow the clues, to flow with the leadings of our memories, to live in spirit rising, to give in to the urgings of our memories, our dreams, our fantasies, our reflections, so that we may find new interpretive connections that will allow us to live and work and dream and write in interconnected ways. Goodall (1996) writes: "Put it this way: have you ever surrendered to your dreams, to your bliss, to your imagination . . .?" (p. 88).

Have you?

If you haven't, *shouldn't* you?

And then Ron Pelias (2004) steps forth and leads us: "I know my heart still has much to learn. And so I go on, trying, one day at a time, to pump, to love, and to forgive; trying to walk, whenever necessary, on broken glass; to rejoice, whenever possible, in the stitch; to carry, whenever needed, the weight of the stone" (p. 172).

Indeed.

I have written elsewhere that we ignore these urgings of the heart at our peril, that our very health depends on this quest to open our hearts to possibility (Poulos, 2002, 2006a). We know from the writings of doctors (Chopra, 2004; Siegel, 1990; Weil, 2005) and other healers (Freud, 1980; Hay, 1999; Jung, 1989; Rogers, 1995) and spiritual writers (Chodron, 2000; Hanh, 1999; Lamott, 1995; Salzberg, 1999) that a healthy life is a spirited life, a life of heart, a life of love. Isn't it horrifying, after all, that so many of us die of heart *attacks*? Isn't that a clue? Wouldn't it be better if we embraced rising spirit, allowed the pumping of the heart to infuse our consciousness and began to live in enheartened ways? Wouldn't it be better, as Jung (1989) suggests, if we paid attention to—even flowed with—our memories, dreams, and reflections instead of ignoring them?

That is what this writing is all about.

The accidental ethnographer, then, is one who, while stumbling along through this world, falls into the habit of attending to signs, to clues, to memories, dreams, and reflections. The accidental ethnographer feels the urgings of the heart, the surging energies of the spirited body, and knows that she or he is called to move with the heart's flow, to live out the promise of the mystery, to write the dreamstory, to build a life of memory morphing into story, to construct spirited meaning, to follow the rising spirit to new and treasured places. The accidental ethnographer is a spirited researcher, building interconnectivity through remembering, through dreaming, through wandering, through writing, drawing on the resources of the heart, of the mind, of memory, birthing story as a pathway to connecting the past, the present, and an imagined future.

Accidental ethnography seeks and embraces *possibility*. It is a way of engaging the world so that life opens up, the world comes alive, and the ethnographer observes, lives, breathes, and dances in that which Levinas (1969) called "infinity" and what some ethnographers, like Goodall (1996) and Eisenberg (2001), call "mystery."

In infinity, in possibility, in the mystery of the spheres, lies hope.

But the infinite is also a place where anxiety may intrude.

In the face of infinity, the accidental ethnographer becomes acutely aware of limitation, especially as it resides in the power to write this grand, mysterious world into being through story. In the face of infinity, the accidental ethnographer must stand, heartfully and courageously, and face down the anxiety. The accidental ethnographer hears a call of conscience and, quite simply, *must* answer that call (Hyde, 2001).

So . . . facing infinity requires *heart*.

Facing infinity requires *courage*.

This is why the accidental ethnographer writes: The accidental ethnographer *must* write. There is no other way out of this predicament.

Accidental ethnography is the engaged practice of living the heart's call to action.

Accidental ethnography means that we humans *must*, in our very nature as *homo narrans*, follow the urgency of emerging story (Fisher, 1987).

This is the call emerging from the springs of *this* story:

To surrender to the bliss, to flow with the imagination, to rejoice in the little discoveries and to carry the weights of the worlds we inhabit—worlds imagined and real, dreamed and written, fantasized and spoken and stumbled on.

To follow the urgings of the heart out into the forests of our imagination and there to drink of the springs of spirit rising.

To follow a trace of a trail to an unexpected place.

To open ourselves to the signs that our memories, our dreams, and our reflections are offering us, and to follow the clues life offers us to new lands of interpretation.

To fly, to fall into the river, to stumble, to tumble, to plunge face first into the spring, to yell and to cry, to laugh, to sing, to run up the golden hillside . . . to go wherever the moment takes us, chasing possibility, always chasing possibility.

To be, whenever and wherever possible, an accidental ethnographer—one who embraces and lives out the promise of the little memory-eruptions, the dreamstories, and the imaginative world-building moments that come on us, drawing us toward that mysterious, uncertain, but genuinely interconnected world of the heart that awaits us.

To stumble on a treasure, and to see it for what it is, or what it might be.

To live fully and openly, always and everywhere searching—
searching courageously, heartfully—for meaning, for connection, for
a breath of spirit rising.

Come along, won't you?

It is time.

Exercises

Whether you are just beginning to practice ethnography, or looking to
enhance your ethnographic practice, it is my hope that the exercises
at the end of each chapter will refresh and invigorate your writing.
It is not my intent to provide some sort of lock-step approach to
writing accidental ethnography, but rather to nudge you, to suggest
possibilities, and to open doorways. Of course, writing a manual
for practicing accidental ethnography would be silly, as what I am
advocating is *stumbling into possibilities*. Accidental ethnography
is, well, grounded in fortunate accidents of everyday life. But I do
believe you can work to attune yourself (or at least be ready or
available) to the openings that may occur during your ethnographic
life. Or, at least, you can work to be more mindful of the possibility of
such openings. I hope you can make good use of these exercises.

Writing Exercise 1: Field Notes for
Accidental Ethnography

At the 2004 convention of the National Communication Association,
I was asked by Bob Krizek to co-facilitate a pre-conference workshop
on writing ethnographic field notes. Our task was relatively
straightforward: to lay out the various "methods" of observation
that we employ as we practice our craft and to lead groups around
to various places in Chicago to practice taking field notes. At the end
of the day, we would come back to the conference hotel to reflect
collectively on what we had just experienced.

Having been trained in a naturalistic style of field ethnography,
I was certainly competent to take on this task. And, of course, as an
emerging scholar, I was flattered to be asked to share my "methods."
So I readily accepted the challenge. Yet, as I began to craft what
I wanted to say about methods of taking field notes, I began to realize
I needed to articulate a key feature of accidental ethnography: It is not

a method, nor is it particularly "methodological," at least as we have come in the field of communication studies to think and talk about those things. If anything, it is somewhat *anti-method*.

Or, maybe it is *pre-method*.

But I do have a way of approaching this task that you might find helpful. I hope you will NOT think of this as an absolute way of approaching the crafting of ethnography but rather a matrix of options, designed to help you become attuned to your world. These practices may help you become available to the signs, whispers, and openings (accidental and otherwise) that might show up in your life. Cultivating the kind of attention called for here may help you enhance your ethnographic practice.

Because I believe we ethnographers are studying humans-in-culture, I have come to understand my way of doing ethnography as the practice of a reflexive but culturally situated human engaging with other humans within a bounded space at a particular time. Swirling around me in this complex life-world are culturally driven and sometimes culturally bound identities, ideologies, traditions, rituals, symbols, meanings, premises, rules, practices, moments of encounter, and so on. It is my job, as ethnographer, first to *notice*, then to *record* or *document*, and then to *interpret the meanings* of these things. I seek to come away with a richer understanding of the cultural and communicative forces at play within the particular space-time nexus I have chosen to enter. I see the field notebook as a starting place and a resource book for the richer reflections and permutations that will occur and emerge as I convert the notes into texts of various sorts.

In the end, I seek to construct a compelling story of the lives of characters in space and time.

In some sense (perhaps many senses), it is an artifice (a conceit?) of the researcher that somehow he or she is entering alien territory and becoming a studied observer of a new or "foreign" cultural space. What we are really doing in ethnography is paying attention to the goings-on of everyday life in a hyper-reflexive, focused way. I see the process of my fieldwork as unfolding in six key phases:

1. Entry: On entering the site, or space, of observation, I spend a few minutes "centering." I try to breathe deeply, first focusing on gaining comfort and a sense of calm perspective. I work to not be caught up in what's going on . . . yet. As I want to seek clarity and balance in my observation, I seek first to simply be at rest before I move into action. I want to become mindful, *then* observe. Once I feel centered, I start to take in what's around me.

2. Reaching Out/Reaching In:
   a. Thick description of the site: I start with a detailed description of the space or place, the people and their actions, and so on; my focus is on the world "out there" beyond me, but I am always and everywhere intrigued by the questions: Who and where are *we* in (this) space and (this) time? Here, I work toward coming to understand how space and time and relationships *here and now* shape and reflect the human stories of those present. I strive to notice *everything*, while knowing that there is bound to be something I'll miss.
   b. Thick description of my own emotional responses to being in the site: Where am *I* in all this? What do I bring to this place/event/culture? What is my heart telling me? What emotional and other affective responses do I feel? What is the relation between my experience and this site? Who am I *here*? How do I *feel*?
3. (Balancing) observation and participation: As I become a mover and participant within the space or site, I strive to observe human life with clarity and focus, bringing my life-experience into play in the process of observation. I do try very hard to be an ultra-absorbent, new, improved sponge. I focus and absorb. So I tend to write down everything I see, hear, smell, taste, touch, and intuit. I especially write down everything I hear or overhear, what people say and do, how people move about the space, any encounters I observe or experience. I write my observations in one hand (e.g., cursive), then my (autoethnographic) reflections, feelings, and responses in another (e.g., print). Or I alternate pages.
4. Encounter-as-dialogue: "Genuine conversation"—following Gadamer, rather than "interviewing." I engage in *conversation*. This is conversation we "fall into," rather than "conduct." As I become a participant at the site, I fall into conversation as a natural by-product of being located among humans at a particular time and place. I drop the notebook here, but pick it back up immediately afterward to record what just happened.
5. Reflection-as-response: From time to time, I "retreat" from participation and actively reflect on the lived experience of observation, dialogue, and action. What is going on here? Here I offer questions, variations, possibilities, interpretations, feelings, openings to new ways of seeing/experiencing the site/culture/space.
6. Storying praxis: Here is where I convert the field experience and the field notes/data into compelling stories of people-in-action. This is the magical, alchemical moment of ethnographic praxis. At some point, I just cast aside all my notes and write. They were for preparation anyway. I sit down and I write from what I know, write from the heart, write what comes. This is the organic moment where all I know—now deeply embodied knowing—comes forth into being in a new way.

Clearly, in doing all this, I make choices and when I choose to focus on one thing, I am bound to miss something else. I think the trade-off here is that I get a richer understanding of what captures my attention. So I'm making sense of my own (admittedly limited) experience *in situ*, but I also take time, in the reflection-as-response phase, to reflect on what I may have missed, left out, overlooked, etc.

I strive, in doing field notes, to capture EVERYTHING I can.

Students often ask me, "What do we write about?"

My response: "Everything. All of it. Write the details, write what you see, hear, smell, taste, feel. Write your thoughts, and their conversations. Write it all down."

At the outset this all seems very raw, and I believe that it should. It *is* raw, and open, and messy. Like the world you are experiencing. That's OK, I think, because the work of converting the notes into various written texts is the work of alchemy, of finding the "gold" in the many moments of unfolding that are out there in that messy world.

So, as I sat down to consider what I would present at the pre-conference on field notes, I naturally began by writing field notes about the experience of preparing for talking about field notes. What follows are those notes, verbatim as I wrote them in my field notebook. I share them because I think they can be helpful, especially to those of you who are just starting out on this journey into ethnographic writing. You will notice immediately that they are written in a "stream of consciousness" style. That is simply because this is how my field notes often take shape—following the flow of my thoughts as they come. I also share them because they begin to hint at what I think is the beginning place of accidental ethnography. I'll have more to say on that in a moment.

Some Field Notes on Field Notes

He was asked to speak about field notes at an ethnography conference on field notes, which made him wonder what it was about field notes that was so special that it merited a conference that lasted a whole day but he was glad they would be *doing* field notes more than *talking about them* since field notes seemed to him to be a doing thing rather than a talking about it thing, which led him to wonder why they had asked him since he was sort of an accidental ethnographer anyway, at least the way he learned to do ethnography was by accident because it was the only thing to do in the circumstances that presented themselves, which is to say he stumbled into research sites quite by accident and because of circumstances the way he learned to do field notes was on the sly since his first ethnographic writing was about a place that wasn't really a place at all though it was *in* a place but it wasn't a *site* as much as a *happening* called the *shvitz*, a wet drippy sauna with lots of soap and water where elderly Jewish men went to hang out and kibitz, which was of course no place to take field notes so he found himself slipping out to the locker room grabbing his notebook and writing furiously hoping no one would see but writing notes so he could remember the amazing conversations he was hearing and he wrote them down and they saw him writing notes but acted like they didn't and much of what he wrote in those note-taking moments was cut out of the final version of the article but it was all really good stuff even though at least the conversations were often most likely a performance for him since the observed in this world *might be* as reflexive as the observers. And as all this unfolded, the *shvitzers* struck up conversations that wandered all around and made him think of how important it is to be present at your site and at the same time to write as much as possible so nothing is lost to the mists of slipping memory. And then he was startled back into the present, and these reflections made him immediately think maybe these ethnographers at this conference were throwing a *happening* billed as a *conference* on field notes because field notes like ordinary conversations can become so ordinary as an activity that the process is taken for granted, which means it's probably extraordinary somehow.

As he arrived at the place where the conference was to be held he wondered again how he happened to get into this position but he remembered the email asking him and he was a little flattered until he figured out quickly that they had probably asked Dr. Bud, who had said no why don't you ask Chris which was ironic because what Chris had to say about field notes was probably in one of Dr. Goodall's books, which led him to wonder if the people who would be at the happening had read Dr. Goodall's books, especially the "little red bible." Maybe they had, maybe they hadn't, but maybe they had read something by Art Bochner or Carolyn Ellis or Nick Trujillo or Sarah Amira de la Garza, which led him to think of poets like ee cummings and T.S. Eliot and William Blake and Maya Angelou or a guy named Michael somebody from North Carolina who writes poetry about things like August in the South with words and images so vivid that you feel you are there in August even when you're not, and he didn't know why but he liked poetry and read it whenever he could and then he wondered if maybe these ethnographers had read other ethnographers like Robin Clair or Bob Krizek or John Van Maanen or maybe Lisa Tillman-Healy or Rob Drew or Lyall Crawford but

then he wondered if they had read novelists like Walker Percy or
Graham Greene or William Faulkner or maybe Kafka or even Michael
Parker who doesn't talk very much but sure has an ear for talk, sure
can write dialogue like it sounds in real life. Or what about all the
great philosophers from Plato to Levinas to Buber to Augustine to
Kierkegaard to Tillich all of whom were in love with language and
that led him to think of Mark Twain and Albert Camus and Jean-Paul
Sartre and Kurt Vonnegut but what about those ethnographers like
Gerry Philipsen or Clifford Geertz (probably they had read Geertz) and
Dell Hymes and then he wondered what about Ron Pelias's new book,
which is a really good book with many gems but he kept coming back
to Walker Percy and was thinking of the mystery of the search and in
this case the search for what he would say when it came his turn to talk
and he damn sure hoped he would say something intelligible about
such a personal ethereal nonlinear anti-procedural organic process that
defies gravity and rules and intelligibility because it is so dynamic and
open and mysterious and ambiguous and responsive and what could
he say but that it's a part of his organic writing process, which he has
never planned and only barely understands even though he does it
every day because his fingers make him.

Of course, all that did was distract him into thinking about
whether any of them had read anything *he* had written, which
made him wonder if they had liked it or if *like* is the right word for
intensely personal writing about stuff that matters but then of course
he worried that after all that work and sweat and blood and tears
maybe nobody reads it and maybe we all just pretend to read each
other's stuff because we are so busy trying to write ours and dying
to get tenure that we run out of steam for reading even though we
know that we won't be able to write worth a damn if we don't read
good stuff, which made him wonder whether we might have a
conference on *reading* ethnography someday but then maybe it's been
done after all there was a panel on that subject a couple of years back
and Bud was there and he was there and Ron Pelias was there and
John Warren and Denise Menchaca and others and anyway the topic
pressing in on him now was part of *writing* ethnography and so he
had to figure out something to say about field notes that would make
sense and that was worth hearing so here goes.

Which led him back to Dr. Bud and made him wonder what Bud
had said about field notes and he figured that since Bud had fingered
him for this assignment that maybe turnabout was fair play so he

looked in the little red bible for clues and even found a few but of
course he knew that everyone in his audience had read Bud's book
or should have or surely would soon so instead of repeating that he
kept thinking about Walker Percy so he looked there for more clues
and he came up with this, knowing that what his teachers taught him
was here somewhere, and knowing especially what his teacher of
qualitative methods in graduate school would say to every question
raised in class about how to do something: "*It depends. . .*"

And first, he thought he might share some framing ideas by Walker
Percy who wrote a book called *The Moviegoer* which everyone on Earth
should read and especially ethnographers because it's a good story
about a conflicted character who is on a search and who happens to be
a good keen observer with quirky ideas about what it means to wander
about the world living a mystery and who struggles to communicate
but is always hoping to find clues that will help him to understand or
at least go on. And, anyway a good story about a conflicted character
or characters is better than anything he could think of. So, to quote for a
moment, here is what Percy (1960) has to say about the *search*:

> This morning when I got up, I dressed as usual and began as usual to
> put my belongings into my pockets: wallet, notebook (for writing down
> occasional thoughts), pencil, keys, handkerchief, pocket slide rule (for
> calculating percentage returns on principal). They looked both unfamiliar
> and at the same time full of clues. I stood in the center of the room and
> gazed at the little pile, sighting through a hole made by thumb and
> forefinger. What was unfamiliar about them was that I could see them.
> They might have belonged to someone else. A man can look at this little
> pile on his bureau for thirty years and never once see it. It is as invisible as
> his own hand. Once I saw it, however, the search became possible. . .
>
> What is the nature of the search, you ask.
>
> Really it is very simple, at least for a fellow like me; so simple that it is
> easily overlooked.
>
> The search is what anyone would undertake if he were not sunk in
> the everydayness of his own life. This morning, for example, I felt
> as if I had come to myself on a strange island. And what does such a
> castaway do? Why, he pokes around the neighborhood and he doesn't
> miss a trick.
>
> To become aware of the possibility of the search is to be onto
> something. Not to be onto something is to be in despair. (pp. 11–13)

And so, Percy, through the words of Binx Bolling, teaches us to notice that which so often goes unnoticed, those ordinary things and events and moments in life that could otherwise pass by under a cloud of ordinariness but which, if we see them, may indeed turn out to be remarkable. His search is a search for the extraordinary by looking deeply and directly into the ordinary. Stare it in the eye. Sight through your thumb and forefinger. Poke around the neighborhood. *That*, it seems to me, is an important field note strategy.

Later, Percy (1960) writes about various methodological quirks he has developed while on his search, including two primary semi-accidental processes known as repetitions and rotations. A *repetition* "is the re-enactment of past experience toward the end of isolating the time segment which has lapsed in order that it, the lapsed time, can be savored of itself and without the usual adulteration of events that clog time like peanuts in brittle" (pp. 79–80). In other words, after having done something, wait a while and then go back out there and do it again and see if your experience, once repeated, has a different flavor or texture to it. Or not. Either way, focus your attention on the time in between and see if the experience of time passing in between events has changed you. Or the place. Or the event. Or the site. Or the experience. Or someone else. Or something else. Search for clues that it has. Or hasn't. *That*, it seems to me, is an important field note strategy . . .

A *rotation*, on the other hand, is "the experiencing of the new beyond the expectation of the experiencing of the new. For example, taking one's first trip to Taxco would not be a rotation, or no more than a very ordinary rotation; but getting lost on the way and discovering a hidden valley would be" (Percy, 1960, p. 144). Again, a vital strategy for writing field notes. Take a rotation. Get lost. Go somewhere by accident. Happen upon a site. Get lost. Open yourself to discovering a hidden valley. Or a new alley. Or two. Or three. *Another* important field note strategy?

Along the way, Binx speaks of a phenomenon he calls *certification*. Certification of a place or a happening or a site occurs when one recognizes the place in a representation of that place. Seeing your neighborhood in a movie *certifies* the place as a place that is "Somewhere and not Anywhere" (Percy, 1960, p. 63). Certification, in the context of writing, would be the act of creating a world on paper in such a way that those who read it will recognize their own world in what they read. Thus, that world will be *certified*. In your field notes, you strive toward a rendering of people-place-event that will, in the end, become certifiably powerful. *Another* important field note strategy?

So, somehow, this reading and this writing and this circumstance we are in now takes us back to the idea of a *method* for field notes, which as Gadamer and others have pointed out, may be a fool's errand because it's knotty at best and a rather strange idea anyway, given that we are all so different, to try to claim that any *method* that works for one of us may work for others. So, remember, as you hear these ideas, that it all *depends*.

Everything depends. It depends anyway on the circumstances and the space and the time and probably on the smells and the sounds and the sights and the tastes and the feel of the place and the people, and most of all on you the writer of the notes and your own experiences that led you here in the first place and made you who you are today in this place at this time as a person who writes because you have to and so write notes to make sense and to seek meaning and to maybe kid yourself into thinking you understand but it's OK if you do or you don't understand because it's all a great mystery anyway and it's all a wandering conversation, and that's the best part.

But here, he said, is what I do, or at least what I think I do. Be a sponge. Not exactly SpongeBob, who is none too bright, but who is spontaneous in a way and that is good but most of all be *absorbent* in an open, smart way. Cultivate a beginner's mind. Be like a little kid. Go to a playground and watch little kids for a while. Little kids are sponges. Do that. Absorb your environment. That's what play is—being where you are, in the moment, absorbed and absorbing. So play. Play deeply. Be where you are. Hear, taste, touch, smell, see—as deeply as you can. Live your life-moments like you are eating the world's best cheesecake, which you are.

Take up a search. Poke around the neighborhood. Look deeply into the ordinary, searching for clues to the extraordinary. Know it's all a mystery, and embrace that. Embrace the search knowing that the end of the search may just be a new path to a new mystery—a rotation, not a conclusion. Anyway, you are not seeking answers but openings to possibility. Know that. Do that.

Live! The life of an ethnographer is different from that of any other kind of researcher. You don't put on your ethnographer hat when you get to the office and take it off when you get home. Ethnography is a full-time job description—24/7 as they say. So LIVE! Participate in your world. Fully. Hear, taste, touch, smell, see—and talk. Tell stories. Live an ethnographic life!

Be Forrest Gump. Tell stories even to people who don't want to hear them. Travel through your world with innocence and openness. Try for a day to be a little less *smart* than you are, and instead be *open* to the stories that are hovering in the air, waiting to be told. *Search* for stories, and listen to them. Listen to stories told by people, even people you don't like or whose stories you don't want to hear. Listen. Attune. Engage.

Like Bud Goodall (1994, 1996, 2006a, 2006b), seek clues that will help you engage the mystery and maybe even understand a little slice of it. Look for signs and symbols. Look for intersections. Look at them carefully. Read them symbolically. Search for turning points, bends, curves, forks in the road. If you see a fork in the road, take it. Keep searching.

Carry a field notebook with you, wherever you go. Write what you see, feel, taste, touch, hear, smell, and intuit, wherever you are whenever you are there. Or here. These are field notes. Write what comes as it comes to you in the "field," which is, after all, just another word for your life. There are no rules here, but I use field notes to remember, to render, to deliver, to help me navigate, to make my mysterious inner and outer worlds a little more concrete and to *detail* it, but also to help stir the mystery a little, if only to help stir the mystery that is the life of my eventual reader. Of course, sometimes, especially when dealing with strange phenomena like memories and dreams and secrets, I strive to make it understandable, or at least readable, though not exactly ordinary.

Listen carefully for conversations and write them down, especially good conversations, which are so cool and so hard to remember and so very hard to write so that they sound natural if you have to reconstruct them, so capture them as they come.

Write! Write the details. Write it down. All of it. Maybe something you write down will be worth something later even if you don't think so now. And know that you will very likely miss something important anyway. Don't we all?

Then: Read your notes and reread them. Every day. Pay attention to the *story* that is emerging.

Write. Every day. Do something like this, which is what I do: Get up, plug in the coffee, and walk to your computer before you are awake. Write what comes out. Let your fingers do the talking. A lot of good writers say they have writing rituals. Come up with one. Make it so. Write. Write some more. Absorb. Absorb some more. Go back to your place or your research site or just be there or here or wherever you are, wherever that is, and talk to more people, listen some more, read some more signs and symbols and clues, taste the air and smell the food and breathe it all in, and write some more notes. Hang out and write some more notes.

Evoke. Write life into story. Provoke. Write passion into being. Stoke. Write fire into life. Write like you care, because you do, and write so others who read it will care. Because they do. Or should. And, anyway, even if they don't read, which they should, write it so that you think they would dig it if they could find the time to read it. You have to write it that way anyway. So do. Write with *heart*, which, as Ron Pelias (2004) puts it, is a part of you that should, at least, pump, love, and forgive.

Don't choke. Even if you don't feel like writing, even if you think you can't write, or have nothing to say, write. Write about *that* if you have to. But write. You don't have to write every day. Just the days you plan to breathe.

Know that good writing is really good editing. Take your field notes home, read them, chew them up and spit them out, read them again and rewrite them again and again. Turn them into something beautiful. Attend to the story that is emerging. Let your fingers do the talking.

Finally, *imagine*. Build the mystery. Consider the phenomenologists' (Hyde, 2001; Levinas, 1969, 1981; Merleau-Ponty, 1962) advice, which is to imagine the world were different from the one you are hearing, smelling, tasting, touching, seeing, or even intuiting. Imagine. What if the pile of stuff on your dresser really is a site filled with extraordinary clues? What if your site, your neighborhood, or your accidental alley, your wrong turn, was full of clues?

Imagine *that*.

Of course, you'll eventually want to imagine something like a final product (a book or an article or a paper) coming from all this. So there are probably those of you who will want to be more systematic about it all, at least at some point. So I offer this: maybe you can be. But first, try to let go of systems and outlines and order and just fall into the writing.

Perhaps something beautiful will come of it.

Writing Exercise 2: The Search

Locate yourself in a familiar place—a comfortable room in your house, your office, somewhere you have spent a lot of time. Sit comfortably. Try to relax. A little breathing might help here. Look around your environment, and *notice* its familiarity. Gaze at every corner, every object, every nook, every line, every color. Listen carefully—are there little familiar creaks and shiftings and pops around you? Now sniff the air. What smells—old and new, musty and clean—are available? Now, stand up and walk around the room, touching things. Notice the textures, the relative hardness and softness of various surfaces, the warmth and smoothness and old familiar coolness of walls and windows and pieces of furniture. Then, taste the air. Chew it.

Now, shift your attention. Do you notice anything about this place you had not noticed before? Is there anything extraordinary about this ordinary space you are inhabiting? Then: Step outside, and repeat the above exercise. Next, take the time to walk around. Poke around your neighborhood. What do you notice? Do you notice anything that you had never noticed before? What have you, until now, taken for granted about this place? What have you failed to notice until now? Is there anything remarkable about this place?

Finally, step back into your home or your office and sit down to write about the experience. Here, you will want to begin working at careful *description* of the places you inhabit regularly. What have you seen, heard, smelled, touched, tasted? Your goal, as a writer, is to draw your reader into your world. How would you evoke its presence, its texture, its flavor, to someone who had never visited it?

Queries

1. What was the experience of going through these exercises like for you? Did you have any "Aha!" moments during any of them?
2. What rituals do you practice in association with your writing? How do you orient yourself to the writing process? What "gems" can you share with others about what works (or doesn't work) for you?
3. How do you engage in fieldwork? What can you share with your colleagues about your process of composing field notes? Of turning field notes into stories? As you begin to "poke around" your home, your

neighborhood, your world, what have you begun to notice, and how might these awarenesses become part of your writing journey?

4. Have you had any "accidental epiphanies" or other moments where a sight or sound or smell or anything triggered a thought, a memory, or a pathway for your writing? What have you made of these moments in your ethnographic life-writing? Write a story about one of these.

Chapter Three

Dreaming Autoethnography

In the end, the only events in my life worth telling are those where the imperishable world erupted into this transitory one.

—C. G. Jung, *Memories, Dreams, Reflections*

Dreamworlds

The dream has fallen on hard times. Especially in the academy. Skepticism abounds. We don't talk much about the meaning of dreams these days. We think of them as mere chemical reactions, or the productions of REM sleep or, at best, random indecipherable images and story pieces that we shake off as we sip our morning coffee. We dismiss our dreams with a wry grin or a puzzled frown or even a fearful shudder. Then we move on.

But in the ancient world, dreams were often interpreted as messages from the gods. Hermes, the thief-trickster-messenger of Homer's world—a god who first shows up on the scene as a *child* (a way of thinking about a god that, to my way of thinking, invokes all the openness and spontaneity and innocence we need in our gods)—was an interpreter of signs, a purveyor of dreams and images and flashes of insight (Brown, 1947; Jung & Kerényi, 1949). In the world of Hermes, these were matters of the greatest import; they were the pathways between the ordinary and the divine, between life and death, between the unconscious and the conscious, between immanence and transcendence, between ennui and ecstasy. I want to suggest that we who study and write about the human social condition ought to take our dreams more seriously. In this chapter, I move from the world of story to the world of dreams and back again, making a storied case for the inclusion of dreaming into the methodological repertoire of the accidental ethnographer. I dream my way into writing and find, along the way, all sorts of signs, clues, and pathways to follow. I offer suggestions for the integration of the dream/story into the larger storied life of the (accidental) (auto)ethnographer. And, following the suggestions of my own dreams, I begin to center the praxis of accidental ethnography within the context of an unfolding family story of pain and loss, of secrecy and silence, and of the potential for the dream/story to bring light to this project.

Breakthroughs and Openings: Dreaming the Sacred

I wake, shivering, in the dark. A bead of sweat trickles down my forehead, burns a little as it hits my eye. Tomorrow—no, wait, *today*—is my birthday. It's not really a happy thought. It's getting harder to sleep. These days, I rarely make it through the night. But I'm getting used to it. And, anyway, my dreams are . . . well, I don't want to think about my dreams.

My hands are shaking. I'm weak, nauseated. I breathe heavily. How did it come to this? I get up slowly, knowing there will be no more sleep this night.

I pace the floor. I have this nagging feeling that there is something I am supposed to do, but I can't get there. What is it?

And I'm haunted by the memories—or, really, by the parts I don't remember. I know, vaguely, that I have been places, done things. Shadowy images lurk at the edges of my consciousness. A fog of uneasiness swells up as I think about how little I remember. The darkness folds up close around me. I realize that if there is a dark moment in life or a time of day when it is darkest, it must happen at 2 A.M. Always at 2 A.M. I am haunted at this hour.

Thresholds

Sometimes, what we need to make sense of the dream is a story to connect it to. It's a story we need—sometimes mine, sometimes yours, sometimes someone else's—but always a story.

And every great story involves a *crisis*.

Leo Tolstoy's short story, *The Death of Ivan Ilych*, chronicles the life of a conventional man, a judge who gets too caught up in a life of role-performance. At the end of his life, he contracts a fatal disease. While lying in bed, he reflects on his life, and for the first time he realizes that he has no real connection with people, that his life means little, and that he won't be remembered. Confronted squarely with his human failures and his impending finitude, Ilych falls into Despair.

Ivan Ilych is slapped directly in the face by the absurdity of an existence in which one is consumed by a search for the unattainable. He realizes, too late, that he has become mired deeply in the muck of toil and the quest for recognition in a world that withholds success and the approval that goes with it far more readily than offering it. Worse, he has often been a poser, a phony, a person who believes appearances and style trump depth and substance. He has certainly focused more attention on impression management than he has on developing his own virtue (Freeman, 1997). Some would say he has lived a life of bad faith (Sartre, 1958).

He was too busy engulfed in deception to note the quick passage of time and the loss of connection that were the inevitable outcome of his overactive impression management. In the end, overwhelmed by his own falseness, he is bereft (Freeman, 1997). And now his life has been cut off! Looking back, it seems he has lived only for a brief day, rather than a life. A life cut off: How to make sense of *that*?

So, at the end of this day called a life, Ilych confronts his own failure. He knows he has been on a fool's errand, that the meaning he sought in the dream of success was an illusion. At the end of this day called a life, he meets a horrible, painful, meaningless, pointless end.

Finally, on the verge of being taken by death, he finds he cannot sleep. On his deathbed, Ilych finds himself stone cold awake, stiff as a stick. And he discovers, in his agony, that he cannot stop screaming! In his final days, he suddenly realizes that he no longer has choice. He is not free; he will die: "From that moment the screaming began that continued for three days, and was so terrible that one could not hear it through two closed doors without horror . . . he realized that he was lost, that there was no return, that the end had come, the very end, and his doubts were still unsolved and remained doubts" (Tolstoy, 2003, p. 154).

Have you ever wondered: Am I to be pulled into doubt, overcome, dragged into an untimely grave? Will I lose my breath inside the black hole of Anxiety? Will I literally die of Despair?

The absurdity of our human finitude offers us a profound moment of choice. Confronted by the onslaught of time-bound existence, on the verge of Despair, one is *called out* into the open.

Exposed.

Vulnerable.

This is a moment of great peril.

As Hamlet puts it:

> To be, or not to be: That is the question. Whether 'tis nobler in the mind to suffer the slings and arrows of outrageous fortune, or to take arms against a sea of troubles, and by opposing end them? To die: to sleep; no more; and by a sleep to say we end the heartache and the thousand natural shocks that flesh is enemy to, 'tis a consummation to be wish'd. To die, to sleep; to sleep: perchance to dream: ay, there's the rub; For in that sleep of death what dreams may come, when we have shuffled off this mortal coil, must give us pause. (Shakespeare, 2003, *Hamlet*, Act 3, scene 1)

In the end, Ilych faces Hamlet's question, directly: To be or not to be? On his final day, his consciousness fogged by pain, his eyes squeezed shut in agony, Ilych has a vision.

Or is it a dream?

Or is it "real"?

In his dream-vision-life, at his moment on the threshold, in that liminal space between waking and sleep, between life and death, his young son visits him, holds his hand, looks him in the eye, cries a little. And Ilych's Despair breaks in a moment of Hope, brought to the threshold by the presence of this significant Other, this small child who loves him. Then, before he can form a response, Ilych expires, falling forever into that dream. He shuffles off his mortal coil.

But, in the storied dream-presence of the child, we have a clue. The child opened up a place of possibility. The child draws our attention to the threshold of possibility. The child, standing at the threshold, ushers Ilych into a new world.

Thin Places

In Celtic lore, the world has "thin places"[1] (Gome, 1996), where one might experience a disruption in the ordinary temporal-spatial plane we inhabit. These thin places may provide an entry point, a sort of portal to another realm, a realm of spirit. Going to these places can release us from the everyday world and open us up to a new world of possibility.

Sometimes, the story goes, we experience a moment of sacred opening, a breakthrough from the mundane world to the spirit world. These moments often occur in sacred places—cathedrals and mountaintops, lakes and shrines, caves and crypts—the famously thin places of this world. A visit to Stonehenge or to Charlemagne's grave can have this effect.

Religious historian Mircea Eliade (1957) called the experience of a thin place a *hierophany*. A hierophany is a manifestation of the sacred, a moment in which one *knows* (intuitively) that something special, something powerful, is available to experience. The boundaries of ordinary space and time disappear, and we move into a sacred spirit-realm, a realm of space-time where the ordinary, everyday rules of embodied life are suspended, if only for a moment. Our ways of thinking—and being and moving and knowing—to which we have grown accustomed simply do not apply.

We enter a liminal space-time (McLaren, 1988; Turner, 1969).

We are betwixt and between.

If we are lucky, hierophany leads to epiphany. Ivan Ilych comes to a thin place as he finally confronts his death. In that moment, as he sees his child—sees him for who he truly is, that next possibility— Ilych has the epiphany that allows him to cross the threshold. As we come on some new awareness—as the "Aha!" seizes us—we may well move into a deep knowing wherein the heart opens up to new, spirited possibility as it transcends the ordinary boundaries of this everyday world.

Once in a while, these experiences just come on us, as though we have wandered into some thin place in ourselves, unaware. In my own life, it is these apparently random experiences of the thin places that fascinate me. It is as if, instead of seeking the experience of the sacred, I find it breaks in on me.

Perhaps the thin places are really places within us.

Perhaps we wander into the thin places when we are ready.

Perhaps, if we are ready, epiphany will wash over us like a sudden rain shower.

I find myself stumbling into the thin places of this world with surprise and awe and a rising spirit. The story that unfolds here is about those special eruptive moments in the thin places of life.

Secret Places

I have this strange recurring dream—a dream of mystery, of shadows and secrets, of leaks, and, in the end, of deluge. In my dream, my family has just moved into a large house with a complex, multi-tiered roof—a roof of so many angles and gables that I am both fascinated and frustrated when I look at it. The roof appears to buckle in places, but it is so high and complicated that it seems to move around, fading and weaving, evading my attempts to make sense of it.

Inside the house is a forgotten room, one that appears to have never been used. The room is off in an odd corner of the house, one that you don't naturally go to very often. Perhaps it is easy to see why the room was ignored or forgotten, as it doesn't seem to have a function. The unfurnished space is rectangular; the floor is sunken about a foot below the level of the other rooms, and the carpet is that older sculpted stuff—a 1970s style, greenish and damp. For some reason, in the dream, this room bothers me. It is as if the room, perhaps intended to be some sort of extra den or maybe a reading room, was simply built to support one of the complicated roof structures. And yet, it seems to me, it is both calling out to be used and, at the same time, difficult to locate or put to use.

In the end, I can never think of a use for it. But I am drawn, from time to time, to locate it and ponder its possible uses.

Perhaps it is something besides everyday use that draws me here. In a shadowy alcove in the wall on the far corner of the room is a door to a closet. The closet seems to hold a secret—one I desperately want to discover. But the door is locked.

There is no key.

At some point in the dream, I go to bed, and immediately begin dreaming of my childhood. But my dreams are interrupted. I wake to the sound of running water, *inside* my new house. At first it is just a little drip, as though someone just didn't turn the faucet tight enough. But the sound grows, until it sounds like a small stream is running through my house. I get up to investigate, and inevitably—once again—I'm drawn to the forgotten room.

I see the source of the water there, but before I can discover the meaning or the import of this, I become aware of the sound of a torrential rainstorm pounding the odd roof of my new home. At that moment, the closet door flies open, and I fly awake, stunned and overwhelmed by the deluge of secrets that floods my consciousness.

I get up, stumble into the kitchen, plug in the coffee. I move to my computer, drawn to write.

My writing weaves about, buckling, wavering, evading me. But I know I must write. At the thin place between dreaming and writing, I enter my day.

And gradually, I find myself wandering into a story. It is a story of a young man, a seeker, who is looking about for some purpose, some way to put himself to good use.

Like the forgotten room, he is difficult to pin down.

He is haunted by his dreams.

He is haunted by his memories.

He is haunted by secrets.

Most days, he gets up, stumbles into the world, and just tries to make sense of it all.

Most days, he is simply lost in wonder, not at all sure how to make sense of his life, his world, his search.

What is he to do?

He is on a search; that is all he knows.

What does he seek?

He doesn't really know what he is looking for, but he does know that he feels best when he is in-between—at the thin cool moments just before dawn, in the magic hour just before twilight, at that moment just before the movie begins, or in that lull between words in a conversation. In these moments, he finds comfort. In these moments, he finds possibility.

Sometimes, he likes to go to a baseball game, entering the stadium in the ninth inning. He feels at home toward the end of a ballgame.

One day, he steps out of his house, on his way to a ballgame. Before he gets to his car, the sky opens up and washes the world clean with a torrential rain. He stands at the curb, looking up, filled with wonder, letting the rain wash over him, making him clean, clearing his mind and his heart. And he lets the rain wash his secrets away, and he watches them go rolling down the street into the storm drain.

And just as suddenly, he knows what he must do.

So he walks back into his house and begins to write his story.

The story, like the dream, is a story of between-ness, of beginnings and endings, of secrets and storms, of wonder and puzzlement, of mysteries and possibilities. The story, like the dream, ends in a deluge.

And then there is the writing . . .

The dream, and the story that it birthed, follow me around all day. By mid-afternoon, I know I must do something with it.

Communication Studies 460: Communication and Ethnography. 1:00 P.M.
I stride to the front of the room, pause, decide to tell the story of
the dream. Slowly the story unfolds, and I notice I have their full
attention.

A rare and precious moment in teaching: Every eye in the room is
fixed on me. So I ask:

"What does the dream say to you?"

A long pause. Then, finally:

"That the secrets will come out eventually," says Karen.

"Yes." I look around the room. "What secrets do you carry?"

Another long pause.

"I have many," says John.

"Yeah, me, too," adds Danielle, "But I'm not telling them."

"Why?"

"Vulnerability."

"Yes, very true. It's a vulnerable place, revealing your secrets.
But in letting the secrets out of the closet, there is freedom. In the
deluge, you are also washed clean, free of their hold on you, free of
maintaining them, free of them."

"Yes, but that's risky. You could be rejected for that."

"True enough."

Ashley: "But what are the consequences of holding them inside?"

"You might dream a lot," says Stephen.

Laughter.

"Yes," I say, "Or worse. You could be overwhelmed. The deluge
may be too intense to handle. . . . So what does my dream tell me
I should do? Just keep dreaming?"

More laughter.

Melissa: "I think you should tell us your secrets!"

"Ah . . . how about this: Maybe we should tell *each other* some
secrets," I reply.

Dark Places

I dream I am walking down a path in a forest. It is very dark in here.
Night has fallen, and the world is muted, nearly silent. There is an
occasional rustle, a snapping twig, a light scurrying sound, a thin
breeze tickling a pine needle. But, except for these faint rustlings
and my own heavy footsteps, mostly it is silent. The air is thick, my

breathing short. I do not know where I am going, only that I must go. I blink and squint, as the path grows faint, then seems to branch in several directions.

Which way? I stand still, at a loss, not knowing what to do or where I am going. I search for a sign.

Suddenly, I feel something—a presence—just behind me. As I turn, something very large and very much alive, breathing hotly, knocks me to the ground, its full weight landing on my chest. My breath is gone in an instant, and everything goes dark.

When I come to, I am lying in a clearing in the forest. A full moon rises above the edge of the trees, shedding light on the ground about me. In the center of the clearing a small campfire flickers. The ground about me is bare, and I am lying on my back, naked. My hands and feet are tied to pegs sticking out of the ground. I cannot move.

All about me I hear people whispering. I cannot hear what they are saying and I cannot see their faces. They sit in a circle, just outside the ring of light created by the fire and the moon. Their faces are veiled in shadow.

I cannot hear what they are saying but somehow I know they are talking about me. I strain to hear, and occasionally a word slips through, hits my ears, makes sense.

"Test," whispers one.

"Broken," says another.

"Just wounded," replies a third.

I try to call out to them, but my voice won't come.

"Help," I cry silently.

And suddenly, I find I am overcome by deep sadness, by a grief the likes of which I have never experienced in waking life. A sob breaks like a wave up through my heart, flows into my lungs and gasping, breaking, retching, heaves up into my throat. A long, low wail finally escapes my lips. And then the pain, pain like I've never felt, pain so intense I do not know if I can survive, roars up through my body.

I *am* pain!

I want to scream, but I cannot. I want to sob, but I cannot breathe. I am pain. . .

Then, suddenly, standing over me is a warrior. I cannot see his face, but I do see the spear in his hand. With a sudden jerk, he raises the spear over my chest, and jams it full force, into my heart.

Oh, the pain!

I open my mouth to scream, but instead the world becomes all blinding white light. I want to scream, "NO! WAIT!" But I am so taken by the light that my scream falls short, and what comes instead is "Oh, I see."

I sit bolt upright in bed, knowing the secret of the spear.

One day, many weeks later, I sit down to write, and a story just seems to come upon me, out of nowhere.

That's what stories seem to do.

The spear holds a secret. It is a secret I must come to know if I am to move beyond the spear, heal the hole in my heart.

I must move beyond the life of the spear.

What stories does the spear have to tell?

The spear has pierced many chests, dropped many warriors in their tracks.

What can the spear teach us?

In the story, I am sitting in a room surrounded by people I know. My parents are there. My siblings and my children are there. My wife Sue is sitting next to me. Many of my neighbors, from various locations throughout my life, are there. My friends from childhood, from high school and college, from my work life, from yesterday and today . . . all are there.

We sit around a large, round wooden table. In the center of the table is the spear. We are telling stories—stories of the times we have shared, stories of the good and the bad and the in-between, stories of our rich and varied lives.

There is laughter, and tears, and rapt attention as the many stories unfold.

Then, suddenly, the spear draws our attention, and we fall silent. A strong voice from across the room, speaking directly to me: "This was the spear that took you down. Did you notice? It is your *own* spear. Why did you feel the need to wield it?"

"I do not know what you are talking about."

"I think you do. You have defended yourself. You have spoken strongly and forcefully and passionately. You have scarcely considered others as you have stormed through your life. And then the spear was turned on you. Tell us about *that*."

"I still don't know what you are talking about."

"Oh, come on."

And all the people around the table chime in: "Yes, do. Come on. Tell us. What is the meaning of the spear? What did you see when the spear hit its mark?"

I hesitate. Then: "O.K. Wounded. I was wounded. I just remember that I always felt like the world was unsafe, like people might jump you. Once, when I was about thirteen, I was standing at my locker at school. This guy named Rusty came up behind me, kidney punched me. I turned, and he dropped me with a fist to my jaw. Then he stood over me, laughing. It was all so random. I didn't understand why he didn't like me. His friends were all there, laughing. I never knew why they did that. But I never again wanted to expose myself. So I carried the spear—*the spear of words*—the spear that would protect me from danger."

"Right. Fine. We've all been through our own little hells. But what did you see in the dream? What was the bright light?"

"Look. I don't need the spear any more. The life of the spear has run its course. It is no longer useful."

"And?"

"The light was the light of connection. No need for defense. Just connection."

"Yes, but what did you see?"

"What I saw was all of you . . . here."

At the end of this story, I remember the dream that started it.

Responsive Places

Communication Studies 305: Persuasion in Western Culture. 2:00 P.M. Today's agenda is the power of story. We sit in a circle, and begin by sharing significant stories from our lives. There are only three rules. When the storyteller speaks, we all listen. We do not interrupt. Everyone takes a turn.

My students begin to take turns, haltingly at first. As the stories begin to flow, I notice that they are gradually beginning to tell their stories *responsively*. The next story picks up on something in the previous one: "Since you told a story about your family, I will, too." And the stories just begin to flow.

It is now John's turn. He is generally a quiet young man. I have trouble reading him sometimes. He sits for awhile with his head bowed, and then says: "I'd like to tell a story about my great uncle Norman, the man who taught me how to pray *and* how to cuss."

He tells of his uncle, a man who took him to special places, a man who told him stories, a man who taught him about reverence and irreverence, and about all those places in-between. He tells us how his uncle would take him fishing, teaching him the finer points of angling and the nuanced tones and meanings of cussing—the sharper tones of a bruised shin, the softer whisperings of a cast gone astray, the thin harsh mutterings of a tangled line, the triumphant shout of a fight well won.

And then they would go to church. And later, back to fishing.

And, finally, he tells of how his uncle died a few years ago, taken by cancer. He watched his uncle slip into that thin place between this world and the next. And he says that, as that final moment approached, his uncle began to pray. And then he cussed. And then he smiled, and died with a knowing smile on his lips. As John tells this part of the story, a tear runs down his cheek. I turn to look around the room, and there are many tears on many cheeks. And a few small smiles.

And we are released into the thin place between sorrow and joy.

Edgy Places

I dream I am standing high on . . . what is it? A tower? Yes, a tower of some sort. I do not know how I got here, but it is very high, and I am very close to the edge. Below it is dark, and my eyes spin a little, losing focus. I can just make out the faint outlines of sharp rocks on the ground below—far, far below. This would not be a pleasant place to fall from.

The wind is blowing, hard. My heart is pounding, hard. I can hear water below, and the wind around me, but mostly what I hear is the pounding of my own heart. Thump-thump. Thump-thump. Thump-thump. Like a deep bass drum, its rhythmic loudness distracts me for a moment.

I sway a little, losing my balance. No! No! Don't let me fall! My arms spinning madly in the air, I—

I sit up, in bed, awake, sweat beading on my forehead.

And I know.

And I shake my head, and the knowing falls into the abyss.

I walk to my computer, sit down to write. For a long time, nothing comes. I know I must write *this* story. I am called to do this. I am to write from the heart, write deeply and vividly, write performatively, evocatively, autoethnographically, with passion.

And this: I can also be playful . . .

But my fingers hesitate over the keyboard for a long, long time.

Sometimes, when I am sitting like this, I wonder: Do I have anything left to write?

Have you ever felt wrung dry?

Wordless?

Empty?

Played out?

But I know, if I wait long enough—*with focus, intent, and determination*—a story will come. The stories always come . . .

I am standing on the edge.

Below is darkness, but above is the light. I am between the two, between darkness and light, wavering on the edge.

Will I stand?

Or will I fall?

And then I wonder: What would happen if I leap?

I raise my arms, and leap, upward and outward. I soar out over a lush green valley. I turn my eyes to gaze upward at the light . . . and I fall into a deep sleep.

Shadowy Places

"Everything with substance casts a shadow," write Connie Zweig and Jeremiah Abrams (1991, p. 3). In this case, they are speaking not just of objects in nature, but of *subjects* as well. Philosophers, writers, psychoanalysts, and poets—from Plato to Nietzsche, from Robert Louis Stevenson to Joseph Conrad to Alice Walker, from C. G. Jung to Marie-Louise von Franz, from William Blake to Robert Bly to Maya Angelou—have played with this theme. Human selves, so the theory goes, cast a sort of shadow—a shadow that lives in the unconscious world of each of us. This is the "dark side" of human being. The shadow consists of those parts or aspects of ourselves that we cannot, or sometimes will not, face—"that part of us we fail to see or know" (Johnson, 1991, p. 4), that we do not like or that is socially ugly or unacceptable.

"The shadow goes by many familiar names: the disowned self, the lower self, the dark twin or brother in bible and myth, the double, repressed self, alter ego, id" (Zweig & Abrams, 1991, p. 3). The shadow is that dismissed part of us, that part that we do not wish to acknowledge. The shadow is the "heart of darkness" that beats in each of us.

Perhaps the darkness is so dark that it scares us.

Perhaps the darkness is just too much to bear.

Whatever the case, each of us, according to Jungian theory, harbors a Mr. Hyde—a shadow self—somewhere within the skin, the cells, the consciousness of the Dr. Jekyll that is the everyday persona-ego that we show to our world.

Sometimes, that shadow descends on us, catches us off-guard. And, for a moment, or for many years, it can grip us, holding us in its sway. The problem, of course, is that this kind of "seizure" can make it very difficult to walk in the ordinary world of functioning humans. We may take on negative living patterns, developing neuroses or engaging in addictive habits or building destructive communication patterns. Once these patterns are established, once we begin to live lives of deception and betrayal—what Brian Spitzberg and William Cupach (1998; Cupach & Spitzberg, 1994) have called "the dark side of relating"—the patterns are difficult to break. In any case, according to Jungian literature, if the shadow is not somehow met, faced, owned, and dealt with, the "buried" side of us—the side that we may ordinarily find horrifying, the side from which outbursts and other dark emanations can come—may erupt.

Sometimes, the shadow descending on the person will take the form of Despair. Hope fades, becoming just a trace, a wisp, of a . . . memory. Gloom settles in. Once Despair takes hold of the human heart, once terrible sadness grips us, we may slip away into that place from which we find no easy release. If we are not careful, Despair can kill us. Indeed, as Despair grips us, we may find ourselves . . .

> battling madly, if you will, for possibility, because possibility is the only salvation. When someone faints, we call for water, eau de Cologne, smelling salts; but when someone wants to despair, then the word is: Get possibility, get possibility, possibility is the only salvation. A possibility—then the person in despair breathes again, he revives again, for without possibility a person seems unable to breathe. (Kierkegaard, 1980, pp. 38–39)

There is, in the end, but one way to conquer Despair. We need to breathe again. We need to feel *possibility*.

Amid many personal traumas—most notably the deaths of my uncle, my grandfather, and my aunt in quick succession—my own family found itself stunned, wrapped in shadow, lost, and, eventually, engulfed by Despair. And the family stood by, silent, splintered, unable to speak, unable to act, engulfed in shadow, barely breathing, teetering always on the brink . . .

Engulfed by a *collective* shadow, a *family* shadow, we scattered, desperately seeking a way out of the darkness. Some of us tried drugs, or alcohol, or food, or sex . . . to salve our wounds. Some of us disappeared, fell into our work. Others collapsed on the couch and let the television suck our vision, and what remained of our breath, away. The rest of us experimented, stayed busy, got addicted, ate too much or worked too much or drank too much, ran helter-skelter along our various paths of escape.

It was not entirely our fault.

We just did not know what to do.

Our family had lost the will to live. We were, in fact, each trying in our own silent, desperate way, to escape the shadow.

Even if that meant hastening our own deaths.

Each day, we died a little.

But the shadow did not lift.

And so, in the darkening corners of our lives, we began to harbor secrets. At first, they were just small secrets—things like where we were going, or where we had been, what we had been doing, and so on.

But the family shadow offered fertile soil for growing secrets. We grew our secrets in the dark, like mushrooms. And, like those little fungi growing in dark, damp places, our secrets began to spread their spores into all the little corners of our lives. Soon, nearly everything we did was done furtively, in a secret, private world. Small transgressions, held close, morphed into epic secrets. Little lies became the foundation for deeply dishonest lives. It seemed that, over time, we had lost all sense of what to say and what not to say. Soon, we had all lost track of what we had told—what we had opened up to the light—and what we had held in the shadow.

Engulfed in shadow, how do you discern the difference between truth and lie, between story and secret? Even if you begin to understand, and see that something needs to be revealed that has been held close, how, after so many years of skulking in the darkness, do you begin?

Silent Places

In some religious traditions—in the ancient practices of the yogis, Taoists, and Buddhists of Asia; among the mystics of Judaism and

Islam; among the various orders of nuns and monks of the Christian church; in the practices of the Society of Friends (Quakers)—silence has a sacred quality. For Quakers, sitting in silent communion is how they access the "light of God" that is in the universe and its people.

In his book, *Reclaiming the Tacit Dimension*, George Kalamaras attempts "to authenticate silence as a mode of knowing" (1994, p. 1). In my own work, I have attempted to probe the communicative capacities of silence (Poulos, 2004a). Indeed, silence can be a powerful force of peace and goodness in the world.

But there is another kind of silence we must acknowledge—a dark silence, a silence of truths unspoken and stories untold. It is a silence held in the shadow of emotions too painful to bear, too deep to speak or speak to. Perhaps at first it is a protective silence, one that allows us to escape the overwhelming grief that threatens—or seems to threaten—a very painful rending of our hearts. But, as time goes on, and the silence deepens, it becomes an inescapable silence, a silence of doom. This shadowy silence is what descended on my family in the face of our tragedy. It is a silence from which we have never fully recovered, a silence that threatens to engulf us and destroy our *courage to be* (Tillich, 1952). It is the silence of despair, the kind of despair that Kierkegaard considers a "sickness unto death."

Of course, one might well see this shadowland as a land of opportunity—or, as Kierkegaard put it, as the opening to possibility. We can find meaning in the darkness . . . Jung certainly saw it this way, as have Viktor Frankl (2006), Stanley Hauerwas (1990, 2005), C.S. Lewis (1998), Rudolph Otto (1923), Paul Tillich (1952, 1957), and countless poets and purveyors of tragedy, from Homer to Aeschylus to Shakespeare to Blake to Eliot. The problem for the family was not the descent into shadow itself. The problem was staying there, engulfed in that shadow world.

The Psalmist tells us: "Yea, though I walk through the valley of the shadow of death, I will fear no evil" (Psalms 23:4).

But my family *did* fear that evil.

We feared the valley we inhabited.

It was a dark valley, too deep and long and treacherous to navigate.

Our silent cries for help—our addictions and our transgressions, our lies and our dark secrets—fell on deaf ears.

Our voices were muffled by the misty silence that enshrouded our very consciousness.

There was a veil of silence that ate us alive.

Our problem was that, in all this tragedy, in lives taken too soon, we did not know how to find *meaning.*

How do you find meaning in Despair?

Some may retort that Despair itself is a kind of meaning. It is also a trap. The dark closet of Despair is too confining; it is no place to live for long. To function in this human world requires, at some point, transcendence of Despair. Our problem was that our family had no roadmap for navigating these experiences. It is my hope, in writing this book, that I can show how the practice of accidental ethnography can help all of us who have experienced life in the unmapped territory of family secrets to find a way out of Despair. It is my hope that through the practice of accidental ethnography—of shedding light on the dark places of memory, dream, imagination, consciousness through deeply engaged storytelling—we might learn how to navigate the terrible blows of fate that disrupt our existence. It is my hope that where we once saw only sadness we might find renewal, hope, and possibility.

Darkness and light, sorrow and joy, shadow and image, secret and story: These are the dialectics we will, inevitably, encounter in our lives. It will be important to remember, along the way, that neither side is "bad." We simply must walk through some of the more difficult places to see the other side. We begin, of course, by dreaming autoethnography, finding possibility in that thin place where the dream fades into day.

Dreaming Darkness (Again)

I wake up. It is very early; the sun has not even begun to hint at the coming day. The sound of my own wailing is what startles me into consciousness. As I sit up in bed, I feel something on my cheek. Reaching up, I realize that whatever it is, warm and damp but now drying, has been there a little while. It takes me a few moments and a couple of shakes of my head to understand what has happened. I have been crying in my sleep, aloud. Hard, bitter tears; tears of the deepest grief; tears that run like a hot river of lava through my very soul. At this moment of realization, the feelings come storming back into my heart, and I remember the dream. I nearly cry out. . . . Can I bear this pain, this loss? I choke back the next wail, but just barely.

Oh, what a dream, I am thinking. What a knife of a dream . . .

In my dream, I am sitting on the edge of my bed. I have just learned that I am about to die—that, in fact, I only have a few minutes left on this Earth before my breath is taken away forever. I am sitting with my dear, dear family: Eli, my oldest son, just now a young man, fifteen, on my right side; Noah, my precious bold child, all of eleven, on my left; Sue, my partner and dearest friend these many years, sitting behind me, her hand on my shoulder. I am explaining to them what is happening, that I will be dead soon. They are crying. I am crying. As I say goodbye, my final farewell, the pain runs so deep and so strong that my breath is taken away. I think that this is my death rattle, which just shoves the blade of loss even deeper into my heart. . . . I feel as if I'm being run over by a semi-truck of sadness, of grief and loss and pain. I sob, and sob, and sob.

As I sob, I am thinking of all the wonderful times we have had together, and of the times that might yet be. "I have no regrets," I tell them, choking back the sobs for a moment. But this is not true. I regret—so deeply, so poignantly, I regret—this very moment of loss, this destruction of possibility . . .

"But I am sad," I say.

I am so, so sad.

Together, we regret this: Possibility has vanished like a puff of smoke on an ill wind.

We will not be together again, perhaps for a long, long time . . . perhaps we will never see each other again.

"Goodbye," I say, "I love you."

And they cry and cry and cry.

As they cry, I feel the deep agony of their grief.

I cry with them.

I cry *for* them.

We can only sob our loss.

There are no words for this moment.

After a long flood of tears, there is a pause.

You can only cry so much.

As we come to a halt, catching our breath, Eli says, "Remember that time at the lake when . . ."

And a story escapes his lips. It is a story of togetherness, of connection, of happy times in the long days of summer amid the short years of childhood. That story reminds Sue of another story, and me of a third. Then, it is Noah's turn. So we sit and tell stories, for a long time.

One favorite story that we tell, over and over, is about a long, hot summer day where we happened, quite accidentally, on a strategy to pass the time. We tell it because it makes us laugh. The story begins as Noah and I sit idly by the water, talking. Eli is lying on the dock a few yards away, sunning himself.

Noah says, "Hey, dad. Think I can hit him with a crapapple?"

"Crabapple?" I ask.

"Yeah, that's what I said."

We laugh.

"I wouldn't if I were you," I reply.

A smirk comes over his face, and he goes to pick a few crabapples off the tree a few yards away. Before I know it, he is pelting his brother, with great accuracy, as I watch to see what unfolds. Eli jumps up, and steps off the dock, falling into the cold water, "Oh, you're dead!" he shouts.

What follows is an epic battle that lasts until dark, filled with scheming and stealth and laughter. At one point, Noah chimes in,

"Hey, Dad. Remember when I hit you square in the back of the head with a crapapple?"

"Oh, yes, I'll *never* forget. You *will* pay," I say.

We laugh, and I tackle him. We roll around laughing, and then start telling the story again.

Each of the stories we tell is about *us*, about our family, our traditions and our love and our joys and our sorrows. The stories are a welcome breath of joy and meaning, an interruption of the sadness of this otherwise terrible moment.

"Remember when we found that waterfall by the road?" Eli says.

As I listen, I long to live on.

I long to live on, not because I am selfish, not because I want what I want. I long to live *for* and *with* them, these beautiful humans, my significant others who have made my life and its meaning and our joy possible. I long to live on so that, together, we can build and tell and live more stories.

After a time, we tire in the telling, and fall silent. And in our silence, grief returns like a wave on the shore, eroding our joy. We fall back into mourning. Of course, we all knew this day would come, but, of course, we all hoped it would be later—much, much later. We all mourn our loss, sinking into pain and regret and despair. I sob and sob and sob . . . and I feel a new tide of feeling rising in my throat.

. . . I am filled to bursting with grief. I cannot hold that feeling in; it shoves its way up through my throat, forces my jaws open, erupts in a long, loud wail, and, suddenly, I am awake.

There will be no more sleep for me this day.

But there is a clue here.

To make a shadow, there must be light.

Light Places

To make a shadow, there must be light. And for light to be meaningful, it must transform the dark. I have walked in darkness and have emerged into the light. In both places, I have found what I needed, at that moment. In both places, there is the suggestion of the other side. The other side is always needed; it makes its counterpart possible.

I dream I am in a golden meadow. The light around me is so rich and colorful that I am filled to bursting with joy. At first, I cannot make out the source of this light. It seems to come from an unexpected place . . .

From the ground?

From all around me?

From me?

It is as if the whole world, the universe even, is smiling with me, bathing me in light. Oddly, there are no shadows in this place, only golden light and golden grass and golden flowers . . . and golden air. I am warmed and soothed and calmed and invigorated by this light. I feel it washing over me, and through me, and around me, and the joy is intense, so intense I do not know whether to laugh, or to cry . . .

And then, suddenly, I am in that thin place between joy and sorrow and the sorrow washes over me and I fall into that sorrowful place and I look up and there are clouds where before there was only sky and I look down and where golden light was before there are only shadows and I feel the sadness of it all. So sad is this life on Earth, so fleeting, so drenched with loss and grief and sorrow, and a wave of pain and tears washes over me and I feel so sad and I do not know if I can hold it in and a deep painful sob reaches up from within me and as I am about to release it I find myself back in the middle, and I lean a little and fall to the other side.

Then I am back in joy, feeling the power of joy, bathed in joy. And I know the truth of this ephemeral bliss, know it is so beautiful and

so wondrous and so full and so true and so powerful, and also know
that it will pass, now know that it is only one side of being.

And, suddenly, I spread my arms and run toward a hill on the far
horizon and I know that once I reach the top of that hill I will wake
up and I do not want to wake up but I know that there is something
special something important over that hill and so I must keep moving
so I do and I am so happy so sad so open so tired so free so . . .

And as I crest the hill my eyes open wide to the new world that
will unfold below and there she is, running up to the top of the hill
from the other side. Our eyes meet, and joy is on our lips. Just then
I wake up, eyes wide open, and I sit up slowly, a knowing smile
spreading across my lips . . .

Relational Places

That evening, I walk into my Relational Communication seminar,
where we have been studying the work of Martin Buber.

"Let's talk about relation," I begin.

We struggle for an hour to make sense of Buber's thoughts, to
draw a light between the poetry of his words. "All actual life is
encounter," writes Buber (1970, p. 62). Suddenly, we seem to grasp
his meaning, seem to understand, but then, just as suddenly, meaning
eludes us, slips away.

Then it hits me: the dream. We must follow the dream.

So I tell them my dream of the golden meadow. In the dream,
I slip from joy to sorrow and back again. I want to stay, but cannot.
There is something I need to know, and so I run to the crest of the
hill. And all that my spirit was seeking rises and engulfs me as
I see her, my dear Susana, my love, running from the other side to
meet me.

In that moment, we both know the eternal alchemical magic of
encounter.

The experience of encounter transcends words.

Hopeful Places

A light breeze, barely noticeable, kicks up as a faintly visible orange
sun peeks from behind the clouds. Somewhere a leaf, left over
from an autumn mistake, flutters. A light fog begins to lift. It will

be a beautiful day in North Carolina, one of many that suggest the impending arrival of spring, beginning in mid-February.

It is a beautiful suggestion, and I await the reality with anticipation. The spring—ah, spring! When life shoots forth, beckoning to the sky . . . what dreams of spirit wait in your early light, accompanied by fresh symphonies of birdsong? Spring is the time of possibility, when I crest the hill at the far end of the golden meadow, and come to know.

And one day, mid-April, it comes, and I walk out into my yard and lie on the grass. I feel the world emerging around me as I lie here, staring upward at the blue-blue sky, draped by the pink dogwood blossoms, and I drift into a light sleep. . .

Later, at a new thin place of transition—at the cusp of two seasons, as spring waxes into summer—my dreams turn to sultry days and the places and moments of relaxation, of release, that come with summer's freedom. But I also dream of sweat and steam and a dark heat that seems to inhabit the ground, rising relentlessly upward into the cooler night air. And in those thin places between world and summer heat, gases rising from the asphalt, I find myself alit with the wonder of it all and open my heart to hope.

I am a prisoner of hope . . .

Thin Places (Revisited)

What do we know when we experience a dream?

What sort of knowing do we come to when we write?

What do we learn when we teach?

I have dreamed and taught and storied whole worlds into being, into meaning, into connection . . .

In these thin places, between dreaming and writing and teaching, there is much to learn, much to explore, much seeking to be done.

There is a kind of knowing waiting for us in the thin places of this world.

And yet, I wonder, after all this time wandering these places: What do I know?

Sometimes, I think that what we come to know is . . . all that we once knew, long ago in some thin place between this world and another . . .

And my spirit rises at that thought. Somehow, in these liminal spaces, I feel free.

Could it be that Plato was right, that we move toward birth with full spiritual knowledge, knowing all that we need to know, only to have all but a trace erased at that moment when we emerge into this world?

Could it be that our task on this Earth is to fall into those thin places where new worlds may erupt into this world, where the spirit can soar to new heights, where knowing and spirit can come together in epiphany?

Could it be that we may yet crest the hill at the far end of that golden meadow?

Could it be that the River Lethe, the River of Forgetting, brimming as it is with the secret dreams and the secret knowledge and the secret spirit of a life washed clean . . . returns its gifts to us with a hint and a trace . . . in our dreams, as we write, as we teach?

Could it be that we are called to dream and teach and write from the thin places of consciousness, so that we may one day share the gift of breakthrough with those Others who inhabit this world with us?

Dreamstory, Familystory

According to scholars of family communication, the family's engagement in storytelling is a central form of family-making praxis. Family stories are vibrant and critical communication events that produce family culture, define family history, feature family uniqueness, develop identity, and display and establish family values (Langellier & Peterson, 1993; Pelias, 2004; Rehling, 2002; Trujillo, 2004; Vangelisti & Timmerman, 2001; Yerby, Buerkel-Rothfuss, & Bochner, 1995).

Meanwhile, a family that lives in a pattern of unhealthy silence and secret-making simply stumbles along in the dark.

What, then, to make of a family shrouded in silence, shadow, secret, pain?

Can anything be done to release the family from the grip of its collective shadow?

In my family, our stories had deserted us. We had lost our capacity to make sense through story. The shadow had blocked the sunlight of story-making. As a family, we lived for decades in a stricken state. We were stunned by grief and pain and loss. The knife of death stabbed us, and . . . left a deep wound, a hole . . . in our hearts.

Into that hole, a shadow crept.

Then one day, out of the mouth of a babe . . . came a light in the darkness.

In September 1998, my grandfather, James N. Leckie, Senior, died. He was ninety-four years old.

One day, two weeks after Grandpa's funeral, my youngest son, Noah, age three, sidles up next to me. He looks me in the eye, and says, very seriously, "Dad, tell me the story—how Grandpa Lucky[2] [*sic*] died."

Taken aback, I sit down on the floor next to him. I tell him, "Well, one day, Grandpa, who was very old, got sick and died."

He replies, "NO! Tell me the STORY! The WHOLE story!"

Stunned, I look into his bright brown eyes.

"OK, son," I say. "The whole story . . . well, you know, Grandpa was a very strong man. When he was younger, he was a cowboy in a rodeo. He loved to ride horses. And he was a farmer. He liked very much to take care of his cows."

"Did they have milk?" says Noah.

"Yes, they had milk."

"I'm allergic to milk."

"Yes, you are. Anyway, one day, he decided to retire and move to Florida. You know, he had a swimming pool in his yard."

"Cool!"

"Yeah, it was pretty cool. Anyway, when he got very old, he moved into Mema and Papa's house. He had his own rooms there."

"Yeah. He liked to watch TV!" says Noah.

"Loud!" I say, and he laughs.

"So one day he got very sick—he got pneumonia and he had to go to the hospital," I continue.

But Noah breaks in, "NO! First tell about how he goes to the beach with us and plays that mouse game."

And so I tell about all the good times Noah knew with Grandpa, about our trips to the beach and the little games he would play with the kids, about how Grandpa had to walk very slowly, with a cane, and about how he was very good at sleeping while sitting in a chair. And when we get to the part about the funeral, and the horses who appeared suddenly to watch, standing, hovering over the fence, Noah grows very quiet. He starts to cry. I hold him.

The next day, Noah is standing beside me in the living room. He says, solemnly, "Dad, tell me the story of how Grandpa Lucky died."

I wonder if I can get off the hook here. I don't want to talk about it. I start to tell it the way I had started the day before.

But Noah grabs my sleeve. "No, Dad! The WHOLE story!"

And so the story lives and grows. Each day, it grows longer, more detailed, as Noah insists on hearing the WHOLE story. One day, it hits me: This is not the story of how "Grandpa Lucky" *died*, but of how he *lived*. His death is just one small moment in the WHOLE story. Of course, there is no WHOLE story, because the story grows and shifts and lives on. It unfolds and becomes as much a story of Noah and me as a story about Grandpa.

Still, every day for three weeks, Noah makes the same request. He wants more. I find myself searching for details.

I call my Mom, explain my problem. I need to find out more about Grandpa's life. She tells me some stories. I can tell she likes this. Then she suggests I call my uncle Bud, her brother, to find out more. He is, it turns out, a master storyteller. So, in the end, I am able to tell Noah the story of "Grandpa Lucky"—the WHOLE story. Every day for three weeks, we sit in the living room, and the story unfolds.

Another clue.

Is this the glimmer of dawn?

As Noah issued his insistent call of story (Coles, 1989), I was forced to investigate the life of my grandfather. I did not know the whole story, the story Noah needed. I needed my family to fill in the gaps. As I talked about Grandpa with various members of my family, it became clear that they *needed* to tell these stories.

And I began to dream of story.

I do not know how my family's story will turn out.

I only know that we must begin to craft it anew.

Reflection

As I move into my day, I wonder at my dreams, at the power of the unconscious forces that shape and infuse our dreams. Dreams, if you listen to them, if you read them carefully, can cut through all the hubbub and haze and shadowy ambiguity of everyday life. I sometimes turn to my dreams to clarify the issues that arise in my research and my writing. My dreams "cut to the chase," as they say in Hollywood.

These are the stories from thin places, produced in that liminal state between shadow and light. These are the possibilities formed

out of the shadowy unconscious, and they are open to us—*sometimes.*
We find our dreams illuminated in the thin light of dawn. In the gray,
misty, filtered light of dawn, possibility casts no shadow.

And in that moment of possibility, I find myself, seemingly by
accident, drawn to writing. There is always the writing. But, as I write,
I am aware that I must not only draw the dream across that thin place
from shadow to light, but also help illuminate it for you, my reader.
Still, in doing that, it seems to me that I must seek not *explanation*
but *impact*. I strive to evoke the sense of emotional reality that makes
the dream meaningful. I am reminded of Laurel Richardson's (2000)
call to ethnographers. The ethnographer, according to Richardson,
should offer works that make *substantive contributions*, that shimmer
with *aesthetic merit*, that rebound in *reflexivity*, that deliver *impact*, that
express—poignantly and evocatively—a *reality.*

How can I rise to such a high calling?

I have dreamed a clue . . .

I stand, and I thank my dream, and I sit down at my keyboard to
write these words.

How did my dreams become so magical, so *alchemical*, as Jung
put it? By what transformative magic can our dreams deliver
possibility? What new meanings emerge from our dreams? How is
any dream a helpful narrative, delivered by Hermes, the messenger
god, to illuminate our lives?

In the rich literature focusing on ethnographic method, scholars
from Bochner (2001) to Denzin and Lincoln (2000) to Ellis (2004) to
Goodall (2000) to Pelias (2004) to Richardson (2000) to Trujillo (2004)
have written in various ways of the *nexus* of observation-evocation-
imagination-story-heart. I think we should add another dimension to
our growing ethnographic nexus of possibility: dreamstory.

Let us recall the offerings of the unconscious.

Let us recall that threshold between our conscious and unconscious
life-worlds.

Let us recall the signs, the symbols, the missives of Hermes.

Let us recall our dreams . . .

For in the gray mists of dawn, the shadows begin to fade. If we are
to loosen the grip of shadow, we must attend to those betwixt and
between moments—those moments on the threshold, when shadow
is fading into early light. We must attend to our dreams, for they can
be the key that opens the door to a new story.

Dreamstory.

For writers and readers of ethnography, the writing of dream blending into story—of the unconscious enriching our consciousness—is a rich, textured nexus of evocative possibility. Dreamstory takes us toward a liminal, shimmering space—a place where, when shadow fades in the mists of dawn, we find new clues to enrich our understanding of this human journey.

Returning briefly to the story of Ivan Ilych, we find that the dream (vision? actuality?) of the presence of the child can be written into a new story of emergence from despair into the light of hope. As Mark Freeman (1997) argues, Ilych's life can be *reconstructed* into something meaningful only through a grasping a sense of virtue, as it stands above and beyond a life that follows, lockstep, the social norms of a particular day. And in that grasping of what really constitutes the good life, *narrative integrity*, an idea that I will later tie to what I call *narrative conscience*, may be possible. But it is only through the dream of the child—the innocent, good, caring child—that the doorway to that possibility is open. It is through dreamstory that narrative integrity, rebounding in narrative possibility, comes into our collective consciousness.

Further, for a family shrouded in the shadows of loss, possibility awakens on the threshold. In my dark dream of death, we came to a point where we could bear the pain no longer. So we told a family story. In my dreams of family storytelling, we begin to heal as we *story* light into shadow, as we *story* Despair into Hope, as we *story* Life into Meaning, as we *story* Dream into Daylight.

In writing the dream into the light of day, maybe the shadow will lift, if only a little.

Maybe my dreams will fill in the blanks.

Maybe, together, we will dream a new story . . .

Maybe . . .

Process

When my students read my work, they often remark, "Your dreams are so vivid! How do you even remember them?" My first, instinctive answer may seem glib, but I think it is honest: "I don't seem to have a choice."

Embedded in the question is a deeper issue about the process of intentionally accessing, working with, and developing stories out of our dreamworlds. Of course, some of you may think it strange to advocate the inclusion of dream material in ethnographic work at all. After all, the dreamworld can be a dark, strange place. The human mind does some weird stuff as it dives deep into the unconscious. Last night, I dreamed about a talking dog. Weird. I have no idea what to make of it. However, at times, my dreams do seem to carry a deeper meaning connected to my waking life, my history, my memory, and my need to transcend my legacy of family secrecy. At these times, my dreams are insistent, and, as I said, I seem to have no choice but to pay attention.

My students want me to teach them how to be *available to* their dreams so that they might actually come to be aware of them and their deeper meanings, and then, perhaps, make use of them in their autoethnographic writing projects. My own particular ways of accomplishing this are really quite simple. When I go to bed at night, I try to set myself up to engage dreaming. As I lie down and begin to relax, I consciously attune myself to the hopeful possibility that I may fall into a dream. If it happens, it happens. If not, there will always be another night.

I keep a dream notebook by my bed. If I wake in the middle of the night, stirred by a vivid or disturbing dream, I pick it up and write quick field notes about the dream, its content and context, and any details that may later trigger my memory. Sometimes, with a particularly insistent dream, I will get up, go to my computer, and write the whole thing. Again, at these times the writing just *takes* me. I am, like in my dreams, simply along for the ride. I then go back to sleep, hoping to reenter the dream, or find another.

When I rise out of bed in the morning, I typically pick up my notebook to see if there is anything there to be mined. Then I set myself up to write whatever comes, beginning the writing process before I am fully awake and conscious. I try to enter into writing as soon as possible, when I am still in that liminal, thin place betwixt and between dreaming consciousness and waking consciousness.

And sometimes, I strike gold.

Mostly, the dreams just take me where they want me to go.

So, I try to let the writing do that, too.

In other words, if having a vivid dream requires some sort of unconscious surrender of control, perhaps writing a vivid dream requires a conscious surrender to the process of writing.

I am fully aware that this way of approaching it may not be helpful in the sense that it offers concrete, specific advice about how to proceed. But that is exactly the point. The issue is not procedural, at least not in the ordinary sense of that word. There are no specific steps that must be taken.

That is the essence of dreaming accidental ethnography.

The process is, instead, a process of *letting go.*

Let go, and see what dreams may come.

There is a thin place somewhere, just waiting for you to stumble into it.

Exercises

Writing Exercise 1: Accessing Your Dreamworld

Keep a dream journal (field note book) at your bedside. If you wake up from a dream, write field notes on the spot. Then, whether you have written anything in your journal or not, spend a few moments reflecting on your dreams (or potential dreams) before you get out of bed in the morning. If at first you cannot access or remember them, stick with it. Over time, you will train yourself to remember. Reflect. Breathe. Reflect some more.

Who knows what dreams may come back to you?

As you begin to remember them, write in your field notebook. Try to recall details like sounds, colors, characters, important events, turning points, images, metaphors, and so on. As you write, withhold from the temptation to interpret—at least for now. Just try to remember.

Some bizarre images or moments are bound to intrude here and there. There may be no way to make sense of some of your dreams, at least not in the language of waking consciousness. But, again, just hang in there. You never know what you might find.

At some point along the way, you will inevitably be visited by a particularly powerful or meaningful or significant dream. Then, as you become ready to translate your dreams into meaningful, vivid, evocative stories connected to your everyday life, you will want to surrender to the dream, and surrender to the writing process. Just let go.

And go!

Writing Exercise 2: Composing the Dreamstory

I have found that the interpretation of dreams is tricky business.
But I have found ways of accomplishing the task that seem to fit
with my own storied/symbolic dream world. The frameworks and
vocabulary of Jungian psychology have been enormously useful in
this interpretive enterprise. The Jungian understanding of unconscious
processes—the world of the human shadow, the personal unconscious,
and the deeper layers of the collective unconscious (including myths
and archetypes)—that we all share offers an intriguing set of resources
for coming to fuller understanding of my dream world.

Jung's books, *Memories, Dreams, Reflections* (1989) and *Man and His
Symbols* (1964), are enormously helpful for dream interpretation, as
is any standard dictionary of symbolism (e.g., Biedermann, 1992). In
Memories, Dreams, Reflections, Jung outlines his notion that dreams
are the doorway or threshold to the unconscious. For more on this,
see Chapter Five. But in the end, it is up to me to make sense of
my dreams in the context of my life as I understand it. I do this by
crafting story, as narrative sense is often the only kind of sense I can
make of anything I experience.

So, I think it behooves any writer who wants to connect a dream
story to her or his life story to work diligently to bring the dream
alive in story form, in much the same way as you might make any
scene from your life come alive. Your task is to invite and draw
your reader into your world. To do that, you'll need to focus your
conscious ethnographic attention on the details, the images, the
themes, the plots, the characters, the spaces and places, the time
sequences, and the metaphors that infuse your dream world. For
example, in examining and writing about the dreams I've written into
this chapter, I begin by reading them as stories about characters who
are doing something meaningful. From there, I look carefully at the
thematic, spatial, and temporal meanings that invigorate the actions
of the characters.

The next time you have a particularly vivid dream, do this: Write
it as a story, as if it had actually happened in your waking life. Use
your own imaginative sensibilities about how to construct the story in
such a way that it becomes a vivid reality for your reader. Once you
have written the dream, share the written story with five or six people
you trust. Just ask them to read the story. Then ask them for their
response. Who knows what interpretations may come?

Queries

1. What recurring dreams or dream themes are you aware of?
2. How do you currently respond to your dreams? Do you think about them? Talk about them with others? Try to interpret them? Write about them?
3. How do you think your own ethnographic story might change if you incorporated dreamstory into your writing practice?
4. Do you keep a dream journal? If not, would you consider starting to keep a journal at your bedside for recording dreams? Why or why not?
5. What do you make of the intersections between dreaming consciousness and waking consciousness? How do you navigate across that threshold? Do you ever write before you are conscious?

Notes

1. I am indebted to David Bills, pastoral minister of New Garden Friends Meeting in Greensboro, North Carolina, for this reference.
2. Noah always called his great grandfather "Grandpa Lucky"—on the assumption, we gathered, that anyone who lives to be that old *must* be lucky.

Chapter Four

Out of the Shadows

There is no guarding against memory. That's the devil of it. It slips in before you can catch yourself, closing your throat, startling your heart. . . . Anything can trigger it—the unexpected convergence of a particular sight and sound, a specific smell, a song. Anything. And there is absolutely no way to protect against it.
—Anne D. LeClaire, *Entering Normal*

Perhaps it is in what we don't accept about ourselves—our aggression and shame, our guilt and pain—that we discover our humanity.
—Connie Zweig and Jeremiah Abrams, *Meeting the Shadow*

Beginning

As an accidental ethnographer who finds himself stumbling over the many rhizomes pushing up through the soil of my consciousness, I find I *must* write about the dark contours of a life of secrecy, about the perils and the promises of secret-keeping and secret-breaking, and about the healing power of storying our secrets into the light. I must write about the ethics of revelation and about the deep connection that can come when someone musters the courage to tell the story.

I begin with stories. These are stories gathered out of secrets, born of hints and whispers and clues, of small story fragments that have slipped out or seeped into the lives of people I have known. These are the stories of a family—or, at least, part of one. These stories trace the family members' responses to sorrow, loss, trauma, and conflict that arise in their lives.

The stories here are necessarily incomplete, and therefore, perhaps, inaccurate. But they are nonetheless stories that, like fading dreams in the early morning light, hover on the edge of consciousness, poised to tell us some truths about who we are. As such, they are not stories of particular people, but rather stories about *all of us* who, in some way, have experienced trauma and have stumbled through life in its wake,

alternately striving to pick up the clues offered by the sometimes quiet, sometimes overwhelming eruptions of memory. These are stories about the heart of forgetting and of secret keeping, and of the illusory and tenuous and temporary protections that forgetting and secrecy offer. In the end, I will suggest that the power of story trumps the power of the secret and that the ethical move for the researcher of human social life is to tell the story in ways that will move us toward healing.

☐ ☐ ☐ ☐

The trouble with secrets is how they keep you separate.
—Anne D. LeClaire, *Entering Normal*

Life, Interrupted

Audrey. Her name means "noble strength"—or so they told her once. But she hasn't thought about her name so much as lived it.

And then, one dark day, she falls into silence.

It comes like a rush of wind, the kind of wind that threatens to crack the windows, blow the door in, snap a pine, and send it crashing into the roof.

"Push!" someone yells.

And she pushes.

And she feels the baby emerge.

She has done this before. A daughter—the light of her life—was born just a year ago. So she waits in anticipation of that magic moment when she will meet this next child and hold him close to her heart.

But soon she realizes there is no sound, no first gasp for air, no crying. Just silence.

That's not right.

The nurse turns to her, holding the tiny lifeless body of an infant, and says, "I'm sorry."

No! And she feels the wind rushing out of her body. Gasping for air, and searching for light, blinking back tears, she begins to sob quietly.

Dead.

Before he was even alive.

Dead?

Now what? It was a tough pregnancy. She was sick most of the time. But she never imagined *this*.

Later that day, as she lies in bed, staring at nothing—her baby gone, gone, gone forever—she vows never to speak of this.

"This will be our secret," she tells her husband, Thomas. "We will bury him, and we will never speak of it again, to anyone."

And so, two days later, she stumbles out to the little graveyard for a private ceremony, attended only by her, her young husband, and their Methodist pastor, all dressed in black. They listen to the minister intoning the proper words:

Yea, though I walk through the valley of the shadow of death, I will fear no evil.

She cries quietly, for the last time.

Ashes to ashes.

And they lower the tiny box into the ground, scoop dirt on it, and leave.

Dust to dust.

And they never again speak of this.

It is a very dark year. But the darkness begins to lift a little after a time, and life begins again. A baby is born the next year, and this one is big and strong and healthy, a son joining their two-year-old daughter, helping to blot out the memory with their laughter.

Life goes on. The years pass, and memories fade. And the secret just lies there, buried in the ground in a tiny box. Almost sixty years later, she sits alone in her living room. She is old now, very old, and very nearly blind. Macular degeneration. In front of her is a large TV, and she sits too close to it, the volume turned way up. At her side is a bottle of sherry. She began drinking about ten years ago. At first, it was very controlled. Just a little cocktail at five. Soon, it was cocktails at five and seven-thirty. Then it was a pre-cocktail glass of sherry at two. Before long, it was Bloody Marys for breakfast, sherry at ten, noon, and two, Manhattans at five and seven-thirty. Lately, she has taken to drinking her sherry all day long, straight from the bottle. Why dirty a glass?

Her liver is beginning to harden and to float a bit. She knows she will die soon. She doesn't care. In her mind, she will go to meet her baby, the one she never met. Her heart is broken. A few weeks later, she is dead. And no one ever speaks of her secret or of the alcoholism that killed her.

The official word is that she died of "heart failure."

Don't we all?

This will be our secret.

Sleep, Interrupted

It settles down on him like a warm, thick blanket of fog, lulling him to sleep. In sleep, he is free. He does not dream. As long as he sleeps, the rage fades away. His demons do not appear. As long as he sleeps . . .

Sleep.

The television helps. He comes home, pours a watery Scotch on ice or cracks a beer, settles into his chair, turns on the TV. Within minutes, the fog settles in, his head droops to his chest.

Sleep.

Some nights, he just sleeps straight through, missing dinner. Others, he gets up, stumbles out to the kitchen, eats in silence, and pads back to his den. And the fog settles in. . .

Sleep.

When he was young, his mother sang him to sleep.

Sleep little baby, don't say a word . . .

His name is James. Named for a king, they told him.

When he was little, he often wished he *was* a king; *then* they would treat him right. King James! But they just pushed him around, called him "Squirt."

Still, he was a happy—if nervous—little kid. He grew up in a small town, had many friends. His family was weird, and volatile, and loving. And controlling. And manipulative.

Papa's gonna buy you a mockingbird . . .

His father was distant, an immigrant who believed that a man should work. Most of the time, he was not home. He worked.

And if that mockingbird don't sing . . .

And when his father came home, he would shuffle into the den, settle into his chair, turn on the radio . . .

Papa's gonna buy you a diamond ring. . .

And nod off. That's how he remembers his father—sitting in his chair, head bobbing, falling into sleep . . . first to the radio . . . in later years to the TV . . .

And if that diamond ring don't shine . . .

He remembers it like it was yesterday. The sound of glass shattering, followed by the guilt, quickly replaced by fear. He knows he will get it when Papa comes home. He rubs his backside, almost feeling the whipping before it even happens. Briefly, he contemplates running away from home. Instead, he spends the afternoon sitting under a tree in the backyard, sweating profusely.

But Papa says nothing about the window. He just walks into the dining room, takes a look, and goes out to the garage. He returns with a piece of cardboard and a roll of tape, covers the hole, and walks out of the room.

He never says a word. That cardboard remains in that window for thirty years, and no one ever speaks of it. A constant, visible, lasting sign of his transgression stares at him during every family meal . . .

A silent reproach.

A few weeks later, they are eating dinner. Sal and Joe are arguing loudly. Mom sighs. Papa, spooning greens onto his plate, turns to the boy and says,

"Take some greens, boy."

"No thank you."

"What did you say?"

"No thank you, *sir.*"

"Take some greens."

Muttering, the boy takes the platter, spoons a few greens onto his plate.

After dinner, the family goes for a ride in the car, the three children crammed into the back seat. He, the youngest, perches on the hump in the middle.

"Move over, *Squirt.*"

"No! Don't call me that! *You* move over!"

"Quiet!" yells Papa turning to glare back at them.

"You be quiet," the boy mutters under his breath.

Papa glares at him.

Wait until we get home.

The threat is palpable. They finish the ride in total silence.

That day, the belt cuts into his skin. He bleeds in silence, a tear streaming down his cheek. And the pain wells up inside him, chokes off his voice, takes him to a dark place from which he feels he may never emerge. His skin begins to feel warm as the rage starts to seep into his blood. Sweat forms on his brow. Shaking now, he wants to break something, to beat someone. Hard.

But he never says a word to anyone about the quiet rage bubbling deep inside.

A little secret.

Years later, he jumps up from his chair in front of the TV, startled awake by someone yelling out in the yard. He pulls the curtain aside, peers out into the darkness. His teenaged sons are out there, going at each other, fists flying.

Drunk.

And the rage wells up, pouring into his limbs. Fists clenched, he storms out into the yard, yells at the top of his lungs, "STOP!"

Fuck you.

What did you say?

Fuck you, sir!

STOP, I said!

No response. The fists just keep flying. So he jumps in, punching away. He will pound the rage out of himself, out of them, out of their lives. The boys pull back, startled. They have never seen him like this.

Shaking, fists still clenched, he says through gritted teeth, "Inside. Now."

Silently, they walk into the house. And they never speak of this night again.

Our little secret.

One night, years later, he wakes with a start. Someone has turned off the TV. He looks up, and sees his sister standing there, just staring at him, an inscrutable look on her face.

Sally?

And, just like that, she is gone.

That was so long ago. Why is she here, now?

And, at that moment, the memory pours in like a thick fog, only this time he sees it coming, sees each molecule of the fog with great clarity, so that it no longer seems to be fog at all, but just bits of water, floating about in the air in front of him. He is transported back in time . . .

Thirty years ago, standing in his living room, feeling uneasy.

Something is not right here.

He grabs his keys, heads out the door, steps into his car, drives slowly in the general direction of her apartment.

Not like her. She calls. She always calls.

Yesterday, it crossed his mind, but only for a moment.

Sally didn't call.

The next morning, the phone rings. It's Sally's boss. She didn't show up for work.

Not like her.

He pulls up to the curb in front of her apartment, which is in a converted old plantation house. A pretty nice place. He gathers himself, pulls up out of the front seat, slams the car door, takes a deep breath as he stands, looks around, spots her car in the lot. The stairs up to the front of the building seem steeper today, longer than he remembers. By the time he gets to the large front door, he is winded. He pauses, then pulls the heavy door open, turns into the hall, trudges up to the second floor.

He pauses again, in front of her door, knocks lightly. No answer.

Sal?

Almost a whisper.

Sal?

A little louder.

SAL!?!

Louder still.

He tries the knob, and it's locked. He jiggles the knob again, this time vigorously. A little "CLICK!" and the door swings open, groaning on its old heavy hinges.

Not right.

He walks back toward the bedroom, like he is being pulled there. The bedroom is empty, the bathroom door ajar. He pushes it open, tentatively, his fear mounting.

Not right.

And there she is, naked, sprawled over the edge of the tub, a little trickle of blood at the corner of her mouth.

Dead.

His only sister, she is—was—forty-six years old. Now she is gone. At the hospital, the doctor takes him aside, tells him it was her heart. It just sort of exploded. She probably never knew, except for a brief moment of pain. She went very quickly.

Oh, Sally! Why didn't you call?

For a moment, he feels a tightening in his chest, feels her pain. And that old rage surges up. He clenches his fists, tightly.

That evening, he pulls into his driveway. It's been a long day. He steps out of the car, and walks inside. The family knows, and soon they will all ride up the road to his mother's home for the wake and the funeral. He wants to talk about it with someone, to lay it all out, to let go of the pain and the frustration and the rage, bottled up all these years. But they never speak of these things, never bring the pain to light, never talk about the sadness or the anger or the hurt.

Our little secret.

Instead, tonight, he will slip away. Sitting in front of the TV, an open beer on the table next to him, he feels the fog descending. His head droops . . . and . . . he hears his mother's voice, crooning softly . . .

Sleep, little baby, don't say a word . . .

Frozen

For her, it's a chill down in the bones, like that coldest day of winter when, no matter how much you bundle, the shivers reach deep inside. At times, she looks at her feet, and feels frozen in place, like she has stepped into an icy puddle, the ice closing in around her ankles, holding her tight, locking her into position. At these times, the only thing she can think of is to keep moving, stay busy, never stand still. If you are not still, you cannot be frozen in one place . . .

When she was born, her parents, Audrey and Thomas, were filled with joy. They named her Claire—which means "bright"—because they said she lit up their lives. She is very bright, indeed. In the mid-1950s, she marries James. They quickly have two sons, naming them Gabriel and Isaac. In raising them, she hopes to stay busy, to forget her past.

In the 1940s South, life for her family was relatively prosperous. Though her family lived in the country, her father was a professor, raising his farming roots to a somewhat higher social station. The small town where they lived was a place of genteel society, a place where ladies learned proper manners, and gentlemen were polite and distant.

She is a young girl of fourteen or so, but she has begun to bloom. She now carries the full, curvaceous body of a woman twice her age. Her piano teacher is a middle-aged gentleman, a bit on the quiet side, a somewhat stern taskmaster. His wife is pleasant and keeps an immaculate home. Each Tuesday, she walks over to their home after school. It is a large, freshly painted plantation-style place with a wrap-around veranda, complete with white porch swing and rockers to match. As she enters the house, the smell of cookies baking in the oven catches her attention. Her stomach growls lightly in anticipation.

She smiles and says hello, then walks over to the piano, sits down, pulls out her music. She senses him standing behind her, watching over her shoulder as she begins to play. After her warm-ups, his hand reaches out, rests on her shoulder. A bit startled—he has never touched her before—she stops playing, turns to look at him. And before she knows what has hit her, his tongue is in her mouth, his right hand cupping her breast.

She freezes, in shock, uncertain what to do. And just as quickly, he has left the room, and his wife enters, carrying a plate of cookies. The girl stands, stiff as a board, and finds herself frozen in silence. For a long moment, she is unable to move or to speak. Then she gets up, smiles faintly at the man's wife, and tentatively accepts a cookie and a glass of lemonade.

And then she is running, running down the street, running all the way to her house, running. She runs into her room, sits on the edge of her bed, reaches up and touches her cheek. A single tear is sliding across the smooth, unlined skin. She sits and stares at nothing, not moving, crying quietly.

Shame.

She does not know what has happened, does not know what to say or do. But she knows it is not right. So she screws up her courage and walks down the hall to see her mother.

"Mama, I want to quit the piano."

"What? What are you talking about?"

"I just don't want to play any more."

"Oh, you'll play, all right. We paid good money for those lessons."

"But, Mr.—I can't go back there!" Tears stream down her cheeks as the shame, and a new feeling—anger?—yes, anger!—rises up.

"What on Earth are you talking about, young lady?"

"He—he touched me. And he kissed me!"

"How DARE you! That is a fine upstanding family in this town! I'll not have you talking such nonsense!"

"But, Mama!"

"You will go to your room now. And you will go back to your piano lesson next week. And your mouth will stay shut. I don't want to hear any more about this. Do you understand?"

And she turns on her heel, stomps down the hall, slams her door.

Shame, mingling with anger, shrouded in silence.

Our little secret.

And they never speak of this day again.

A few years later, when she goes off to college, she quits piano. And she never plays again. Many years later, she is standing in the hospital waiting room, looking out the little window. In a room down the hall, her mother is slowly dying, her systems shutting down one at a time. As she gazes out into the parking lot, the faint sound of a piano tune, piped in over the hospital's Muzak system, tugs at the edge of her consciousness. And, out of nowhere, that old feeling of shame surges up. She stands frozen, staring at nothing. And suddenly there is a hand on her shoulder. She turns, startled. It is her Mama's doctor.

"I believe the time is close. Do you want to be with her?"

She nods, turns, and walks slowly down the hall to hold her mother's hand while she dies. Along with her mother, something else dies that day. It is the knowledge that, in her time of need, her mother denied her.

Three days later, having buried her mother and reluctantly left her aging father alone in their South Florida home, she is on an airplane on the way back to her home in North Carolina. Her younger son sits next to her, and they begin talking of days long past, of the young man's childhood and teenage years. He speaks of having felt alone for much of his life, with no one to talk to, no one to confide in. He compares that feeling to the feeling of loss that comes with death. And she feels herself freezing up, falling silent, unable to speak any more. And there is also that faint twinge of anger, mingling with shame.

A year later, she and the son are sitting on her porch. The conversation turns to the past, and she feels that familiar feeling welling up.

Chilled.

Frozen.

"So I just felt like you and Dad were clueless, like you didn't know what I was going through, like maybe you didn't care. Anyway, you never asked."

The shame and anger rise up, and she can't take it any more. She explodes: "How DARE you! We were good parents! I was there for you! You have no idea what it's like to be abandoned! You don't know what you are talking about! How DARE you!"

"But, Mom . . ."

"YOU are the one who is self-centered and clueless! A year ago, you start talking to me about all this stuff, this stuff you don't need to keep bringing up, and my mother has just died, and all you can talk about is how bad it was and how we weren't good parents and how your life was no good. That was years ago! How DARE you!"

He does not know where this has come from or what to say.

She stands there, her fists clenched, frozen in place.

And she finds that, just as sudden as her outburst, the feeling of shame comes over her, blotting out the anger. She just stands there, enveloped in silence. And they never speak of this again.

Frozen.

Little Flashes

Gabriel. The strong one. Firstborn son of James and Claire, grandson of Audrey and Thomas.

It comes on him in brief, blinding flashes, like the flash of a camera taking a picture you don't want to see.

One night, he and his little brother make a plan. He is sixteen. His brother is fifteen. They will find someone to buy it for them: a quart of cheap Scotch, a case of beer. Then they will make their way out to the mountain and party! They will drink until they can drink no more. As he approaches the young man standing on the corner near the front of the liquor store, there is something familiar about the guy. Is he smirking?

Flash! His cousin, sixteen, sitting on the porch, smoking a cigarette, smirking.

They get the beer and Scotch and drive out to the mountain. The next thing he remembers, he is in the drunk tank at the police station. The holding cell is a little room, only maybe four feet by four feet—a closet, really, with a steel bench and a steel door, no window. Arrested for public drunkenness, he comes to in a fog of nausea and fading memory.

Flash! A small, cramped room, clouded with smoke, reeking of stale beer. The cousin's face, leering, smirking, laughing.

"Let me out of here!" he yells, and pounds on the door.

A cop's voice responds laconically, "Shut up in there!"

"Let me out!"

Crisp steps on the concrete floor, then, the swish of a nightstick being pulled from its holster, and three quick raps on the door. A clear signal . . .

"Let me out!"

A year or two later, he finds himself sitting alone in the basement. From upstairs come faint sounds of dinner being prepared—clanking pots, scraping chairs, cabinet doors catching on the latch. He sits with a drink in his hand, a splash of cheap Scotch he swiped from his dad's cabinet. He is wondering what he will do next.

Flash! He is about eight or nine, maybe ten. He's standing in the corner, naked, embarrassed, his back against the wall. His teenaged cousin is sitting on the bed, smoking a cigarette. No! I don't want to see this. Go away. Let me out of here!

And, just like that, it's gone.

Then, a few years later . . .

It's midnight on an ordinary weeknight, sometime in the mid-1970s. He is drunk, stumbling loudly around the house, looking for something but unable to focus. His young wife comes into the room, says something in a sharp voice, dripping with sarcasm, her words bleeding with barely suppressed anger.

Flash! Pain! No! Oh, it hurts! Stop! No! Strong arms hold him in an icy grip, bruising his biceps. He is thrown to the floor. A heavy boot slams him in the ribs. No!

And he cuffs her jaw: SLAP! The unmistakable sound of a hand striking flesh. Hard.

His little brother walks in, says, "Try me instead of her."

So he does.

Soon fists are flying everywhere. A hard right cross, and a head slams against the floor. Brother on brother, on the floor, pounding out the rage.

The fists are flying hard now. Die! Die you son of a bitch!

Flash! The cousin stands up, walks over to him, stares into his eyes. He averts his gaze, and the cousin takes a long drag on the cigarette, blows a smoke ring in his face. "That's right, kid. Keep that mouth of yours shut."

The younger brother, now lying silent on the floor, in the fetal position, begins to lose consciousness. But the fists just keep coming. Blood on the floor, blood everywhere. Will it stop? Fists flying. Will it ever stop? Then someone else is in the room, pulling him off, shouting. "Stop! Stop man! You'll kill him!"

The brothers part company and do not speak for several years.

Four years later, now a landscaper who works long hours in the hot sun, he feels his strength building. His biceps are tight, powerful. Sweat drips down his brow. He wipes it away with a quick swipe, lifts the pick, slams it into the hard clay. There is something very basic about digging in the dirt, something primal and suggestive. At six that afternoon, as the sun begins its long fade into twilight, the humidity lifts a little. Such relief, no matter how small, is welcome. It has been a good day. He is tired. He is walking along a sidewalk, on his way to his truck, smoking a cigarette, thinking of nothing . . .

Flash! That room again. It's dark. He sees only outlines. The shadow of his cousin, getting up from the rumpled bed in the corner, naked, smirking, a dark look in his eye. He is standing up against the wall on the opposite side of the room. He feels nothing. His body has gone numb. No!

On the way home, he stops at the liquor store, buys a fifth of Jack Daniels. He will drink it that night—*all* of it.

As he sits on his couch, glass in one hand, cigarette in the other, the fog descends. He feels free. Jack will blot out the memories. The warm liquor courses down his throat, catches a little. His limbs begin to tingle, then go numb.

Flash! Searing pain as his cousin pins his arms, digs a knee into his back, and climbs on. . . . NO!

Shaking, he stands, slams his fist into the wall, grabs the bottle and chugs.

NO! Let me out of here!

Years later, he is standing on his front porch, watching his young daughter play in the yard. She is digging idly in the little sandbox he built for her. He is sober now and has been for a few years. He is happier than he has been in years, but, as he stands there, it seems that the shadows are starting to return. He feels uneasy. He glances over at the corner of the house, notices that the end of day shadows are pushing their way across the lawn toward the crawl space under the house. That's how he feels inside—like the shadows are creeping in on him, about to hit the foundation.

Is that water he sees seeping out from somewhere under the house?

Flash! Pain, this time deep inside him. His cousin struts into the bathroom. He listens silently to the sounds of a long leak, flushing toilet, the shower being turned on.

Her blond hair shifts in a small breeze, and catches the long rays of the sun with a glint. She glances up at him, grimaces at the cigarette in his hand, goes back to her digging, but this time with a little more force. The plastic shovel in her hand twists, and the handle cracks with a SNAP! She looks down at it, and a tear wells up in her eye, streams down her cheek. She cries silently.

Flash! He hears a loud SNAP from the bathroom, followed by his cousin cursing. Something has broken. He doesn't care. But deep inside him, a new feeling wells up, overcomes the numbness . . . shame rumbling into anger, anger into rage. He begins to shake. And a tear streams down his cheek.

One morning, sixteen years later, he awakens with a start. What was that dream?

Flash! The cousin's face looking back into the room, smirk still in place. "Get dressed. Get out. And keep your fat little mouth shut, or I'll do you again. This whole thing—well it's our little secret."

He groans as he climbs out of bed, his muscles stiffening. He is starting to notice, these days, that he moves a little slower in the morning.

Our little secret.

His work is hard, physical. And it takes its toll on a body. But he also knows that he gets up slowly because he has little to look forward to. Hope has slipped from his grasp, begun to roll off him like rain on the super-parched earth after a long drought. He can't soak it up. He only barely notices its presence any more.

Flash! The cousin grins widely, an evil glint in his eye, pumps his hips once, tosses him a shirt, walks out of the room. "Get out. Now."

The memories are coming more often these days. The flashes are more blinding. He fixes a cup of coffee, decides a shot of whiskey won't hurt, will give the coffee the jolt it needs.

Flash! He pulls on his pants slowly, shaking. He walks out of the room. He does not look back.

Torrents

Isaac: The laughing one. He is the second-born son of James and Claire. His smile is rare but bright. When it appears, the world changes. But something has choked off his laughter.

It comes on him in torrents, a dark thunderstorm crashing in on him, washing away his defenses, pouring over him in his dreams, the water seeping and soaking, eroding his dammed-up strength, then breaking through the levees he has built in his heart. The dam bursts, and there he is, overwhelmed by shame and rage and grief.

He remembers being a small boy, about four years old. It is the middle of the night. In his dream, he is being pursued, by something large and scary—a ravening monster. He runs through a dark forest, as fast as his feet can fly. But the monster is gaining. Suddenly, he comes on an opening in the forest and finds himself standing on a cliff. He turns, and there is the monster, bearing down on him. He must choose: Jump or be eaten. He spreads his arms to leap, and, just at that moment, the monster throws him to the ground, leaps on him. And he wakes up screaming, terrified.

Gradually, he becomes aware of something warm and moist near his lap. He gets up, pulls off his pajamas, strips the sheets off the bed, takes them to the hamper, lets the lid close on the damp secret— THUMP. And shame seeps into his heart.

That summer, the family is on a trip across the country to spend the summer in North Dakota. His dad has to do some kind of training out there. He feels the tension in the car, senses that something is about to go wrong. It is hot. The wind whips at his hair, but even with the windows down, there's not much relief from the oppressive, relentless heat.

Beads of sweat form on his dad's brow. He has that look—that dangerous look. He's close to his limit. The boy stirs as his brother takes a poke at him, squirming, moving both to get away and to see if he can make an advantage out of position. Dad, face now reddening in anger, turns, and:

"That's it! It's quiet hour! One more sound out of either of you, and I'll show you something to make noise about!"

"Ugggh."

Next thing he knows, he is standing on the side of the road.

"You want me to leave you here, is that it?"

"No."

"What did you say?"

"No *sir*."

"Bend over, and grab your ankles."

The dad pulls off his thin leather belt with a flourish, and alternates blows between the two brothers. One/one—two/two—three/three. Whack/whack—whack/whack—whack/whack. There seems to be more force in his blows than usual today. And the boy feels a mix of shame and anger welling up inside. But he has learned not to make a sound, not even a whimper. So he takes his licks in silence, and nurses his silent rage.

Shame. Anger. Silence.

That night the boy's dream picks up where it left off. The monster has grabbed him, thrown him to the ground. Now it is beating him, with a belt. Whack. Whack. Whack. The pain surges up in torrents, crashing thunder and flashing lightning, pounding the roof of his consciousness. And he wakes up screaming even louder than before, this time in rage.

He looks down at his lap. Wet again. *Shame.* And he gets up and begins the ritual of late-night laundry.

One day when he is twelve, he is playing basketball on the blacktop by the school with a group of boys he doesn't know too well, doesn't like much. But he is competitive and loves to play. They play rough, though. Street basketball, no fouls. As he guards one of the boys, a kid named James, an elbow flies up, whacks him hard on the chin. He falls back on his butt, jumps up quickly, says,

"You bastard! Foul!"

"O.K. You get a free throw. We throw you down, for free."

Arms—too many arms, too strong to resist—throw him to the blacktop, pin him on his back, spread his legs. He looks up, and James is slowly, methodically taking off his sneakers, slipping on his boots. Then he gets up, lifts the right one high, brings it down hard, right on target. And the boys walk away, laughing, as he lays there, blinded by pain and rage, clutching his wounded crotch.

That night, he dreams the scene again, in exact detail. And, as the boot comes down, he wakes up, screaming. And begins the ritual of late-night laundry, shame mingling with pain and rage.

Several years later, now in his teens, he has abandoned sports for new pursuits. Much of his time, he spends alone, smoking a bit of weed, nursing a beer. Who needs people anyway? They just smoke your stash, drink your beer, and leave. Better just to sneak off into the woods, or lock the basement door . . .

One morning, he stands in the living room of the family's large Victorian house, nursing a wicked hangover. It is a hot August Saturday, around 11:00 A.M., and he has just climbed out of bed, stumbled upstairs. He's trying to remember the night before, but the details are fuzzy. Suddenly, the front door bursts open. There stands his dad, face reddening, brow dripping with sweat. He has been mowing the lawn.

The young man smiles, says: "What's up, Dad?"

And without a word, his dad walks into the living room, knocks him to the floor, walks *through* him as though he doesn't exist, even steps on him, stomps into the kitchen.

Ah, a message, he thinks, as he lies on the floor, though not exactly a clear one. At first he feels a wave of shame. Then the rage boils up, and he decides to clarify the situation:

"Fuck you, dad."

"What did you say?"

"Fuck you, *sir*."

"Out! Get out of my house! Out!"

"It used to be my house, too, *sir*."

He storms out, does not return for two days. When he does, it is to silence, in silence. He never does find out what happened that day. They never talk about it.

A little secret . . .

Secret rage and shame.

Twenty-five years later, now in his late thirties, he stands in the kitchen of his parents' house, sipping a seltzer. The front door bursts open, and there is his dad, all sweaty and red-faced, fists in a clench.

Something familiar about this scene, he thinks.

"What's up, Dad?"

And the dad walks into him, shoves him aside, no longer able to knock him to the floor so easily. This time, no clarification is needed.

But they never speak of these things in this family.

These are private, secret little moments.

Secrets that won't go away.

What a shame.

Shadows . . . and Secrets . . . and Stories

What are secrets? Why do we have them? Why do we keep them? What purposes do they serve? We do know this: "A life of secrecy begins with the first secret" (Goodall, 2005, p. 499). And from that small seed of secrecy, all sorts of dark forests may grow. In the case of this family, the first veil of silent secrecy led to a family pattern of keeping secrets close, of repression and displacement and avoidance (Jung, 1989).

The family in these stories is an afflicted family, a troubled family. These are dark, painful stories, to be sure. There is much pain, in the form of missed opportunities for connection, misunderstanding, abuse, violence, and the deep, abiding sorrow that comes with being harmed by those with whom we are supposedly most connected— our siblings and our parents, our sons and our daughters, our "significant others" (Mead, 1934). There is something that permeates this family structure, a sense of "dis-ease." In response to trauma, in moments of shame and pain and anguish, in times of anxiety and suffering, in loss and in grief, this family does not, perhaps cannot, turn outward for support. So they fold inward and hold the dark little secrets close to their hearts. But the heart cannot hold these things forever.

A heart that holds on to darkness is a breaking heart. The memories won't be contained. The floorboards are buckling. The memories whisper in ears, flash eyes, wash over stomachs, tear at hearts. Caught in the tense dialectics between memory and forgetting, between secret-keeping and storytelling, the family defaults into silence. At times, they feel deeply. They feel as if they have pulled over to the side of the road, broken down: retching, grieving, drawn down into a spiral of pain and shame and rage. At other times, they are just numb, stuck, unable to move, unable to feel, unable to speak. Frozen, unable to grieve, isolated in pain, afflicted. So silence seeps into secrets, and secrets blend into more secrets, and silence begets more silence.

In this family, as in most families, such affliction is not isolated to specific individuals, but hangs instead as *shared* disruption—a living, pervasive *anxiety*. Like a thin veil of fog on a grey morning, such affliction can be damp and cold, chilling even, freezing people in place. It can also be nerve-wracking, pushing people to escape, or to stand stock still, or to fall into silence, addiction, sleep, disorder. Family affliction is, at times, simply overwhelming. Worse, it can be difficult, perhaps impossible, to discern where one person's problems begin and end, and how and where these problems fold into *family* problems—and how and why, in the end, people decide to hold them in silence and secrecy, whether simply struck mute, or choosing not to communicate, or just holding it in, afraid that letting it out will destroy . . . something.

Sometimes the fog lifts a little, and a little story erupts into a flash of clarity; at other times the fog descends, and people grope about trying to make sense of the shattering, shivering ordeals they have experienced: death, loss, sexual abuse, physical violence, alcoholism, anxiety, depression. And, as is common in such families, for several decades now, this family has worked to control the presentation of a family identity in everyday life. The tactics employed to achieve "cover" for the affliction—for the dis-ease—involve a large repertoire, ranging from simple silence or repression to the social performance of achievement, to little white lies, to acts of selfless service for the "less fortunate," to very intricate deceptions, to everyday glossings and embellishments of the truth, all morphing into a closet full of secrets that must be contained but that, at the same time, will not stay put. In all these tactical maneuvers, taken in the service of "impression management" in the face of impending stigma, we humans often stridently and tenaciously and actively attempt to hold our secrets close, in the shadows, in the closet, in the fog, under the floorboards, damp and cold and hidden.

These are, after all, dark, dark secrets. Or so the family believes. The need to keep secrets even pervades everyday language and storytelling *within* the family. Thus, in the family portrayed in these stories, for example, alcoholism, an affliction shared by many family members, is rarely referred to directly in ordinary conversation; references, if they arise at all, tend to be oblique and elliptical. Yet everyone knows the truth. Alcoholism, which the literature on recovery labels a *family* affliction (Black, 1985, 2002; Bradshaw, 1995; Satir, 1967, 1972), is like an elephant in the living room that the family agrees not to mention, in case that might somehow make it depart, or at least seem less large. The family is afflicted because, try as they might, they cannot get the alcoholic to stop drinking. Along the way, they fall into the painful, tortured, and ultimately doomed task of managing the impressions of others so that those others will not learn of the alcoholic affliction. In so doing, they fall into dysfunctional patterns of communication, spiraling unresolved conflict, and general torment. And, along the way, the darker details—the little clues and whispers and secrets that hint at the diseased, rotting heart of the family—are left out of the stories. *Denial* is the primary symptom of alcoholism (Bradshaw, 1995).

According to the Swiss psychiatrist C. G. Jung (1989), within each of us is a part of the self, a "shadow," that consists of all the repressed and unconsciously harbored dark energy that has emanated from moments of grief, dysfunction, illness, trauma, and so on that make their way into our consciousness. In Jungian psychology, one of the great tasks of life is to learn to face and integrate these shadow-energies. If we are to become healthy, functioning human beings, the theory goes, we must face our darker selves. And in facing—and to a large extent, accepting, even *embracing*, that darkness—that Mr. Hyde who lives within each of us Jekylls—we can come to peace and wholeness.

Most people, as Jung points out, do not wish to undertake this voyage into the darkness within. Still, the unconscious can only stand so much pressure. So these things have a way of bubbling up to the surface. Indeed, much of Jung's psychotherapeutic practice demonstrates this principle; the practice of Jungian analysis is aimed at uncovering these dark energies within the patient, and most of his patients presented themselves to Jung because of apparently *spontaneous eruptions* of these energies in their lives. Something as simple as a bad dream, or a whisper of a memory that causes a stir in the patient, or even something as debilitating as the development of an ongoing addiction (an eating disorder, alcoholism, drug addiction, etc.) could be considered such an eruption—a manifestation, in tangible form, of both a dark energy at the core of the person engaged in the practice, and of the loss of control by that same person over the eruption.

In any event, one cannot forever escape the intrusion of the shadow into everyday life. The secrets come up—in the wind, in flashes, in whispers, in torrents, in waves. And so, as I began my ethnographic journey a few years ago, memories, dreams, and secrets began to slip into my writing, first as hint and innuendo, as thin little threads of storied experience, as little uncontrolled vignettes creeping into my stories of communication in everyday life. At first, I purged these little fragments from my writing during the editing process. After all, I reasoned, even though they might be "real" or honest or important, they were only fragments anyway, and they might be, at best, self-serving and at worst, life-damaging. They might put certain people, or characters in the stories (or, at least, the public "faces" of these people) at risk of humiliation. And anyway, I questioned whether these little fragments of secrets seeping in really served the story. So I had better, I thought, carefully consider the potential impact of what I write before I proceed along this path.

But the memories cannot be contained. They *must* be made into stories (Kuhn, 1995). I, as writer of ethnography, face a predicament: These stories cannot be told, but they cannot *not* be told! What to do with all these memories morphing into secrets, secrets morphing into stories? How can I reverently, respectfully write these stories into life, knowing that I am exposing to the light of story many things that have lived in the shadowy crawl spaces of my family's collective lives? And, most important, what might this uncontained, uncontrollable, seeping, searing, flashing, torrential in-burst of memory, falling out of secret, crafted into story, do *to* or *for* those whose stories I tell?

What is the "ethical" thing to do? Ethnographers and other qualitative researchers who come into direct contact with others—especially intimate others like family members and friends—while researching human social life are faced with compelling questions of ethical responsibility. Do I reveal the secrets and stories others reveal to me? Why or why not? If so, how?

Carolyn Ellis (2007) argues for a relational ethics of care in autoethnographic and personal narrative research. A relational ethics is an ethics that raises more questions than it answers, that calls the researcher, at every turn, to search, to question, to confront self, other, and secret directly, dynamically, with heart, with care. As she puts it, "Central to relational ethics is the question 'What should I do now?' rather than the statement 'This is what you should do now'" (p. 4).

A relational ethics is an ethics of wonder. Faced with revelations of secrets, trauma, and darkness from the depths of the human spirit, we are confronted with questions about how we might act in a "humane, non-exploitative way" (Ellis, 2007, p. 5), while we "honor our relational responsibilities yet present our lives in a complex and truthful way for readers" (p. 17). There are no easy answers to these struggles. Each case is different, driven by different exigencies, different relationships, different purposes, different fears, different needs. But each case calls us to reach toward care.

How dare we speak or write of the pain, loss, anger, and fear that may come of trauma? Like the thin wisps and blinding flashes of memory, and the tiny, seeping-whispering rhizomatic secrets that grow from them, ethical questions like these are elusive yet insistent. Like particularly haunting dreams, these questions break into consciousness during the writing process, nagging and tugging at the corners of awareness, insisting on being taken into account but offering no easy or simple or neat or appropriate responses.

If we could just craft a code of ethics to cover every situation confronted in research! But, of course, life—like the memory and secret and story I am tracing here—is too complex for all-inclusive covering laws. So, we are left with decisions, flawed as they may be, about how to render stories and characters and lives, about how and why and when and where to reveal matters of the heart, of the soul, of the shadow.

We are left with conscience. Conscience, as Emmanuel Levinas (1969, 1981) points out, is a force driven by the particular face and presence of the Other who inhabits my world—in this case, the Other about whom I may write a story. Conscience is invoked by the face of the Other. Its exigencies are shaped by the case at hand, by my dynamic relationship with this Other. The possibility of a "fitting response" (Schrag, 1997, 2002) to the "call of conscience" (Hyde, 2001) is invoked as a choice by our shared human agency, endowed with the creative, co-constructive force of human communicative practice. Our communicative acts, including our storied acts, constitute our shared social reality. These are not choices to be taken lightly.

And yet, if Walter Fisher (1987) was correct in his assertion—that we humans are, fundamentally, *homo narrans*, driven by the very roots of our co-being to tell our stories—and I think he *is* right—then I must find a way to give these stories to the world. In the stories told here, I have chosen to "thin out" the stories, to tell them skeletally, so to speak, to trace the barest of bones of the stories. The stories are, like the memories and secrets out of which they are born, only *traces* of the *whole* story. I have also chosen to "fictionalize" the stories so that the characters are not exposed. Their "truth value" has to do with how the stories penetrate the heart, and speak to the heart of the matter—the heart of darkness that can hold any one of us in its sway. If you see some of yourself in any one of these stories, then something important has happened; if you see your family here—even better. Identification is the first step toward getting at the truth of these stories. More will be revealed about what an accidental ethnographer might do with all this in the next chapter.

Meanwhile, these writing choices are built, in part, to protect identity and to mitigate the possibility of stigma. They are also, in part, conscience-driven *responses* born of my dynamic, caring relations with the particular humans in these stories. I do not wish to hurt them. Indeed, I hope that by telling these stories I can help as many people as possible to overcome the horrors that face them. I hope and believe that stories have the power to heal and to help us all move outward into the light-filled world that vibrates beyond the cold, damp, and intricately shadowy realm of pain, loss, suffering, grief, and secrecy that may threaten to overwhelm us as a result of traumas large and small. I hope that readers will find some resonance in the heart of these stories; that many readers may see parts of themselves here; and that some may make different choices about how to live their lives after reading these stories. At the very least, the presence of these stories suggests a simple—albeit not an easy—healing choice that may be made in the face of trauma. Rather than secret-keeping, we might do well to turn to storytelling as a means of overcoming the pain, shame, loss, grief, anger, and sadness.

The stories, as rendered here, are, like all stories, *partial* accounts of experience. In their current form, they render the problem but represent no "ease" from the "dis-ease," no solution or fitting response. I want to suggest, then, that the stories themselves are the beginning place for that fitting response; they provide an opening to the continuing building of a life grounded in story-weaving practice, wherein the family might well be liberated from the harboring of secrets into a life-affirming crafting, weaving, and blending of new and greater stories—stories that shed light on the shadow, stories that release the secrets, stories that smooth the floorboards in that closet of the unconscious. Stories might well be the only way to gain a footing whereby the smell of death and grief and pain—of trauma, of hurt and loss and shame and rage and dark, secret, silence—might begin to dissipate.

In a sense, these are not stories of particular people but rather of *all* of us. All families have secrets; all families feel pain and loss and trauma. If we can open our hearts to the power of story and begin to read the clues that stories offer in our quest to follow the mystery of human life, we may well transcend the dark powers that threaten to buckle our floorboards.

And, in *that* sense, to tell the story may well be the *only* ethical thing to do.

Reflection

If you think dreams are tricky to write about, wait until you get to buried memories and deep, dark secrets. These things are notoriously slippery. Not only do unspoken and unspeakable things *become* secrets, they often seem to work very hard, with the help of the human players in the scene, to *stay* that way.

And yet, as *homo narrans*, the storytelling creatures (Bochner, 2001; Fisher, 1987; Goodall, 1996, 2005), we humans are naturally, deeply, and magnificently oriented toward story-making. Indeed, we arise in—and out of—our stories. We are, as co-narrators, ever in the act of creating new realities, narratively. We are also called, by our very storied being, to be participant-listeners in the stories of those others we encounter.

In the discipline of communication studies, our ethnographers—particularly those who traffic in the "new ethnography" (Goodall, 1996, 2000)—have, in recent years, offered deep insight into the dynamic and mysterious narrative contours of our co-being. Bochner (2001) offers a cogent account of the virtues of a narrative approach to understanding human life. He carefully pushes us to focus on the deeper meanings of narrative, urging us beyond the critical and theoretical *analysis* of narratives for instrumental academic purposes and toward the crucial *heuristic* insight that narrative truth is at the very core of our human being; we simply *must* engage our narrative meaning-making faculties if we are to survive as human beings in a human world.

Meanwhile, Pelias (2000, 2004) passionately and evocatively reminds us of the heart's involvement in these transcendent moments of story-making. And Ellis (2007) tells us that our story-making must, inevitably, involve us in a relational-dialogic ethic of care that brings us together, in dialogue, with the characters who inhabit our lives and our stories—we *must* embrace this ethic of care, she argues, or our story-making praxis can threaten, even sever, the ties that bind us. Goodall (2005) offers the notion that we all live out a "narrative inheritance" that provides us with a framework for understanding our identity through the storied lives of our forbears. He writes: "I use this term to describe the afterlives of the sentences used to spell out the life stories of those who came before us. What we inherit narratively from our forbears provides us with a framework for understanding our identity through theirs" (p. 497).

Indeed.

Many ethnographers[1] have explored and expanded our narrative knowing of human social life in deep, enriching, and fascinating detail. This rich, emerging tradition of ethnographic and autoethnographic work always reminds me of that storied *center* of our human being. It also reminds me that there are close connections between the narratives we tell, the narrative trajectories we live out, and the dialogic action we might fall into on any given day. All of this is grounded in a life of the heart (Pelias, 2004; Poulos, 2004b). All of this is born of one of the primary forces that gets carried through our narrative inheritance: *narrative conscience.* Together, we weave a story-making praxis that infuses consciousness, and thus makes its way into a storied narrative conscience (a "knowing together") that is the energy that allows us to go on in a community of humans. Narrative conscience is the storied eruption of imaginative possibility that pours forth into our lives as a primary pathway to all forms of "knowing together." Narrative praxis is the center and ground of conscience-building in all cultures and communities (Campbell, 1948; Fisher, 1987). Narrative conscience, then, is grounded in and emergent from a way of being in the world that foregrounds the vital importance of the story as the center of human social life and the storyteller as the weaver of the fabric of shared social existence (Taylor, 1996).

But the building of the narrative is an organic process, arising spontaneously from our co-being. To be sure, stories are a *response* to previous stories; each story is a link in a chain of story-utterances that bind us together through the ages (Bakhtin, 1981, 1993). Thus, no story emerges in a vacuum. Still, as often as not, we simply *fall into* story; story is perhaps easier to stumble into than dialogue, as we appear to be "wired" for story (Bruner, 1987; Fisher, 1987; Goodall, 1996, 2005). Stories just emerge, naturally, as a primary way that we relate with each other. On any given occasion, we may find ourselves in a story, standing at the threshold of a new world, which is itself a threshold for joint action or shared possibility or dialogic engagement.

And so, as I turn to you, responding to your presence in our world, I turn to you for a story. I turn to you, opening myself to your narrative capacities, hoping that the tale you weave will be a tale of resonance and import. In turn, I offer you my story. Together, we craft the story of "us"—the story that will guide us along the way on the next phase of our life journey.

Renewal

On one recent day, I find myself falling into story. I am sitting on the porch with my mom. It is a lovely early spring day. The dogwoods are just beginning to burst forth in that wash of color that always takes me aback. The abundant birds that make their way to North Carolina this time of year offer a soft symphony, as background to our gentle conversation.

My mom, now seventy-two, was a world traveler by the time she was eleven years old. She is a natural storyteller with a welcoming face. Sitting with her, I can just listen, watching how she smiles even as she talks, without my attention fading, for as long as she will speak. I am a quieter sort, more introverted, tending to take it all in before responding, but she makes it especially easy to listen.

Then, somehow, we begin speaking of her father, my grandfather. It's just a spontaneous moment in an ordinary conversation. But suddenly we are swept up in some story-trading. How can we not? Grandpa was a most remarkable man, who meant so much to us in this life.

My grandfather, the adventurer, the wild stubborn headstrong impulsive man, the hobo-baker-forester-farmer-professor, the gambler who lived on the edge of danger his whole life, the mercurial man who outlived all his friends and who, in his later years, began to lose it a bit, first with alcoholic binges, then later, after he stopped drinking cold turkey, with moments of lapsed memory or diminishing social inhibitions, who became a bit of a kleptomaniac as he edged toward ninety-four, and who returned to church in his last years of life after an absence of seventy-five years, who lived life to the fullest, who lived a storied life and who, above all, became the symbol of strength and connection in our family, who lived in a way that we all turned to for guidance, not because he had it all right or because he was smarter or better or more capable than any of us but simply and honestly because he lived fearlessly, courageously. He never backed down from a challenge, never quailed in the face of overwhelming odds, never let fear defeat him, never wavered in his conviction that the world was his oyster and thus never lost a battle except for the final battle, which we believe he not so much *surrendered* or *lost* as *decided*, decided to exit on his own terms, decided not to let a bad death take him later but rather after ninety-four years on this planet decided to go to sleep and say "Adios," as he so often said in life when he shuffled off to bed, that being his way of saying goodnight from as far back as I remember.

These were stories of darkness and light, of sadness and humor, and of life's little lessons writ large in the bold hand of this fearless man. Along the way, my mom tells me the following story, a story that offered me an opening to another story:

Mom: When we were in Paraguay, there was a military coup. It happened when we were walking home from school. I think I was eleven, and Bud was nine. Buddy and I were walking along the dirt road on the way back to our house, when someone came riding along on horseback, yelling, "Get down! Get down!" People were diving into the ditch beside the road so we did, too. And gunshots broke out. Dad was in the house and he apparently heard the commotion. I looked up just as he opened the front door. He stood on the porch, looking around, and a bullet lodged in the doorpost next to his head. He just looked over at it, then spotted me looking at him. He walked calmly

over to Bud and me, grabbed our hands, lifted us to our feet, and
guided us inside.

She pauses for a breath. Then she goes on:

I knew I was safe with my dad. I was always safe when he was there.
That night we left Paraguay on an airplane, and we were off to our next
adventure.

Me: Sounds like Grandpa. I remember one time we were standing in a
line at some feed store somewhere, and this big, burly guy who towered
over both of us kind of came in and muscled past us, breaking in line.
Grandpa just tapped him on the shoulder and said, "We were here first."
The guy just laughed and said, "Oh yeah?" Grandpa looked at him
intently, and said, "Oh yeah." The guy looked him in the eye, kind of
flinched, and retreated to the end of the line. Something passed between
them there . . . a clear message. But Grandpa never flinched. What a guy.

Mom: Yes, that's Daddy. He was a little guy, but very strong. The
strongest man I've ever met.

Me (*smiling*): Strong, and bold, and stubborn. And a little crazy.

Mom (*laughing*): Yes. Remember the time he stole the woodpecker
statue out of the neighbor's yard?

Me (*now laughing, too*): Oh, man.

Mom: You know, he was about ninety-two, and I think he was losing it
a little. I asked him why he took it, and he said he figured he wanted it
more than that guy. I made him take it back.

We fall silent for a moment, slipping into reverie about this man we
loved so dearly. Then:

Me: Say, Mom . . . I like how we tell stories about Grandpa and family
and so on. Do you think we could do this more often? I think it
somehow helps me . . . be part of this family.

Mom: Sure, that sounds fun.

Me: I like this.

Mom: Me, too.

Me: I think our Grandpa stories really teach us about life. About *us*.

Mom: Yes.

Me: Thanks.

In any given story, if we listen closely, we will hear a tale of conscience. In her story of my Grandpa, my mother just *knew* she was safe, as long as her dad was in charge. That is a powerful knowledge, reinforced by the narrative re-configuration of it; this knowledge, passed along through story, draws, of course, on my own storied knowledge and experience of my grandfather's character, and, at the same time, writes his qualities—his courage, his strength, his care—forever into the larger story of a life, and thus of lives.

And this story leads me to another story, a story of a life unfolding, a story of courageously embracing the dialogic and narrative possibilities of family and communal life. In the newly unfolding story, I find myself a father, called on to protect and guide my own children. And so I live the legacy of my grandfather's story. It is my narrative inheritance (Goodall, 2005).

In living out my narrative inheritance, I have found myself in situations that would have, without the storied example of my grandfather, baffled me. I have had to stand with my children when they were hurt—physically, emotionally, socially—and I have had to help them draw up the *courage to be*—the power to stand fast and strong, in the face of the deep anxiety that can come with pain, with the threat of loss, with threats of all sorts. I stood and held Eli when he was less than two years old, as the doctor sewed his gashed lip, and I have helped Noah bravely face stitches in a torn foot. I have stood with Eli when his girlfriend dumped him, and I have been with Noah after he was teased at school. I have been with them both when death visited our family, when we lost our dogs, my grandmother, my grandfather.

In each of these moments, I was visited by my narrative inheritance: Grandpa's courage. Part of me wanted to run like a squirrel. But I knew that is not what Grandpa would do.

One evening, Eli and I are leaving fencing class. It is dark in the parking lot, and my hands are full of athletic bags filled with equipment. As we approach the car, a man leaps out from behind it, runs up very close to me, and starts yelling about something. It looks and feels a bit like I am being mugged. And then, I look over the man's shoulder, and there is Eli, sword in hand, crouched in a full *en garde* position, ready to protect me. So I drop a bag, look at the man, and point over his shoulder. The man looks, sees Eli at the ready, and decides to depart into the shadows.

Narrative inheritance, morphing into narrative conscience, has taken hold, and we are forever changed. This is a story we get a lot of mileage out of—a story, I am sure, that Eli's grandchildren will someday hear. The groundwork of narrative conscience is laid. And so, as we attune our consciousness to the world we inhabit, we may discover that our old, slippery, faded, dark, shadowy memories, dreams, secrets, or reflections may erupt, unbidden, into our world. Sometimes it works like this: There is that odd but oddly familiar smell, or that little flash of light, or that wave of emotion, or that wisp of a memory, or that dark dream, or that thin little whispering at the edges of consciousness. This is a *call*—a call from our narrative conscience, from that still, small voice that lives within us and that knows, in the end, the right thing to do. The essence of working with this material is, it seems to me, to be *attentive*, as much as possible, to the openings, to the little bucklings in the floorboards that may, from time to time, erupt. If an opening presents itself, then it is a matter of *encouraging* the making of a story.

Sometimes, the simple act of requesting just that will be enough: "Tell me a story, please." Sometimes, the possibilities that lead to the transformation of a secret into a story come from deep and active listening, from careful attunement of consciousness to the openings, from perseverance and from caring engagement with the family. Sometimes, you can work very hard to get at something, and it slips away. Really, you never know what might erupt. The trick is to be *available* to it when it does.

But know that memory and secrecy and story are all tricky to work with. About a year after my mom told me the story above about my grandfather in Paraguay, I reminded her of the story. And she said, in all earnestness, "I don't remember that at all." It was as if this was the first she had heard of it. My mom does not have dementia or Alzheimer's or any other physical dysfunction. Even for healthy people, memory is like that. It is elusive and sometimes situational. So I had to talk her through the story and the circumstances in which it emerged. At the end of our conversation, she said, somewhat grudgingly, "I guess I remember."

A life of secrecy, of "We don't talk about such things," dies hard. Perhaps we will never fully unravel the mystery that lives in the realm of memory, dream, and secret. Sometimes, we have to use our own experience and imagination to fill in the gaps. Yet, despite all the pitfalls, the stories that sometimes emerge from trying to get at the heart of a family's secrecy seem to make it all worth the effort. Indeed, the process can be magical, transformative, filled with power.

A family once beset by trauma and tragedy and deep, dark sadness can, gradually, emerge into the light of story and healing and joy.

So, it seems to me that it's worth a shot. The worst that can happen is that your quest hits a brick wall. Since that wall has always been there, at least that encounter should feel familiar. What I have done is to work hard to recover my own memory, while, at the same time, seeking to be attentive to the memories, dreams, reflections, and secrets of my family members as they leak out into everyday conversation. And, so far, it has worked. I have learned much from this simple attunement of consciousness and the willingness to openly embrace a story when it begins, however haltingly, to emerge into our world.

So delving into secrets may, in the end, be an act of faith, carried by a faith in action. Attunement, perseverance, faith, and good, honest digging: These are the tools of the accidental ethnographer seeking to engage the mysteries of secrecy, memory, dream, and half-story in the family. The writer of accidental ethnography forges ahead, even into the darkness, because she must. The accidental ethnographer enters the forest because he can no longer not enter.

One final note here. The accidental ethnographer is working with material that is, as I have said, notoriously difficult to pin down. In the end, all you have is *your* story, which is your re-construction of memories, dreams, secrets, whispers, fragments, events, silences, words spoken and things left unsaid, and all the mysterious hints and murmurings that come upon you. If the story were told from someone else's perspective, it would be *their* story. So don't be surprised if, when you reveal what you've written to your significant others, they say something like this: "Well, that sounds right—sort of." Or this: "That's not how I remember it at all."

Sometimes, you will have to let go of the dream of "accuracy" or even "fidelity" and just aim for resonance.

Sometimes, letting go is a beautiful thing to do.

Exercises

Writing Exercise 1: Rough Times, Breakthroughs, and Turning Points

All lives have challenges—rough spots, moments of turmoil, trials and tribulations, breakdowns, losses, etc. We lose loved ones, relationships become toxic or get broken, we are forced to move at a particularly bad time, people are mean to us, we are subjected to ridicule, embarrassed, addicted, conflicted, or otherwise in pain or in trouble. These rough spots evoke some difficult emotions—anger, sadness, fear, despair, pain, grief, jealousy, envy, greed, and so on. A challenge for the writer of autoethnography is to go inside and probe and write from within these emotions.

That is your challenge with this exercise. It is time to write about a rough time in your life. Write evocatively, performatively, *from within* the emotional landscape of that part of your experience. The big challenge here is to bring your reader along with you. Does your piece *move* the reader to the emotions you experienced? One of Laurel Richardson's (2000) criteria for evaluating ethnographic work is *impact*. The reader will evaluate your work, asking: Does this piece affect me? Emotionally? Intellectually? Generate new questions? Move me to write? Move me to feel in new ways? Move me to action?

Remember what we've learned so far about telling a vivid story. Take your reader with you on your emotional journey. In the end, of course, you may want to write hope—or at least a hint of it—into your story. If so, you can proceed by asking yourself: Have I moved beyond the rough spot? How? How has this experience changed me and my fellow characters? What is the ray of hope, of breakthrough? Have I transcended the difficult emotions and the struggles, at least for a time?

Writing Exercise 2: Signs, Secrets, and Stories

Have you ever noticed something out of the ordinary? Have you ever been presented, seemingly by accident, with a *sign*? Have you ever heard the faint whisper of a secret? Have you ever noticed something that, until now, you had not been aware of? Have you ever had an experience where a memory—even a very dim fragment of a memory—has been triggered by a sight, a sound, a smell, a taste, a texture, a sensation, an intuition, a human presence, an event, a dream, or a story? Have you ever found your attention tuning into the signs that surround you in your world?

To accomplish this exercise you'll want to read. Read everything ever written about ethnography by Art Bochner, Norman Denzin, Carolyn Ellis, Buddy Goodall, John Van Maanen, and others. Read all the novels of Walker Percy and John Nichols and Anne D. LeClaire and Norman McLean and Michael Parker and Fred Chappell and Ann Lamott and Thomas King and Mark Twain and Kurt Vonnegut and everyone else you can think of; read the poetry of Homer and Robert Frost and T.S. Eliot and ee cummings; read the plays of Aeschylus and Shakespeare, Shaw, Beckett and Pinter and Miller. Read all the great stories of our culture. Then read some more. OK, I'm overstating things. You have a lifetime to read all this work. But read *something*. Good reading makes for good writing.

As you go about the business of living, and as you begin to make yourself, every day, available to the possibility of accidental ethnography, you will want to become attuned to the little signs, the symbols, the clues, the hints, the whispers, and the cracklings and the smells and the sights and the sounds that might lead somewhere. You must become, as Goodall (1994, 1996) would have it, a "detective" seeking the least clue that might lead you toward a meaningful accounting of the signs and symbols and possibilities that infuse your world. When presented with a sign or a clue or even a vague hint, write your way into it. Write until you can write no more. Then write some more. Eventually, you will begin to make sense of it all. The story will come. Faith and courage and perseverance will, in the end, get you to where you need to go. Go!

Queries

1. Do you know a secret that your family keeps—or even the faint whisper that there might be one? Can you piece together the story?
2. How do you—and your significant others—deal with tragic or painful moments in your life? What do you do? What do you say? How do you say it?
3. What roles does silence play in your life? Do you engage in peaceful, meditative silence? Have you ever been hit by uncomfortable, painful, or secretive silence? How do you respond?
4. How do you and your family communicate? Do you privilege openness, or some other standard?
5. How have you made sense, in your writing, of the memories, secrets, signs, stories, symbols, whispers, fragments, and silences in your life story?

Note

1. See, for example, Alexander (2003), Ashton (2004), Bochner (2001), Clair (1998, 2003), Conquergood (1993), de la Garza (2004), Denton (2004, 2006), Denzin (1997, 2001), Denzin & Lincoln (2005), Ellis (1995, 2007), Goodall (1996, 2005), Holman-Jones (1998), Menchaca (2004), Pelias (2000, 2004), Poulos (2002, 2004a, 2004b, 2006a, 2006b, 2008a, 2008b), Richardson (2000, 2005), Taylor (1996), Tillmann-Healy (2001), Trujillo (2004), and Warren & Fassett (2004), to name but a few.

Chapter Five

Evoking Archetypal Themes in an Ethnographic Life

We can keep from a child all knowledge of earlier myths, but we cannot take from him the need for mythology.
—C. G. Jung, *The Archetypes and the Collective Unconscious*

Myths are public dreams, dreams are private myths.
—Joseph Campbell, *Myths to Live By*

The Search for Meaning in a Troubled World

Most of us seek to locate or develop or interpret or even dream up some sort of meaning for our experiences. Many seek it in friendship, in family, in some sort of group affiliation, in engagement and action in a community, in work, at play. Some find their sought-after higher meaning in the rituals and belief systems of organized religion. Others seek it in a more broadly spiritual way, less bound by the rituals and rules of religion, drawn by the spirit of the search itself. These moments and spaces of action and connection can be vibrant sources of possibility and meaning. Of course, these contexts are often fraught with trials and tribulations, and though some find meaning even in their own suffering, others feel stymied in their search as circumstances seem to send them spiraling deep into the darkness of misunderstanding, betrayal, conflict, miscommunication, mistrust, tension, secrecy, or deception—and the all-too-often attendant feelings of anxiety, anger, depression, despair.

But somehow, nearly all of us can admit to the power and resonance and meaning of the great stories that inform and infuse our lives. This chapter is about the potential of a *mythical* vision to invigorate our search for higher meaning.

The Power of *Mythos*

Unfortunately, the myth has fallen on hard times. The word, derived from the Greek root *mythos*, shimmering with the power of creation and the eternal light of Being, originally referred to a great story of deep meaning and eternal significance, a story whose truths transcended time and space and earthbound existence. But with the ascendancy of science in the Enlightenment, myth came to mean "falsehood"—a fantastical story with little connection to truth, a lie.

I will invoke, however, the original meaning of the word, and highlight the patterns of the great myths, seeking the truth, the insight, and the light that these great story-patterns offer us. For example, those who study myth note the pattern of eternal return (Campbell, 1972). In the earliest myths from cultures around the world, we return to the moment of origin, to consciousness, to that great moment when creation unfolded. Usually, this moment involves moving out of chaos into sense, out of darkness into light.

God comes to consciousness and says, "Let there be light!" (Genesis 1:3), and all sorts of remarkable things follow.

And then, in all the great myths, there is a moment when a human becomes conscious, mirroring the moment of creation, light flooding in . . .

In Eden, Adam's consciousness dawns, and it turns out to be a dual consciousness, a consciousness of self and of *conscience* (the dawning is, after all, the result of eating fruit from the tree of knowledge of good and evil). In a flash, he realizes he is *exposed*, and he *knows*.

Of course, despite the bad rap many members of organized religion have laid on Eve, it was a woman who was smart enough to see that Adam *needed* this gift. After all, consciousness of the difference between good and evil is surely a gift—it is conscience born—that still, small voice that guides us toward the good life.

Moving on to other great stories from ancient traditions, we find further guidance for living well in a troubled world. In his short essay, *The Myth of Sisyphus*, Albert Camus finds a possible light-source to awaken us, to pull us out of this problem of Despair, to assuage our fears, to open us to possibility, to hope. He sees hope, ironically, in the story of Sisyphus—whom, you will recall, was punished for his sins, for separating himself from the gods and from humans through his greed, to roll a huge rock to the top of a mountain, only to have it roll back down to the bottom, thus forcing Sisyphus into repetitive toil for all eternity.

Perhaps we can learn from this tragic hero, Camus suggests. He imagines approaching Sisyphus with a question. Of course, one has to be careful in approaching a man like Sisyphus. He's a pretty intense guy. In those moments when he strains to push the rock to the top, as he struggles and sweats and toils, he is too blind to see beyond his rock. Like all who are caught up in heavy labor, he cannot see past what he is doing. For all intents and purposes, he *is* his rock: "A face that toils so close to stones is already stone itself!" (Camus, 1955, p. 89).

According to Camus, we must approach Sisyphus in his moment of respite, after his rock has crested the hill and begun its inexorable descent to the plain below. In that moment, as Sisyphus trudges back down the hill to meet his fate, there is an opportunity, an opening: "It is during that return, that pause, that Sisyphus interests me. . . . I see that man going back down with a heavy yet measured step toward the torment of which he will never know the end. That hour like a breathing space which returns as surely as his suffering, *that* is the hour of consciousness" (Camus, 1955, p. 89).

That hour of consciousness provides an opening. In the moment of consciousness, in coming to wakefulness and full awareness, freedom rises. Consciousness begs a question: How to act? In the end, if we are to understand his plight and his respite, if we are to come to grips with his whole story, we must call Sisyphus out; we must question him. We simply *must* ask: Sisyphus, what will you *do*?

In the end, he chooses action. For it is in action that hope is born.

That moment of consciousness is a moment of *possibility*.

And, in addressing Sisyphus, we have opened the door a crack. *Possibility* . . .

Sisyphus is in crisis.

Crisis: that split in consciousness—the interruption—that comes just before moments of breakthrough.

Have you ever been in crisis?

Suppose you wake up one day, and find yourself walking back down the hill. Suppose you realize that, for this moment, you are conscious of freedom, of possibility; and thus you have been given a "new lease on life." For a moment, at least, you have respite from your suffering. And it occurs to you that you might start over.

Suppose one day you really could start over. Suppose you had a simple but powerful *breakdown*, followed by a *breakthrough*, from which you emerged, still breathing. Maybe even barely breathing. But still breathing. Suppose, in fact, that because of your painful yet freeing experience you felt like a new person with a new life. Suppose that vague sense of anxiety you had carried around with you, the anxiety that sometimes accelerated and took hold of your senses, tilted toward fear, toward stark-raving terror, was, well, fading.

What then? Standing at the threshold, in the darkness fading into light, what would you do? Where might you find the light that may illuminate your world—and thus, perhaps, end your crisis?

In the ancient myths that inform our culture, we see countless examples of this dilemma. What to do when one is at the cliff's edge of life? What to do when finitude and faith collide and despair beckons with its seductive, scary darkness?

In the end, following suffering and lament, Cain removes to Nod and bears children. In the end, following suffering and lament, Job is restored, returning to good fortune and the light of happy family. In the end, following suffering and lament, Jesus returns, offering himself as a beacon light of hope for generations to come.

In the ancient world, it was a well-recognized insight that the energy of *mythos*, of archetypal story-weaving, offers meaning to an existence that may (like Sisyphus's life), at times, seem barren, bleak, and repetitive. Of course, oral cultures throughout history and across great geographical spans have seen—and practiced, even *lived*—the arts of myth-making and story-telling as central activities of human existence (Abram, 1996; Ong, 1982).

In oral cultures, the story is the primary mode of communication. Small, everyday stories inform and infuse daily life, offering narrative structure to otherwise mundane events. Meanwhile, grand, archetypal, culture-shaping myths—stories on a larger scale—are told, heard, felt, and followed as guideposts or pathways to transcendence of ordinary, everyday, profane/mundane existence. And some stories reside in that liminal space between the mythical and the everyday, drawing on the energies that emanate from both poles. In such narrative life practice, the smaller stories of everyday life are a central way of making sense of daily social-human experience, the "mid-size" stories speak to somewhat larger communal issues of human conduct and morality, and the grand myths are gateways to hierophanies (see Chapter Three).

The mythically infused great stories—the guiding myths of a culture—open doors or paths for possibility. In myth, we bump up against "thin places," allowing movement toward the sacred. There is a sense of the Holy that emerges in telling—and listening to—the kind of great story that somehow taps into the universal, that strikes at the heart of what it means to be human. The grand myths show us the way into the sacred, and allow us, at least for a time, to enter— and perhaps live, breathe, and absorb—that which is Holy.

In this chapter, I want to focus on the insights gained by tapping into the archetypal patterns and energies that shape our mythological landscape, and then return to engaging the practice of accidental ethnography as a pathway toward release from the grips of secrecy. One pathway to release, I will propose, comes via tapping into the power of *mythos*. This is accidental ethnography informed by mythical sensibilities, allowing us to approach the problem of family secrecy from a new perspective—a mythically guided, archetypally patterned way of living and writing that recaptures the wisdom of the ancient world as a pathway toward possibility, healing, even redemption.

So: Are there central life-giving and life-guiding themes that are shared by nearly all humans?

Themes of joy and sorrow, of risk and reward, of trauma and triumph, of creation and destruction, of life and death, of connection and isolation, of love and hate, of breakthrough and breakdown, of communion and loneliness, seem to be prevalent in most Western cultures, and certainly in many accounts of human experience. From Native American stories to Ancient African fables to Buddhist parables to Greek or Hindu or Hebrew myths, many accounts of human experience are fraught with danger—and victory. The emergence of archetypal mythical themes within stories small and large is the thread of that sacred energy that is the lifeblood of the human quest for meaning.

Myth is a tie that binds us all.

But in Western culture, there has long been a move toward relegating the mysterious power of *mythos* to the sidelines where, at best, even great archetypal stories serve as "entertainment" or "information" rather than sources of deep inspiration or meaning. This devaluing of myth, inaugurated by Plato and reified by the Enlightenment's push toward rationality and hyper-scientism, has led much of the modern academy to value *logos* over *mythos*, and thus to dismiss the power of *mythos* to guide, inform, and affirm human being.

Nowhere has this shift away from *mythos* been so profound and overarching as it has been in the social sciences, including (ironically) the study of communication. It has, over time, become taboo to speak—much less to write—about the sacred, the spiritual, the grand, the awe-inspiring, or the mythical as we study human social life. Have you ever noticed that communication scholars, so willing to teach and write about "stages of relationship development" or "uncertainty reduction" or "social penetration," almost never talk or write about *love*?[1]

The language of science, of *logos*, has long been the language of parsing, of breaking things down into their parts. With our mouths and our keyboards bristling with little Ockham's razors, we tear things apart, looking for the smallest viable units of knowledge. We speak of "data" —little bits of information—as the building blocks of knowledge.[2]

According to mainstream social science conventions, we are allowed to speak and write *objectively*, or *theoretically* or *analytically* or even *critically*. But what about speaking and writing *passionately*, or even *mythically*? These forms of expression, long considered taboo, are beginning to resurface, however. In recent years, ethnographers and autoethnographers have begun to challenge the ascendancy of *logos* and to bring both *pathos* (the bracing power of emotional life) and *mythos* (the invigorating power of story) back to the attention of academic audiences in the social sciences. In part, those of us who have practiced what Goodall (2000) calls "the new ethnography" have been *driven* by unseen and only partially understood forces to work toward reopening the ancient practice of story-making as a legitimate form of academic discourse. Besides, the stories we need to tell about who we are just keep coming up, asserting themselves into our writing and our lives. To paraphrase novelist Anne D. LeClaire's (2001) commentary on secrets, the trouble with great stories is that they won't stay put.

The language of *mythos* and *pathos*—the language of story, of myth, of the human heart, of emotion—evokes the greater scale of the whole of life in this human universe. It works against the notion of parsing and division, against the practice of *logos* as compartmentalizing and pulling apart and analyzing, instead focusing our attention on a more holistic view of storied human life, focusing attention on making connections and bringing together and interpreting. As Walter Fisher (1987) argues, the language of narrative has a logic to it, but it is a *holistic* logic that forces us, the story-making and story-consuming creatures (*homo narrans*), to acknowledge that we inhabit a larger web of life. In storied experience, we begin to grasp what the Buddhist philosopher Thich Nhat Hanh (1992) calls our fundamental "interbeing." Here we understand that our human world is just part of a larger web of relationships; the center of the web, for humans, is found at the intersection of *mythos* and *pathos*. These are the forces that truly *move* us as people, that shake us out of our slumber, that bring us to life, that pump our hearts, that light the way out of the darkness.

A mythically and emotionally infused narrative worldview sees, touches, tastes, smells, hears, and seeks the mythical story as the grander, more vivid, more empowering and life-affirming energy that evokes and invokes a larger sense of what it means to *know*. This is a knowing-in-praxis, a knowing gained and regained as we actively live our storied/storying lives—a knowing that allows a human to *be* a creature who can make (narrative) sense of his or her world. So knowledge itself is not a *product* transcribed from little bits of data; rather, it is itself a holistic *constellation of practices* woven from imaged/imagined, symbolic, narrative strands that come together to form the mythical web of life itself.

On a personal level, the stakes connected to the question of whether or not we embrace the power of *mythos* are high. Without the holistic power of *mythos*, we are, quite literally, lost, wounded, bogged down in the overwhelming influx of information bits and data streams. On a cultural level, the problem is even worse. Psychologist Rollo May (1991) puts it bluntly: "Without myth we are like a race of brain-injured people unable to go beyond the word and hear the person who is speaking" (p. 23). That is, without a connection to *mythos*, we cannot hear, feel, or experience the full power of what it means to be human; we cannot reach beyond the words to the deeper meanings of existence and experience and personhood of which the words are symbolic expressions.

The alternative to this deprivation is to willingly (or perhaps accidentally) stumble into the power of myth to guide our lives. As our shared "glimpse of infinity," *mythos* is, May (1991) argues, a healing force. In opening "roads to universals beyond one's concrete experience," myth creates faith in possibility. And "it is only on the basis of such a faith that the individual can genuinely accept and overcome earlier . . . deprivations without continuing to harbor resentment through one's life. . . . In this sense myth helps us accept our past, and then we find it opens before us our future" (May, 1991, p. 87).

In this chapter, I work toward the possibilities inherent in drawing on the mythical and spiritual traditions and archetypes available within our broader cultural and historical contexts by invoking symbols, patterns, and storylines from our mythological heritage. I see the evocation and invocation of *mythos* as a way to explore the deep, unconscious, shared patterns of understanding that illuminate the meanings of our lives, relationships, writing, and stories.

At the mythical center of human life lie the bonds of family and the threats that those bonds endure in times of grief; here, I invoke the option of reengaging and re-creating a shared *mythos* for the wounded family. My strategy will be to apply these archetypal themes to an interpretation of the stories from Chapter Four—stories of a troubled family beset by trauma, lost in shadow, and bereft of the meaning provided by *mythos*. Then I will suggest the possibility of renewed myth-making in the family circle as a pathway toward family healing. But first, I must briefly set out the ground for this work to proceed upon, which I find in the archetypal psychology proposed by C. G. Jung (1959, 1964, 1989), and the mythological philosophy extended by Joseph Campbell (1948, 1972, 1991), Rollo May (1950, 1972, 1991), and Karl Kerényi (1977).

Archetypes

Jung, in his alternative to Freudian psychology, proposed a layered, textured, multifaceted understanding of the human psyche. Jung's theory is that humans experience conscious life largely unaware that much of what they feel, think, and do is, at least in part, driven by forces, energies, and patterns that reside in a psychic realm he called the unconscious.[3] According to Jung (1959), there are two layers of this unconscious world:

> A more or less superficial layer of the unconscious is undoubtedly personal. I call it the personal unconscious. But this personal unconscious rests upon a deeper layer, which does not derive from personal experience and is not a personal acquisition but is inborn. This deeper layer I call the collective unconscious. (p. 3)

For Jung, the unconscious world is far more complex than the life-world of which we are generally conscious. According to the theory, the psychic world is like an iceberg—what you experience consciously in your life, as well as what you observe when you encounter a human being, is only, so to speak, the "tip" or surface of a large, complex structure, most of which resides below the surface. As a human, most of your consciousness, or psychic energy, is submerged in an unconscious, and largely unfocused, shadowy realm of fleeting images and story fragments. But, if we carefully examine the unconscious images that erupt, from time to time, into consciousness, patterns can be discerned. Indeed, according to Jung (1959), deep within the human psyche resides a series of patterns, or archetypes—paradigmatic images that give shape and substance to our conscious understanding and engagement of life in the human world: "The contents of the collective unconscious are known as archetypes. We are dealing with archaic or—I would say—*primordial* types, that is, with *universal images that have existed since the remotest times*" (p. 3, emphases in the original).

The primordial/universal archetypal patterns shared by humans lie at the foundation of the unconscious. These archetypal patterns are universal and foundational because they reside in the deeper "collective" realm of the unconscious, a part of the web of "interbeing" that we all share. We are connected in ways that we only partly understand. But, when we see or experience the archetypes, we somehow recognize them as being part of us; they are part of the organizing web of consciousness.

The most prominent forms of the patterns or archetypal energies within this unconscious life-world do, from time to time, erupt into the conscious life-world; they come to us via dreams and myths. The dream is the personal form; the myth is the collective, universal form. Each form shares some aspect of the collective, some connection to the universality of human experience, but the dream is the personalized form, whereas the myth is the grand culture-guiding, culture-shaping story-form. Dreams are like our everyday emotion-laden stories of personal experience; myths speak to a larger communal spiritual experience.

So archetypes, the primordial images and energies that inhabit the deeper layers of the collective unconscious, find their way into the conscious world of human social life; we remember our dreams, we tell our guiding myths. Sometimes, with some luck, we can connect the two threads. Archetypes are the prototypical story-forms that help shape these dreams and myths into recognizable patterns.

These patterns reside at the heart of our collective, tacit, unconscious knowing.

These images and patterns form the basis of myth; they are the root structure of the larger stories that inform human cultures. There is no exhaustive catalogue of these patterns, but certain symbols and story-images do recur across cultures and times. Among the most common of archetypal patterns, across cultures, geographies, and great spans of time, are images, crafted into stories, of the origins of human life, of birth, of home (or, as the Greeks put it, *ethos*, the dwelling place), of wholeness, of courtship and love, of loss and lament, of alienation, of threats to survival and triumph over those threats, of domination and fear, of violence, of woundedness and suffering, of death and destruction, and of a return to wholeness. There is also the recurring motif of the dream-as-message, of the cryptic half-understood whisperings of the unconscious, the wisp of memory, the thin threads of secret—and of the hope and the promise that the listener who carefully attunes himself to the possibility of deciphering these messages can somehow discover a deep and important truth about himself, about life, about love, about giving. These patterns, when recognized, can be helpful in understanding—and perhaps even reconfiguring—the life predicaments of characters caught up in a frightening, shadowy world of pain and grief.

Images of Original Wholeness

Birth. The beginning. Those of us who have been present when a life comes into this world know immediately that something sacred, something beyond us—a miracle, if you will—is occurring. The ongoing circle of life is being enacted, and deeper meanings for our existence are evoked. When my sons Eli and Noah were born, I was the first to hold them as they emerged into the human life-world beyond their mother's womb. In that moment, I was struck with awe and wonder. Here, I held in my hands a tiny, precious gift, which carried with it a responsibility both joyous and solemn. These were the most unforgettable peak experiences of my life. Something primordial and deeply spiritual was going on here. Here I was, witnessing the emergence of a newly embodied human spirit joining us in this life-world. I was in the presence of a new human-in-the-making. The *pathos* of the moment was obvious and nearly overwhelming. But my awe came from a deep well of energy, something I powerfully felt but only vaguely understood at the time.

In the world of myth, the circle of life begins as a trio: mother-father-child. There may be other characters in the story, but these are at the center. In ancient myth, of course, there are lessons to be learned from all three perspectives. Homer and other lyric poets of early Greece emphasize the sanctity of the *ethos*, of home and hearth and hospitality as the center of all that organizes human social life. Humans also need to venture out into the world beyond the family to become whole. More on that later. For now, we focus on beginnings, and on the movement from the mother's womb to the womb of family.

According to the biblical accounts of Matthew and Luke, Jesus came to the world via a miraculous birth in a setting fit for a pauper. Matthew reports that an angel visited Joseph, the father, in a dream; Luke has the angel visit Mary, the mother, while she is awake and alone. Both indicate that "God is with" Mary, with Matthew's angel stating that she will, by intervention of God, bear a son, who shall be called Emmanuel (meaning "God with us"). Mary and Joseph, traveling for a census, are forced to sleep in a barn. There, as we all know, they experience the miracle of virgin birth, with a crowd of visitors (who were also called forth by angels) looking on. They hold the child in love and awe, and all who see him are awestruck.

The motif of the miraculous birth is not unique to this story, nor is the notion of a child born of God—nor, indeed, is the experience of awe at the miracle of life a new or unique idea. Indeed, these are the root archetypes of countless stories of birth stretching across most mythical traditions from the occident to the orient to ancient America (Campbell, 1972, 1991). And, today, family communication scholars point out that birth stories are a primary genre of family storytelling (Sterk & Sterk, 1993; Stone, 1988; Turner & West, 2006a, 2006b). Stories of our births are told, again and again. When families gather regularly in the presence of children—even grown children—stories of birth are almost inevitable.

At a recent family gathering we were celebrating my brother Mike's fiftieth birthday. My wife Sue called out to my mom, "Hey, Mema, why don't you tell us the story of Mike's birth?"

The story that emerged was a story of near loss. Mike's birth came as an emergency Caesarean section.

"The pregnancy was tough. I was on bed rest for the last couple of months, because the doctors thought I might go into labor early. It was driving me crazy. One day, the doctor told me I could get up to take a shower. I collapsed on the floor. They say I lost a lot of blood. The next thing I knew, I was hovering above the operating table, looking down on the operation. I heard someone say, '*We're losing her.*' I looked up, saw a light in the distance. I felt an urge to move toward it. But I also felt I was leaving something behind, something I could not bear to part with. So I went back. The next thing I remember was waking up in my hospital bed. I was alive, and Mike was fine."

She looks at Mike and smiles. "Your dad and I were so happy."

The birth story is often one of a "close call" or near emergency or "near death experience." Sometimes the child, sometimes the mother, sometimes both travel to the brink of death.

The story is sometimes a story of birth and *rebirth.*

My own sons were born amid crisis: Eli was an emergency Caesarean section; Noah was born after long and difficult labor with several mishaps along the way. With much relief and great joy, our children emerged into this world healthy and strong. The stories are told and retold as both celebrations of life and as cautionary tales. And they showcase the awe and majesty of birth while demonstrating that the welcoming arms of family are the proper place for the child to land. The stories that follow often focus on the early stages of childhood.

Stories of birth serve to point out the gateway to life . . . the circle of mother-father-child is a sacred circle residing in a thin place between the womb and the sacred welcoming space of family, a place that serves as the launching pad to the next place.

But what if something goes horribly wrong? What if the birth story is a story of trauma and loss and premature death rather than joy? The great stories of the beginning of family show a center populated by dynamic, active, loving characters. Sometimes, though, the center does not hold.

Rewriting the First Story (Audrey's Story of Life, Interrupted—Revisited)

His wife is named Audrey: noble and strong. With a name like that, you can do *anything.*

His name is Thomas, the one who drops doubt in favor of faith.

A bracing wind kicks up as he makes his way toward the little hospital. He is young, and strong, and stalwart. He walks with decision in each step. He looks like a man who knows where he is going, and why. He pulls the door open, holding it politely for a nurse heading home from a long and tumultuous night shift.

She says, "Thank you, sir."

"My pleasure, ma'am," he replies with a nod, and makes his way through the lobby, past the desk, and toward his wife's little room at the back of the building. He enters the room breezily, a broad smile on his face.

"How's my sweetheart? How's my girl?"

She looks up, manages a small smile. "Fine."

"It will be all right, sweetie."

"I don't know. I'm scared."

He grasps her hand. "Audrey, I'm here. It's OK."

She smiles up at him faintly, but she doesn't really believe her own lips. She feels a shadow descending. And just as quickly as that thought comes, her body throws her into her long, hard labor. She follows along with a heavy sigh, and with the bubble of anxiety that has, until now, sat at the bottom of her stomach, gradually morphing into terrible, overwhelming fear.

When it is all over, he finds himself alone, holding the tiny, lifeless body of his son, weeping quietly. So much lost in such a brief moment. He only dimly understands what happened. He feels the dark surge of rage bubbling up and he wants to strike out at the doctor, the hospital, anyone . . . for this terrible failure, but anger and blame dissipate as the thin mist of deep, unspeakable sadness descends upon him. He feels it all acutely and wonders for a moment if he can go on. Still, he is at heart a buoyant man, who knows instinctively that he must grieve quickly and then put their life back together with the cheer and determination that has, until now, made him successful at everything he's tried.

He is a man who sees a bright, straight line between the present moment and the place he wants to go next. It has always been that way with him. He has never hesitated, and never, until now, lost. At this moment, he knows what he must do. He will throw himself into his work. But family will always be at the center, and his children and grandchildren and great grandchildren (God willing) will remember him as a trickster, a storyteller . . . the playful, happy adventurer he has always been. He is also a strong, determined, no-nonsense man who knows what he wants and goes after it. He will not change, will not bow to the darkness. He will forge ahead, following that bright line.

He turns to her, tries to hand her their poor, dead child. She turns away.

"No."

"But . . ."

"I said, NO!" she exclaims in a fierce whisper.

A long pause as he draws up his resolve. "Sweetheart," he says, "We have to say goodbye. They have to take him. They have to take Victor."

"No," she says. "I will not. And I want you to never—ever—name him again.

"Never talk," her voice catches on a small sob, "never talk about him again! We will *never* speak of this—to anyone."

"But . . ."

"No more. Not another word." And she turns away from him, buries her head in her pillow.

For the first time in his life, he does not know what to do. He has never seen her this way, so sure, so closed, so determined. Something in him knows this is wrong, knows that they must talk and grieve and let go, knows that she is refusing to face the horrible truth, knows this strategy of stoic secrecy will fail.

He is at a moment of decision. Should he press the issue? He is a tough man, but not in her hands. With her, he has always softened, melted like butter in the July sun. He knows he cannot force this one anyway.

"OK, sweetie," he whispers. And turns and walks slowly out of the room.

What to make of this story? The characters are caught in a tragic maelstrom, the dark wind of a broken archetype. The circle of life has been interrupted—horribly, horrifyingly, unfairly. And they are filled to brimming with sorrow.

Poor Victor, he keeps thinking. Poor, poor Victor. You never had a chance.

And he weeps for his son who never had a chance.

But his wife remains stoical, never allowing her pain to be expressed.

Perhaps we should pause for a moment—at this moment of interruption—and explore how a mythic vision might open up possibility in our story.

The Homeric hymns sing the tragic life of Demeter (whose name means "mother"), the goddess of the Earth, of fertility and birth, who suffered the tragic loss of her daughter, Persephone. As the story goes, Persephone was abducted by Hades, dragged down to the underworld (the land of death) to sit with him as his queen. Demeter, searching far and wide for her daughter, suffered greatly from her loss. Unsuccessful in her search, heartbroken, she withdrew into isolation. This, of course, caused serious problems for the Earth, which became cold and infertile. Zeus intervened by sending his messenger, Hermes, to negotiate the release of Persephone. But Hades tricked Persephone into eating a Pomegranate seed, forever binding her to the underworld. Thereafter, she was forced to stay in the underworld for one-third of the year, while she spent the remainder of her time with her mother. During the time of year when Persephone was away, it is said that Demeter sat in cold and darkness, weeping bitter tears (Jung & Kerényi, 1949).

How might this myth provide an intervention—an opening to possibility—for our story? What might we learn from the archetype of the mother about responding to the loss of that most precious gift, her child? First, notice that Demeter's immediate response to her loss is to conduct a search—a search that, though ending in despair, is born of hope and possibility even in the face of great loss. *Searching*—for life, for meaning, for possibility—is always an act of hope. Then, unsuccessful in her search, perhaps quite naturally, she withdraws into isolation.

Here is the most potent and poignant turning point in the story: Demeter withdraws into silent isolation. But someone intervenes—a helper who sees that this withdrawal will not do. So the two, mother and daughter, are rejoined, and they rejoice. Hope springs eternal— and when Persephone returns, the Earth goddess celebrates the presence of her daughter, and the Earth itself springs to life again, bright and green and beautiful.

And thus the Earth becomes free once again to follow its perennial cycles: spring, the time of rebirth, when Persephone reemerges from the long darkness to walk with her mother again; summer, the time of gladness and growth when the Earth is fertile and productive, as mother and child bask in the sunlight; fall, when life comes to fruition and the bounty of the harvest is celebrated as mother and child dance in the fading, golden light; winter, the time of dormancy and the mourning of loss as all good things come to an end, when light (Persephone) fades from the Earth for a time, and Demeter weeps.

These are the cycles of the Earth goddess, and these, too, are the natural cycles of human life. But in our story of life interrupted, the cycles are halted, and the mother fades into darkness and isolation, never to emerge, never to search again, never to truly mourn her loss, never to speak her pain, never to weep.

This story of life interrupted is a sad, sad story. But it could turn out differently.

□ □ □ □

At the door, he pauses, and with sudden resolve, turns on his heel, says: "Sweetie, we need to talk."

"NO!"

Now back at her bedside, stroking her hair gently, he says softly, "But we *have* to. Tell you what. I'll talk, you listen. I'll tell you the story of Victor."

And he weaves an epic tale, a tale of the Victor that might have been, a strong and courageous man of determination leading a life of grand adventure, and love, and struggle and joy and many, many fine stories. It is the story of a long and spacious and gracious and storied life. Victor the hero, Victor the champion, Victor the winner . . .

And after a time, he notices the small flicker of a smile starting at the corners of her mouth.

Images of Breakdown and Breakthrough

Death. For all we know, this is the bitter end of all experience. The threat of death calls us all into anxiety and is the subject of many stories large and small. The energy of death is the energy of breakdown, of loss and darkness and cold, cruel loneliness. In ancient Greek myth, the earliest version of death is a two-faced god: On one side is Cronos the Titan, the all-powerful devouring father-figure, father Time, perpetrator of history; on the other, Thanatos, the great, devouring death energy. The Thanatos face is a dark, hideous countenance, unwelcome and unloved. He tends to visit at the most inopportune moments.

But Thanatos is not all-powerful.

He can be defeated.

His enemy is love.

Love, it turns out, is the healing force that salves our wounds. Thanatos, in the end, is always defeated by the gods and goddesses of love, who show the face of innocence, purity, wholeness, care, and compassion to a broken world.

In the soft arms of loving embrace, we are healed.

In the warm presence of love, we can break through our brokenness, and come to life again.

Rewriting the Second Story (James's Sleep, Re-Interrupted)

James, no longer a squirt—indeed, he is a big man who, on a good day, in good voice, is imposing like a king—wakes with a start. He has been sleeping sitting up for several years now, in his chair in front of the television. He says he is more comfortable this way, but it never seems like he gets a restful full night's sleep. He sleeps in fits and starts, nodding off but never falling into dream.

But this night is different. He had a dream! A vivid dream! His first in over twenty years!

In his dream, he is sitting at the kitchen table in the house where he grew up. Everyone is there—Papa, Mom, Sally, Joe, and all the kids and grandkids, nieces and nephews, cousins and uncles and aunts. They are sitting and standing around the large kitchen table, eating the usual hearty southern breakfast: Cat's Paw biscuits, eggs, bacon, ham, and, of course, steaming grits swirling in butter. For a moment, he just pauses to take it all in—the bright morning sunlight streaming through the window, the wondrous smells, the clanking of forks against the sides of plates, the whirr of the fan in the corner and its light cool breeze against his cheeks, the sparkle of his mother's blue eyes—and the laughter.

Laughter?

How strange. Everyone seems to be talking and laughing. They are telling stories. And there are no knives in their eyes, no barbs in their

words, no arguments, no petty bickering—just stories and laughter—
and *joy.*

Joy?

Even Papa seems to be truly enjoying himself.

Could it be that his family has, after all these years, discovered *joy?*

He wants to ask what is going on, but suddenly Sally's voice
catches his attention. She is telling a story:

*When I woke up that morning, I didn't feel right. I was tired, and sore,
and a little short of breath. But I didn't think much of it, had my coffee, and
drove off to work. It was Friday, and I was on my way home—to Mom and
Papa's place—by mid-afternoon. We worked hard that weekend, washing
the windows on the first floor, and cleaning under the rugs and furniture,
dusting baseboards, scrubbing floors. By Sunday noon, I was pooped. I drove
home slowly, deciding a bath would help with the soreness.*

*I got home, fixed a cup of coffee, and started drawing a bath. And then it
hit me—at first it felt like a sledgehammer pounding my chest, but the pain
went away fast, and I knew this was it. I was tired anyway, and, besides,
once I closed my eyes, I saw nothing but golden light. I was content.*

*Then: a noise. It was James, coming to look for me. I looked down at him,
leaning over my body, and smiled.*

*I love, you Squirt. I love you. It's OK. It's all OK. I just kept saying that.
And I imagined that he heard me. And that he would be happy for me.*

And he wakes with a start, a wide, knowing smile spreading across
his lips. He springs out of his chair with a bounce he hasn't felt in fifty
years. He strides down the hall toward the kitchen.

As he enters, the family is gathering for breakfast. He steps
cheerily to his chair, says, "Boy, did I have a dream!"

And, as he tells his story, the family looks at him, astonished. There
is something different about him.

The light has returned to his eyes.

Light returns in the wake of a dream. A good, soft, gentle dream—
a dream of loving affirmation, even in the face of loss. The idea here is
that we can, in fact, come to a sense of wholeness, even when we feel
a chunk of us has been cut away by death. Breakdown is followed by
breakthrough.

In Greek myth, the two faces of wisdom were Apollo, god of sunlight, healing, and truth, and Athena, goddess of art, peace, and reason. Through the intermediary, Hermes (or sometimes Mentor, friend of Odysseus) they offer their gifts to humanity not lightly but with reverence and care. These gifts, coalesced into one all-encompassing gift to humanity—wisdom, or discernment—may offer a pathway toward loosening the grip of trauma. Wisdom, gained through long experience and much human contact, manifests itself most clearly in the kind of practical-moral wisdom the Greeks knew as *phrônesis*. This *phrônesis* is, as John Shotter (1993) points out, a kind of "knowing from within" a situation, a knowing that allows one to say and do the right thing at the right time.

In the ancient myths, one great exemplar of this *phrônesis* manifested in human form comes from the stories of the wily Odysseus, who travels far and wide and manages to survive mostly by his wits (aided, of course, by Athena's good grace). Odysseus overcomes great obstacles, again and again, while practicing and honing his emerging *phrônesis*, his movement toward *knowing from within* each situation what he must do in order to survive. In the end, Odysseus comes home to tell his story to Penelope, his wife, and Telemachus, his son, thus reuniting the original circle of father-mother-child. It is in the sharing of the story that the circle—once broken—is ultimately made whole again.

And so it turns out that in everyday life, one of the offspring—and, yes, I do mean to use that term purposefully, with its implications of living, moving growth—of *phrônesis* may well be the capacity to know how and when and where to tell a good story. The most active, playful, vibrant child of *phrônesis* is story.

Rewriting the Third Story (Thawing the Frozen One)

Claire: A bright light for the world. She doesn't know how it started, or when, but she has been telling stories for many years now. She just knows that, whenever people are gathered, they seem to find comfort and joy and ease in her stories. Her stories bring light to the rooms she inhabits. These are simple stories of everyday events, but it's the *way* she tells them.

One day, she finds herself standing on her little porch. The sun is beginning to heat up the mid-morning as only a deep South sun can do. Its warmth, at times discomfiting in its intensity, is, at this moment, just what she needs. She stands, soaking it in, feeling it thaw her a little.

And then she is the kitchen, bending down to check the chicken baking in the oven.

We used to fry it, she thinks. But all that fat . . .

Her family is gathering for a meal. It is just an ordinary gathering on an ordinary Sunday. But often these meals are spaces where the tension erupts in little snipes and jabs. These are moments that tighten her stomach, make her feet stiff.

She hopes there are none today.

As the oven opens, the smell shoots up into her nostrils, and for a moment, she is back in Mom's kitchen down in Georgia, sitting at the table after a good, hearty southern feast. This is her young husband's mother, but she calls her "Mom" anyway, in good old-fashioned southern-girl style. They are recently married, and she can't get over the fact that Mom is the best cook she has ever met. The secret seems vaguely to have to do with bacon and lard, but it is the 1950s, and nobody knows or cares about the health effects of that. *Boy, that fried chicken was good.*

And then they are upon her. Her family arrives all at once—the four grown children and their six kids. Soon, they are sharing food, and she is telling stories. They are simple stories of her life as a teacher, an artist, a mom, a grandmother.

She begins talking of her childhood, of how her family traveled to new places while her dad pursued his dreams. And in each story, her mother was a rock. She was the one who stayed home, home schooling her children long before that was a trend, cooking, sewing, cleaning, always on the move.

"I always knew Mama loved me," she says. "She just wasn't so good at showing it." She pauses for a moment, and just smiles at them all, soaking them in. For some reason, they seem content. A rare moment for this troubled family. And she feels a kind of warmth flowing into her veins, thawing her feet. And then she finds herself telling another story.

In the story, she finds relief. In the story, she finds possibility. In the story . . .

Images of Action

In ancient myth, there is an active, dynamic tension between the home world and the public world. So we see the child Apollo, both at home and abroad, performing brilliant, light-drenched Apollonian feats, infused with clarity and insight; Hermes the child inaugurating the mysteries of our world, in a Hermeneutic dialectical tradition[4] of traveling across thresholds, of message giving and trickery (Brown, 1947); Demeter the Mother, the fertile one who gives great bounty as a happy gift to the human community (but who nevertheless experiences deep sorrow when she loses her child, Persephone); Hera the mother who protects her own and makes an annual return to virginity; Zeus the roaming father who sows his seed widely but who both disciplines and protects his children, and loves his wife, sometimes fiercely; and Odysseus the wily wanderer who leaves his son behind but in the end comes home and teaches him how to be a man.

A primary archetypal pattern, documented assiduously by Joseph Campbell (1948, 1972), is the "hero journey." In this grand mythic pattern, the protagonist, or hero, is "called out" by an interruption in the flow of everyday life—a crisis, a moral dilemma, a loss, a war, or the unremitting call of adventure. The hero sets out on a journey, clearly seeking something, some action or meaning beyond the home front.

As the hero sets out on his quest, he is met with many seemingly insurmountable obstacles. But somehow, either through miracle or through the unexpected help of a friend, the hero triumphs. The labors of Heracles are a paradigmatic case, as are the stories of Jonah and the whale, Jesus in Gethsemane, the trials of Psyche, or even the travels of Luke Skywalker. Along the way, the hero must at some point descend into darkness and despair, facing the greatest challenge of his life: To defeat the darkness within his own soul, facing down his own shadow. This he does, by dint of skill, daring, wit, and strength. And so he returns to the world and brings back with him a boon: the knowledge of how to win the battle against the shadow—knowledge that is wrapped up in that most elegant of packages: a good story.

He brings hope.

Rewriting the Fourth Story
(Little Flashes Lead to Big Openings)

Gabriel: The strong one. The survivor.

He wakes up—or really, comes to—early one morning. The sun is just starting to peek in through the kitchen window.

Kitchen? Why am I in the kitchen?

He opens his eyes, wincing at the light. There is a sharp pain behind his eyes, spreading into his temples. Slowly, begrudgingly, he takes in his surroundings. He is lying sprawled on the hard wooden floor. Littering the floor around him are several bottles, some holding the last drops of warm beer, two lying on their sides, now empty of the hot, cheap whiskey they once held. On the floor tucked up next to him is the gun. He picks it up, contemplating his next move. He presses the cold steel up against his temple, but drops it clattering to the ground as the vomit rushes warmly up, pushing out through his lips, splattering his lap and the floor and the legs of the only piece of furniture left, a small chair.

How did it come to this?

The next thing he knows, he is lying on something cold and hard and too short for his body.

What is this place?

He is on an examining table in the emergency room at the local hospital, waiting to be admitted.

"Hey, bro'! You gonna make it?" a familiar voice intones. His brother.

"Ugggh. What's going on?"

"We're waiting. They're going to put you in detox. But you gotta wait."

"Goddammit, tell them I'm dying in here."

"Yup. Did that. They didn't care. Said you have to come down a little so they can sign you in."

His blood-alcohol concentration was .30, over three times the legal limit in his state, just shy of fatal concentrations of .35 or more.

Flash.

Three days later, he is sitting in a meeting, surrounded by others in various stages of detoxification from drugs and/or alcohol. A young woman in a business suit stands at the front of the room, telling a story.

We have nothing in common. Look at her.

Then, she says: "You may think we have nothing in common. But I'm here to tell you I sat right there where you are sitting once. I was just as hopeless, just as lost, and just as sure I could never not drink as you are. But here I am, sober five years now, and my life has totally changed. Not too long ago, I sat right where you are, shivering, in complete and total despair. Today, I am happy."

Flash.

Something in him clicks. Just a little something. The door has opened just a crack, and he sees light streaming in.

Flash.

Five years later, he is sitting at his kitchen table, listening to a new guy, just out of detox. The man has been on a prodigious rant for over half an hour, but he seems to be running out of steam.

"This sucks. I've lost everything, man."

"I know."

"It's just so goddamn hard, man. I don't know if I can do this."

"Listen, man, it's not as hard as it seems. If I can do it, you can."

"But how?"

"Look, it's pretty simple, really. You just have to die."

"Die? What the—?"

"Well, not literally. But you have to go down deep. Feel the pain until you surrender to the process, face all the dark shit in you, and learn to let go of it. Then you can change. And the whole world will be happier for it. Trust me."

"I don't know why, but I believe you, man."

"Yes. Why don't you start by telling me your story?"

"What?"

"You heard me. Tell me your story. That's how we do this."

"But . . ."

"Look. You gotta tell me how it all started, how you fell, fell deep and hard, and how you got here. You are on your way back, man. But you gotta tell the story. That's how you'll get back all the way."

"O.K . . ."

And they both smile a little.

Flash.

In the end, Gabriel lives up to his name. He takes action, seizing his second chance at life. He takes hold of his story and crafts a new trajectory: of recovery, of hope, of transcendence. He enters a program of recovery and learns to live again by sharing his message of hope and renewal with others like him. Thus, he joins millions of recovering addicts and alcoholics who have turned back from the brink of death to live life sober, happy, joyous, and free. It all comes down to that moment of action when he helps the other to take hold of *his own* story.

□ □ □ □

Rewriting the Fifth Story: Torrents Streaming into Laughter

Isaac. The laughing one. He sits on the edge of his bed one dark morning, and shakes off the fog that has invaded his head, again.

He wonders when—or if—the dark dreams will ever stop. He knows their source. Now, after long years of introspection, he knows that he must, somehow, overcome the dark, seething rage that has taken hold of him—rage whose source he knows all too well, rage at the violence and misunderstanding and conflict he has always shared with his father. He knows that he must face these demons, but he is afraid.

And then, one day, out of the blue, she comes to him, says, "Let's have a baby."

They have been married for seven years. The idea of having kids has come up occasionally, only to be avoided or diverted into other pursuits. They spend much of their time working, little of it reflecting or envisioning anything different. So, the suggestion comes as a bit of a surprise, but he somehow knows the time is right: "OK," he replies.

A year later, they are carrying their young son out of the hospital. He is three days old, and it is the first time he has been outside. As they step through the automatic door out into the spring day, a little breeze kicks up. The baby turns softly to the left, sniffs at the air. They smile at him, knowing a breath of fresh air when they see one. He falls back into slumber.

One day, a few months later, she calls him on the telephone at work, leaves a message. "Listen to this," she says. What follows are peals of laughter, a baby's perfect first laugh. The little one has discovered the joys of a new toy—the bouncing chair hanging from the doorway—and has, in turn, discovered laughter. And laughter changes everything.

Their days are filled with the joy and the laughter and the hard busy work of raising children. But it is all great fun, as they go about learning and discovering and naming the world. The young one grows quickly into the kind of boy who can see the humor in almost any moment. Along the way, he teaches Isaac how to laugh again.

Then one day, several years later, Isaac is standing in his own father's kitchen, watching his dad and his second son, born three years after the first, playing checkers. This little boy is as determined and energetic and playful as the first. The boy and his grandfather are cutting up, laughing and talking and having a good, easy time. The game is *fun*. And suddenly a new truth hits Isaac: This person, his father, now a grandfather, is a different man than the one he grew up with. He has achieved what they used to call (in their pickup baseball games) a "do-over." A feeling of well-being descends on him. And he knows that, in fatherhood, he, too, gets a "do-over."

And just like that, he lets out a laugh, rage fading into joy.

That night, he has a new kind of dream. In his dream, the family is sitting around the table—all of them. Audrey, Thomas, Victor, James, Claire, Gabriel, Isaac, and all their sons and daughters and cousins— the whole family—is sitting around the table. And it turns out that they are master storytellers.

A story erupts—and they are, quite suddenly, all laughing. Gales of laughter fill the room, his head, his heart. He laughs and laughs until it hurts—and then he laughs some more. He wakes, not in tears or in terror, but this time laughing aloud!

Isaac: he who laughs.

In the story of the "do-over," we see that all of us have a shot at some kind of redemption. Perhaps the key to that chance can be found in (re)claiming the joy that lives at the near edge of our laughter. Perhaps we can (re)gain a foothold in the world by letting go of our "rock" (our burdens), and, like Sisyphus, learn to roll in a new way. Peals of laughter ring true, somehow. Very true.

Rewriting Stories on the Margins: Secrets Re-Storied, Lives Re-Formed

How can a mythic vision inform the new ethnography? More importantly, what can we learn from a mythic (re)vision of our life stories? In the stories told here, Despair lurks in the corner. Just behind him is Thanatos, leering, waiting for his moment. But the great myths teach us that humans can triumph over Despair, and even defeat Death, if only for awhile. The power of Love (and laughter) emerging in and through and from the power of Story, conquers Despair. The light of Hope enters the darkness, sends the shadows scurrying. The revised stories in this chapter offer beacons of hope for the possibility of rewriting narratives that have gone astray. The deep wounds inflicted by trauma—and the pain, silence, and secrecy that often accompany such tragic, disruptive events— may well be salved by the healing energy of *mythos*.

Perhaps, if we who practice accidental ethnography embrace the energy of *mythos*, we can rewrite the dark, desolate stories that haunt us into shimmering stories of possibility.

Perhaps, if we embrace the energy of *mythos*, we can redirect the evil winds of fate, and return to the natural cycles of living the search for meaning, invigorating our lives through sharing the search.

Perhaps, if we embrace the energy of *mythos*, shedding the light of the ancients on our dark dreams, on our shadowy secrets, on our somber stories, we can be free to sleep again, emerging from our rest with clarity and energy and the knowledge that love triumphs.

Perhaps, if we embrace the energy of *mythos*, the circle, once broken, can be made whole again, and Wisdom can reign in our families.

Perhaps, if we embrace the energy of *mythos*, we, the heroes of our own journeys, can return to our communities with the grand gift of Hope.

Perhaps . . .

Reflection

Imagining archetypal and mythical connections and solutions to our human dilemmas requires deep grounding in the cultural mythologies that undergird our culture, along with a vivid

curiosity and a vibrant desire to seek out a deeper understanding
of mythological meaning. If, along the way, we can begin, even
haltingly, to discover the power that reconfiguring our understanding
of life events in mythical terms might present, we may well find
the energy to sustain us through our extended research and writing
projects. This sort of project requires us to delve into our collective
cultural past, to read widely and explore deeply the *mythos* that
informs our lives.

Sometimes these archetypal patterns seem to be buried deep
within our cultural consciousness. Being part of the deeper layers
of the collective unconscious, they may not, at first, seem readily
accessible to the writer of accidental ethnography. However, I have
found that familiarity with the myths, parables, and stories that
have infused our culture for long years has a way of merging with
my own writing in fruitful ways. Once I become familiar with our
mythologies, I begin to recognize the clues, hints, and signs that
define and inform the stories as they emerge. I begin to understand
some stories as poignant expressions of important archetypes. This
takes some effort, but the fruits of the search have been deeply
rewarding. The meaning carried in these vehicles of cultural
knowledge, if properly integrated, can be powerful.

Here we must be careful not to misunderstand. There are those in
our culture who hold out for a *literal* interpretation of our mythology.
In this way of reading myth, God *literally* created the world in seven
days. Adam and Eve literally ate the fruit of the tree of knowledge
of good and evil and were thus banished from Eden. Noah was
rewarded for being the only good man in a wicked world. And so on.
But it is important here to probe the deeper meanings of our myths.
They are, in the end, stories about what it means to be human, about
our place in the universe, about our separation from God, about how
we might live well. So, although the myths that undergird our culture
are, in a way, bearers of traditional messages about moral living, they
are also stories that suggest openings to new ways of configuring our
own life stories.

Over time, I have come to embrace the possibilities inherent in the
imaginative integration of my own memories, dreams, reflections,
secrets, and stories with those deeper archetypes and stories of
my cultural heritage. There is, for example, in Jesus' parable of the
mustard seed, a vivid sense of human potential, just as there is, in
the archetypal hero journey, a deep and abiding link to the troubled

travels of an ethnographic wanderer. As I have demonstrated in this chapter, there is a great deal to be gained in the rewriting of troubled and troubling life stories with the assistance of mythological knowledge. In the re-crafting of the story, we are, as Kuhn (1995) points out, *reconstructing* lives in ways that offer a chance for hope, healing, and renewal. We open ourselves to the laughter, love, and joy that are our birthright—those happy, light moments that the young child learns early on how to access. Sure, we will cry, too, for there is always the specter of loss. But the simple truth is that being troubled, anxious, depressed, or filled with rage just cannot be sustained over time. We must, if we are to emerge from the darkness, make links between the mythic possibilities that infuse our collective unconscious and the memories, dreams, reflections, and life stories we construct in order to go on. As the story of Job teaches us, life may be filled with travail and heavy burdens, but Hope, in the end, is necessary.

The synergies created as we facilitate these links between mythical trajectories and our own life paths—moving from a broad understanding of the *mythos* of culture into a more specific connection between these archetypal themes and our own stories—may well prove to be transformative. My sense is that if you make the attempt you will likely discover some remarkable possibilities.

So, my advice is to read our myths. Study them. Engage them. Talk about them. Fall into dialogue and story with your significant others. Learn and re-learn, tell and re-tell. Shape and re-shape.

Story-making is an active, dynamic, flowing practice.

Fall into the stream of it all, and see where it all leads.

You might be surprised at what you find.

Exercises

Writing Exercise 1: Family, Friends, and Culture

We are all members of a family or families at some time during our lives. All families are weird in their own, unique way. All have stories and all have their quirks and their graces. There are many ways to consider family and its impact on our lives, but one of the clearest truths about family is that, for good or for ill, they have a significant impact on shaping us as humans. They form and perform a central role in the early years of our lives and they continue to have an influence throughout the life course, whether we choose to admit or to like that fact or not. Our identities are grounded first in family identities. We may branch out from there as we grow up—indeed, this is where friends, who often have an even greater influence on us than our families—come in. Culture, meanwhile, is the "surround" that plays into these shaping and development processes. Culture can be conceived of as the symbols, meanings, premises, rules, traditions, and stories that connect us to others in our community. The convergence of family and culture is a rich nexus of story material.

So: What is your family like? Who are the main characters? What do they do? What are their personal qualities, histories, characteristics, personalities like? What events, traditions, rituals, and stories can show us, your readers, who your family is—and, by extension, who you are? And who are those people you have called your friends? Again, how have they influenced you? How have you influenced them? And what does all this say about your culture, and your cultural identity? What stories do you share, tell, and re-tell in your family and friendship circles? How would you describe—or evoke life within—the various cultures you inhabit (family culture, friendship culture, school culture, ethnic culture, work culture, etc.)? How will you draw your reader into the world of communicative texture and practice that you may well take for granted, but that clearly shapes and reflects who you are in this world?

As you begin writing, explore these questions and seek to tell the reader a central story that evokes an image of your family life. As possible and if necessary, bring your friends into the story also. They have a role to play, even if it is peripheral to the particular story you choose. Finally, your choice of story, and how you show the reader who you are as a member of a family, will reveal a lot about you as a person, as a thinker, as a writer. Think about that. Then write about it.

Writing Exercise 2: Your Mythological Inheritance

What are the myths that speak to you? Do the stories of Gilgamesh (Babylonian myth) or Odysseus (Greek myth) or of coyote (Native American myth) or of the ancient prophets (Hebrew myth) or of Jesus and his disciples (Christian myth) or of the Buddha and his followers (Buddhist myth) or of Krishna and Vishnu and Ganesha

(Hindu myth) or of Allah (Islamic myth) or of Elegua and Olorun (African myth) or of some other mytho-historical heritage speak to you? How, and why, do these stories and archetypal story patterns speak to you in your heart? How might you begin to incorporate understandings and teachings from the *mythos* of your life into the stories you craft? Is there a place for evoking and invoking the *mythos* that lies beneath or behind or within the center of this ethnographic life you are living? Do these mythic patterns help you to understand, or evoke, or describe, or narrate, or interpret what is happening to you? How? Are there mythic visions that can inform your life as an ethnographer?

Your task is to read widely and think deeply about the mythologies of our world and to begin to bring in the themes and patterns you find there as you seek to illuminate the dark corners of shadow and secrecy and quiet desperation that may emerge in your life or in the lives of the characters in your stories. And, of course, there will be times when, after you know these mythologies well, it will just make good sense to begin actively incorporating your mythological inheritance into the stories you craft.

Then: Write one of these mythically informed stories. See where it leads you. You may well be surprised.

Queries

1. What myths guided you in your early life? Can you tell a story about a story that shaped your life, spoke to your imagination, invaded your dreams, or created a space for growth in your life?
2. How does the *mythos* (storied understanding) of your life intersect with the *ethos* (moral understanding) you try to live?
3. What great stories do you know that might serve as interpretive resources for your own ethnographies? Are you currently exploring alternative mythologies that might begin to help you make sense of your life world? What are they? Why do these particular mythic visions speak to you right here, right now at this moment in your life of life-writing?
4. How might you begin to use the resources of your mythological inheritance to craft or re-craft the stories in your life that have gone dark or wrong or into brokenness? Are you aware of—and available to—the healing properties of a mythic vision? How will you begin, in your life, to make yourself available to the *mythos* of our larger, collective life world?
5. What help might you gain from your friends, your family, your colleagues, and your fellow spiritual sojourners in achieving your quest?

Notes

1. There are exceptions, of course, in autoethnographic and performative writing and teaching. Notably, Art Bochner and Carolyn Ellis, pioneers in this way of studying human social life, have long written and spoken of these matters. Art, I am told, teaches a course entitled "Love and Communication." Beautiful!
2. But, really, is that how we come to know the things that matter? In little bits and pieces? Is the knowing that urges us to say "I love you" or "I hate you" actually organized as data—broken down in our minds and in our hearts as the constituent bits and pieces of experience that led to this act of saying?
3. Jung pointedly refused to call it the *sub*conscious (his teacher Freud's term) because he believed that the prefix "sub" implied an inferiority he was not willing to admit. For Jung, the unconscious is a vast, mysterious, and powerful realm that influences our daily lives, not a repository of the "leftovers" of the conscious mind. This distinction is one of the key factors that led Jung to break from his teacher. His ongoing assertion was that Freud had the dynamics reversed. For Jung, the conscious mind was actually an outgrowth of the unconscious, not the other way around.
4. In hermeneutics, the art and science of textual interpretation, named for the messenger god Hermes, the trick is always to navigate the thresholds between story and meaning, between text and context, between life in this world and life in the "otherworlds" of dream and death and unconscious image. Hermeneutics attempts to craft the message out of the raw materials of dream and memory and story and conscience, in order to shed light on the deeper layers of meaning that live between the lines and pages of the text. In honor of Hermes, the hermeneutic tradition serves the capacity of helper, messenger, and sometimes trickster.

Chapter Six

The Storied Life and the Courage to Connect

Remembering a man's stories makes him immortal, did you know that?
—Edward Bloom in *Big Fish: A Novel of Mythic Proportions*

We awake after a sleep of many centuries to find ourselves in a new and irrefutable sense in the myth of humankind. We find ourselves in a new world community; we cannot destroy the parts without destroying the whole. In this bright loveliness we know that we are truly brothers and sisters, at last in the same family.
—Rollo May, *The Cry for Myth*

Remembering and Forgetting (Take One)

It happens like this. It comes on me unexpectedly: a sudden rush of anxiety.

I am sitting at my desk, hoping against hope that I have something to write.

Gotta write this book.

So I sit. And I stare at the big screen in front of me.

Damn. Nothing. So I sit some more. Stare some more. I begin to think: Maybe that's it. Maybe I've given it all I've got.

Maybe I have dried up.

I stare at the screen.

Nothing.

Whatever it is that ignites my writing seems to have abandoned me. I reel with anxiety. I *am* anxiety.

What has happened to me?

Abruptly, I stand up, decide to take a walk around campus. As I walk, I begin to reflect on my whole life history, where I have been, what has happened along the way, where I might go next.

I hear, off to my left, a loud "CRACK!"

And a floodgate opens.

Memories pour in, cascading through my consciousness, overwhelming me, knocking me off my feet. Then, just as suddenly, the torrents of memory are replaced by wisps of uncertainty, of vague forebodings without any references. These surges come in alternating waves and troughs, interspersed with long periods of blankness.

My whole life flashes before my eyes, but the problem is the gaps. There are whole sections of my life that I simply do not remember. Flashes of memory are followed by long, empty, dark tunnels of nothing, which, in turn, give way to torrents of pain, waves of grief, whispers of anger, shards of despair.

I sit down, hard, on a bench, and try to breathe. But my breath catches, and the tears flow harder than ever before. I look back on my life and I am immediately drawn to the trauma, the turmoil, the pain that sits down deep at the center of my being. I have lived a troubled life, victim and perpetrator of the insanity of dammed-up grief, manifested in so many sick and dysfunctional ways across the generations of a family.

In my shrouded, secretive past there is alcoholism and verbal abuse and physical violence and obsession and dark silence and unspoken rule-making and defiant rule-breaking and stark perfectionism and painful addiction and the deep, wrenching, misdirected sadness of a family that was torn apart by too much death, too much grief, too much pain to bear.

And I realize, looking back, that I have forgotten more than I remember, and I think, looking back, that maybe that is a good thing, but I cannot shake the feeling that there is something I must know, something I must reach, some memory I must get hold of, some piece of the puzzle back there, shrouded in darkness and secrecy and silence and forgetting, something I must learn to become whole. Before I know what has hit me, I am lying on the grass, clutching my stomach, sobbing loudly, nearly unable to breathe. And I sob, and sob, and sob.

Finally, it all subsides. A brief pause. After a time, I can breathe again. I stand and walk back to my office, knowing full well that I am not finished, but knowing also that I must breathe for a moment and muster the strength that comes to me only in moments when I am creating something new.

And I sit down, finally, to write this chapter.

In a family beset by trauma, members manage pain and grief and loss in different ways. Some freeze. Some sleep fitfully, hoping not to dream. Some remain silent, falling into despair or anger or bitterness. Some wet the bed. Some drink themselves into oblivion. Some cannot go out. Some cannot stay in. Some cannot drive. Some cannot not drive—but they seem to drive in circles. Some lie alone in the dark, awake, alone, shaking. Some fall into work, or food, or television, or other addictions. Some forget.

In *The Savage and Beautiful Country*, psychiatrist Alan McGlashan (1988) asks a pivotal question: "Since man [*sic*] must remember if he is not to become meaningless, and must forget if he is not to go mad, what shall he do?" (p. 5). The problem before us is to maintain a precarious balance between remembering and forgetting, these vital functions of the human spirit that allow us, in our embodied form, to function in a world of other humans. Losing that balance, we can be gripped, engulfed, frozen by anxiety, despair, hopelessness, secrecy, silence.

The answer to our dilemma lies in engaging a new life practice. In this chapter, I explore the meanings and the ramifications of living the ethnographic mystery in the face of trauma. I suggest the possibility of rising to engage in a courageous dance with the storied, autoethnographic life, thus carrying our core life stories into the center-space of our most significant relationships. Employing an imaginative personal extension of the pattern of a storied text that has appeared in popular culture—the novel and film *Big Fish*—as a way to probe the centrality of story as a connective "glue" for our human social world, I move toward development of an *ethos* of storied family life as a primary means of healing and redemption. Accidental ethnography, coupled with the courage to connect, then, becomes a primary means of dialogic living that can illuminate relational life in ways that other methodologies, practices, and actions cannot.

Big Fish

In the 1998 book *Big Fish: A Novel of Mythic Proportions* (which was adapted to film in 2003 by Tim Burton and John August), author

Daniel Wallace tells the story of a father, Edward Bloom, and his son, Will, who do not exactly see eye to eye. The two speak different languages, grounded in different worldviews. Will, a reporter by trade, thinks and speaks in starkly realistic, concrete, factual ways. Edward, on the other hand, is given to flights of fancy and the weaving of tall tales of mythic proportions, each of which has its own peculiar punch line or "moral." The conflict between father and son in this story is the kind of conflict that has plagued fathers and sons, mothers and daughters, brothers and sisters—indeed all of humanity—throughout our storied, shared history. As Rollo May (1991) puts it,

> There are, broadly speaking, two ways human beings have communicated through their long and fitful history. One is rationalistic language. This is specific and empirical, and eventuates in logic. . . . A second way is myth. The myth is a *drama* which begins as a historical event and takes on its special character as a way of orienting people to reality . . . *myth refers to the quintessence of human experience, the meaning and significance of human life.* (p. 26, emphasis in the original)

When these two ways of communicating clash, the sparks that fly are often harsh, bitter, biting, painful to bear. In *Big Fish*, this conflict plays out via a series of storytelling moments, all centered around the dying father (Edward) and his final stories, told mostly to his son on his deathbed. Will wants his father to be "real"—to tell events in his life as they *really* happened. Edward Bloom, however, insists that his stories, as fantastical as they might be, are, in fact, laden with truth. He does not waver in his task, which is, to him, to tell *stories of mythic proportions* that speak *to* and *through* and *with* truth, whether they are grounded in fact or not.

This stance causes no end of consternation and frustration in Will. He believes his father and his life are completely mysterious, mostly because Edward speaks in jokes and riddles and myths rather than reports . . . and that, to him, is tragic. He wants to know what "really" happened. But to Edward, mystery—and its imaginatively constructed language-grounded friends, legend and poetry, story and joke, myth and fable—speaks to the magic that swirls between the sentences of a life. Mystery is the essence of a great story; mystery is the glue that holds a story together, the spark that carries the listener into fascination, the river of energy that leads the story to new and exciting places, the possibility that allows for deeper, more significant, more meaningful (mythic) truth to emerge.

In the novel, the story unfolds across a series of four "takes" outlining the possible, imagined, or impending death of Edward Bloom. Through these imaginative takes on Edward's death, each of which reveals a different aspect of Edward's character, and each of which includes a vital conversation between father and son, Will finally comes to understand his father and why he is the way he is. In the end, as his father passes on to another realm, Will is able to grasp Edward and his meaning. In the film, Will ends the final story by saying: "That was my father's final joke, I guess. A man tells so many stories, that he becomes the stories. They live on after him, and in that way he becomes immortal."

Each of these four takes on Edward's death begins with this line: "It happens like this." In this chapter, I pick up that pattern, and, through a series of takes, attempt to put some glue to my own life story as a way to get inside this emerging idea of accidental ethnography, from a new angle.

Remembering and Forgetting (Take Two)

It happens like this. A sharp pain in my back bolts me upright in bed. Gasping at the intensity of the pain, I look over at the clock. It is 4:45 A.M.

I walk slowly down the hall, plug in the coffee, and walk out onto my deck, looking out on the morning that is about to emerge. I am alone in my world, except for the few birds halfheartedly beginning their morning warm-up, which always comes before full symphony, and my faithful dog, Jessie, who follows me pretty much everywhere. Everyone else is fast asleep.

A mist seems to be rising from the grass, hinting at the summer swelter just around the bend. That pain in my back is startling, breathtaking even, and it has not subsided. Suddenly, it surges. I sit down hard, trying to breathe. As I have been taught, I breathe into the pain, try to breathe it out.

Cut. I am standing in line in the hall of Clifton Elementary School. Brett Morris, my tormenter, the class bully, has stepped out of the line. He stands facing me.

"Crybaby," he taunts, "You couldn't take it, could you?"

"Bastard," I mutter under my breath.

A fist crashes into my jaw. I am thrown against the hard concrete wall. I fall to the ground, crying. Kids are laughing all around me. No one comes to my aid. I am humiliated. I am twelve years old.

Cut. I am lying on the hard ground, struggling to get up, but he is just too strong. He pushes my head into the floor. I scream in pain and frustration.

My older brother stands up, lets me get to my feet.

I stand up, breathing hard, and looking at him, hard.

Suddenly, he just punches me, hard, in the face, shouts: "I hate you!"

"I hate you more!" I shout back.

I am eight years old.

Cut. I stand on the roadside, awaiting my punishment. I have transgressed. I have spoken.

"Bend over," my father says.

"I don't want to."

"Bend over and grab your ankles."

So I do, and his belt cuts into my skin, into my heart. I cry silently, wondering what is wrong with me, wondering why my daddy would hurt me, wondering what I did to deserve this. And the belt hits again. *Whack.* And again. *Whack.* And again. *Whack.* A silent tear trickles down my cheek. I am four years old.

Cut. I am standing in my living room. Ours is a home of yelling, shouting, chaos, and long periods of silent anger. We have long since abandoned talking through our problems. Ours is a wounded family, a family caught up in a swirling morass of pain and dysfunction. We seem unable to extricate ourselves.

We have found a pattern.

The system has reached equilibrium.

Sadly, we are caught up—trapped, if you will—in a cycle of "pathological communication," a pattern so studiously documented, if only we had known, in *Pragmatics of Human Communication*. We live in a cycle of "symmetrical escalation."[1]

As I stand looking out the window, I am wondering how it all came to this. I look back on the years of my life up until now, and I see—and feel—the fights, the pain, the misunderstandings, the deaths, the truncated grief, the anger, the frustration, the addiction, the defiance, the self-loathing, the silence, the shouting.

Where did it all come from? Why do we do this? Why?

Is there hope for escape?

Last night, I came home late: drunk, disorderly, obnoxious.

I was greeted by my father's rage.

How did it come to this? I wonder.

At that moment, I know I must leave all this, as soon as I possibly can.

I am sixteen years old.

Cut. I am standing in my parents' kitchen. My father is standing across the room, shouting at me, fists clenched. I shout back, just as loud, frustrated beyond my limit. I cannot get through to this man. We are symmetrical equivalents: defiant anger vs. defiant anger. We are going nowhere. We will not stop until someone is hurt.

And, at that moment, it hits me: Someone already *is* hurt.

Everyone is hurt.

I walk sadly, silently out of the room, leaving our fight for another day.

I am thirty-two years old.

Cut. I am back on my deck, breathing hard. The memories are surging up, then retreating, then surging up again. And my back pain follows their ebb and flow. It is time to do something.

But I do not know what to do. I have lived so long in silent grief and overblown anger and terrible loneliness that I do not know how to live otherwise. Will I survive? I wonder.

And just as quickly: Of course. Look at all you have lived through.

And then: another surge of pain and swirling memory.

I sit down hard and begin to cry.

After about ten minutes of deep, unspeakable sadness, I am spent.

But I think something is about to change.

Something is afoot.

I am forty-eight years old.

Remembering and Forgetting (Take Three)

It happens like this.

I wake one morning and remember nothing.

But, from somewhere, it occurs to me that I have a friend who has some experience with what I am feeling. He was in an airplane crash when he was twelve years old—a crash that killed his father, nearly killed him, and sent his family into a spiral of pain, silence, secrecy, tumult, and ultimately, ongoing dysfunction.

And it just so happens that, in adulthood, he has spent part of his time studying to be a counselor.

So I call him.

I tell him about the torrents of memory erupting into my life uninvited, followed by periods of blankness, of no memory at all.

"Post-traumatic stress disorder," he says.

"Say what?"

"You are describing symptoms of PTSD," he says. "Post-traumatic stress disorder."

"Say more."

"Hold on. Let me get a book."

While I am waiting, I try just to breathe. He returns to the phone a couple of minutes later, says, "Here are some of the symptoms. See if you think they fit: re-experiencing the trauma—flashbacks, nightmares, intrusive memories, large gaps in memory, exaggerated emotional and physical reactions to triggers that remind the person of the trauma, emotional numbing, feeling detached, lack of emotions (especially positive ones), loss of interest in activities; avoidance behaviors—avoiding activities, people, or places that remind the person of the trauma; increased arousal—difficulty sleeping and concentrating, irritability, hyper-vigilance (being on guard), and exaggerated startle response. That's most of them, but there are more."

"Say no more," I say.

The next day, I make an appointment with a counselor and begin a journey that will take me straight through the trauma.

Remembering and Forgetting (Take Four)

It happens like this. I am sitting in my shrink's office, talking about all the turmoil of my childhood. I can only talk, and cry, and talk some more. And then, once again, I am spent. But our hour is up anyway, so, just as abruptly as I plopped on his couch, I find I am on my way out the door.

That night, as I lie in bed, it quickly becomes clear that this will be one of *those* nights.

One of my fitful, sleep-deprived, dark nights.

Just can't get comfortable. I toss, and I turn. I fidget. I am about to get up and give up when I remember to breathe.

I lie there for a long while, just breathing. Long, deep breaths in; slow, soft breaths out.

In.

Out.

In.

Out.

And I find myself drifting . . .

I wake with a start and find I am sitting in a darkened movie theater.

I look around, and, as far as I can tell, everyone I have ever known—dead or alive—is there.

Everyone.

Before I can register my surprise, music blasts out of hidden speakers, and the screen lights up.

The camera comes into focus on the center of a long rectangular dining table, constructed of sturdy wood, mission style, in a solid room of the same shape, sparsely decorated with western art, the floor a variegated Spanish ceramic tile. The dining room sits in the center of this sturdy brick farmhouse with solid plaster inside walls, painted a light cream color. On one wall, a large wooden buffet, on the other, a row of casement windows looking out onto the yard and the oversize vegetable garden. A deep green forest can be seen in the background.

I recognize this place. This is my grandparents' house. People are seated around the table, with others standing behind them. At first, I can't make out their faces, as if the camera is out of focus. Then, suddenly, I realize who they all are. My family has gathered. All of them, both sides through four generations, some living, some long dead, are there. I am sitting at one end of the table, my father is at the other.

Something is different about this scene, I find myself thinking, though I can't quite put my finger on it.

And then it hits me. Everyone is talking, but there is no tension.

In fact, everyone is laughing.

This is new.

The shadow seems to have lifted. As far as I can tell, people are telling stories.

My attention is drawn to my dad, who is busy talking to his sister and my two sisters.

"We just loved you so much, Sis. We couldn't make sense of it when you left us. We weren't ready. How could you die? It hurt so much. I think we all froze. It was the last straw. And we never got over it. We missed you so much."

"I know," she replies softly. "I didn't mean to. It just happened."

"It was so sad," says my sister. "So, so sad."

"I know," my aunt smiles. "But it's O.K. You just have to talk about it. Talk and cry and tell stories and get it out—get it out of your system. And then, remember. Always remember. And when the memories get to be too much, tell another story. Send the memories out into the air."

"Right. But how? How do you speak the unspeakable? How do you walk through the shadow?"

"Yea though I walk through the valley of the shadow of death, I will fear no evil. Start with the good stories, maybe even the *funny* ones. And it will flow from there."

"We have all walked through that valley, and at the end, we find . . . us . . . together," I chime in.

"Yes, that's it," my grandfather says.

"What?"

"Us."

"Us. That's what we have, what we need," says my mom.

"Us," everyone says, almost like a chant, in unison.

"Us!"

"Yes," I say. "We have us."

"And our stories," says my sister.

"Our stories," we all chant.

"Our stories."

Yes, I find myself thinking. That is it.

That morning, I crawl out of bed, a smile flickering. I walk down the hall, pick up the phone, call my mom.

"Maybe we should talk," I say.

"Yes," she says. "Maybe we should."

So I call a family meeting, inviting the living directly, hoping the others will join us in spirit.

The Courage to Connect

"The more consciousness, the more self," writes Kierkegaard (1976, p. 1). Although it may be de-centered (Jameson, 1991) or reflexive (Giddens, 1984, 1991) or socially constituted (Schrag, 1986; Stewart, 1995) or saturated (Gergen, 2000) or even lost in the cosmos

(Percy, 1983), the self is still stuck with itself—or at least the *impression* of itself (Goffman, 1959). And that impression, at the very least tied to the existence of others with whom we are present, issues a call to consciousness, which is, as I've argued, a call to conscience—which is, notably, a *narrative* conscience. To be sure, consciousness offers gifts aplenty, especially to those of us who hope to engage what Rollo May (1972) calls "the courage to create." For the writer of accidental (auto)ethnography, the call of narrative conscience reigns supreme.

But so often, we find ourselves inhabiting a thin place, betwixt and between.

Up against the sharp edges of anxiety, we may find darkness looming. Of course, this world we inhabit can be a very scary place.

And yet, there is also joy—boundless, incredible joy—to be had on this Earth.

Shadow, to exist, requires light.

In any event, wherever we find ourselves, once we engage the practice of accidental ethnography, the call of narrative conscience draws us on. And so we come up against the open spaces of mystery, and to the cliff's edge where faith beckons.

That is the challenge—and the great mystery—that confronts us all.

And then, there are all those other people whose paths we cross, with whom we must negotiate our social realities.

"Hell is—other people," Sartre's character Garcin famously intones.[2] But I don't think he got that one right. Or, at least the point, only faintly understood by most of us, is partial, incomplete, not quite reaching its target. Like Zeno's arrow,[3] the problem with the self-consciousness induced by the presence of others is that it may never reach its target.

And then there is the hell that follows, much more painful than the hell of human presence. Hell is—the *absence* of other people! This hell becomes especially acute when we are separated from those we love by the hand of Thanatos. Death visits, and he is a most unwelcome guest, no matter how fervently we pray for a peaceful demise, an end to someone's suffering, or the hope of an afterlife. The truth we must face is this, stark and dark though it be: For now at least, the one we love is gone, gone, gone forever.

Sadly, this hell is often magnified by the way we fall into silence, struck dumb by our grief, lost in the shadows of our suffering. When we fail to *connect* in the face of our loss, we lose more than just the one who has gone to another place. We lose hope, we lose possibility, we lose our very breath.

And, as our breath flies out of us, our secrets are sealed within. Sadly.

But, while there is life, there is still hope.

In the end, Steinbeck's (1939) Rose of Sharon, herself starving, nurses a starving stranger.[4]

An act of hope, an affirmation of life.

What we need, as salve for our wounds, is an act of hope, an affirmation of life.

In the end, what we need is the courage to connect.

And so I close this chapter with a simple suggestion.

For the accidental (auto)ethnographer, the courage to connect can be born in that moment when we dare to write our secrets into stories.

If we begin to write our mythic truths, all sorts of remarkable things may follow.

In the end, from this active engagement of the courage to connect, hope may be born again, and we may come, at last, to where we need to be.

Reflection

I'm startled that I became a writer. I don't think I can control my life or my writing. . . . I don't have that sort of control. I'm simply becoming.
—Kurt Vonnegut, *A Man Without a Country*

Father, we are here to help each other get through this thing, whatever it is.
—Dr. Mark Vonnegut (Kurt's son), *A Man Without a Country*

This is the world of the myth, great and strange, always changing but fundamentally the same: man's ultimate concern symbolized in divine figures and actions. Myths are symbols of faith combined in stories about divine-human encounters.
—Paul Tillich, *Dynamics of Faith*

Full Circle

In the end, we come back to the beginning.

In the beginning, you will remember, there was a child's faith that the path would lead somewhere.

As we get older, faith may become more complicated.

Experience—sometimes painful, sometimes joyful, often betwixt and between the two—makes it so.

And so, of course, does joy.

Thus, we get theological formulations: "Faith," writes Paul Tillich, "is the state of being ultimately concerned" (1957, p. 1).

This is a complicated way of saying that faith is about what *matters*.

Of course, if Tillich's predecessor and philosophical mentor, Kierkegaard, was right, that state of ultimate concern only comes from taking a blind leap into an unknown future, despite the anxiety that erupts, threatening paralysis.

It comes from plunging into the darkness, despite the fear, despite the fact that you may get lost.

So now we stand, back where we began, at the trailhead, poised to reenter the forest.

In the end, my ultimate concern in writing this book—my leap of faith, if you will, or at the least my thin strand of hope—has been, simply, that together we might walk this winding path through the forest of life-writing and somehow make it back to where we started.

In the end, we may, as Albert Camus (1955) expects, find the secret we seek, and come, at last, to truly know that which we knew all along.

In the end, if our secrets mean anything, they must mean this: We are here, primarily, to help each other through this thing called life, whatever it is.

We just screw it up sometimes.

In the end, if our secrets mean anything, they must mean this: We are bound, by our very narrative natures, to seek to unveil the mysteries that swirl in the dark, shadowy corners of the secret "hearts of darkness" that dwell within us all.

In the end, if our secrets mean anything, they must mean this: The cry for myth can pull us out of the dark, scary places in our hearts.

In the end, if our secrets mean anything, they must mean this: Telling the story, despite anxiety, is the path to healing. And, anyway, storytelling is far more potent, far more fascinating, far more engaging than secret-keeping.

In the end, if our secrets mean anything, they must mean this: We are called, as humans, to story our way through life, hoping against hope that the possibility engendered by story will, finally, make us immortal.

In the end, if our secrets can take on the mythical energy they need, then we may find ourselves in a direct encounter with the divine energy that animates this world we inhabit.

This book is a story of faith in the simple proposition that our secrets can, if transformed into stories of mythic proportions, transform us all. Or, at least, they can help us help each other get through this thing, whatever it is.

To conclude this chapter, I focus on the organic process of writing accidental (auto)ethnography as a way of living. Beginning with a story about how I came to be a writer of accidental (auto)ethnography, I fold together the embodied writing of life's dreams, memories, shadows, secrets, and stories as they emerge and offer some practical help for the new ethnographer hoping to open a new way of being through the writing of life.

The Call

September 12, 2001. I stand at my window, wondering what has just happened to our world. All my illusions—of peace, safety, justice, or even ordinariness—have been shattered in a burst of crashing metal, shattering glass, disintegrating concrete, soaring flame, searing flesh. As I go about trying to make this day happen, I find there is little I can do but gather with those who matter to me. I find comfort in the company of my family, my friends, my students, my colleagues, my neighbors.

At first, we are bewildered.

Then, we are angry.

Often, we are simply afraid.

But, as the week unfolds, I begin to hear hints of gratitude, even hope. These are not celebratory moments, but rather small instances of the (sometimes thin) feeling that it is good—even with all this going on—to be alive.

And then, it is Friday, and I find myself breathing a little as the respite of the weekend beckons.

The next morning, I am awakened early by a dark dream.

And I find myself drawn inexorably to my computer.

I sit down to write, and what comes to be over the ensuing weeks—all that comes, in fact—is that I am drawn deeper and deeper into the (accidental) autoethnographic story of this shattering, shivering ordeal that quickly became known simply by a date: 9/11. Somehow, I find both symmetry and irony in the naming of these momentous, terrible events. 9/11: so short and small a turn of number for such a large and long-enduring trauma. That story—my first true autoethnographic piece—was published the following spring in *Qualitative Inquiry* (Poulos, 2002).

I have not been the same since the day I started writing it.

I have found, sometimes to my chagrin, that I can write nothing that is not autoethnographic.

I have found, in fact, that my autoethnography began, along the way, to write me. Like Kurt Vonnegut, I am somewhat startled that I became a writer of autoethnography. It just sort of *took* me, as I was in the process of becoming. And I have not looked back.

I have not flinched.

I have not wished for a different turn of events.

On some level, I have stopped trying to control my writing—or my life.

I have settled in for the ride.

My fondest hope is that you, too, will find your ride.

That, I think, is the essence of accidental ethnography. If you can embrace the possibilities that erupt in your everyday life—embrace them and write them into being, write the words that come into the grandest form words can take (a good story)—then you are on your way.

So, if you seriously wish to engage the accidental ethnographer in you, there may be certain things you can do to cultivate a readiness to see the accidents that erupt as your life unfolds.

Can you seize the accident as opportunity?

Can you stumble into possibility?

Can you fall toward dialogue?

Can you fall into the river, fly with the wind, flow with the tide, relax into the ride?

Can you let yourself be swept away?

Will you?

I don't know.

I can't promise anything.

But I do think that within each of us there is both a secret-keeper and a storyteller.

The question is: Which one will you nurture?

This is not an easy choice.

Believe me, I know.

After all, we are dealing with two faces of human life, a double-edged sword.

You have reached a fork in the road.

To your right lies the dark world of secrecy and silence.

To your left, a story.

Both pathways offer promise—and peril.

The ancients depicted this phenomenon as Janus, the god of gateways and doorways, of beginnings and endings.

How appropriate.

The question is: Which way will you look? Will you look to end the story before it is born? Will your story be stillborn, like little Victor, forever kept secret in a little box buried deep within you?

Or will your story emerge into this world, to grow and thrive and change lives?

It is up to you.

Sort of.

Actually, when I say accidental autoethnography writes me, that I am startled that I became a writer, I sincerely and honestly mean that I didn't *mean* to.

It just *took* me.

And I have been writing ever since.

But what we have here is a question of *availability*.

Are you available?

Are you ready to meet Mnemosyne's daughters—your own Muses?

Are you attuned to the crack of the stick, the faint smell, the offhand remark, the dark dream, the small tune, the soft tone, the strange outburst, or the light breeze that may trigger a memory?

Are you ready to see, hear, touch, smell, taste, intuit the world you inhabit—consciously, mindfully, filled with wonder?

Are your ears and your eyes available to hear the faint whisper of a secret seeping out from beneath the floorboards of your life?

Are you ready to face—and embrace—your dreams?

Is your heart open to transforming the secrets you keep into the stories that make us weep?

Or laugh?

Are you willing to go to the thin places where the memories, dreams, forgettings, secrets, and imaginings might show themselves?

Are you available to show them to us?

Are you ready to embrace the organic process of writing what comes upon you?

Are you strong enough, courageous enough to face your own heart of darkness?

If you can answer yes to any of these questions, you may be ready.

And then there is the craft of it all. I have a few things to say about this. But, first, there must be time to dream.

Awakening

I dreamed last night I was sitting in the *shvitz* again. It has been years since I sat there doing my first field ethnography. I sat with these old Jewish men from eastern Europe and middle America and Israel, sweating in their super-heated sauna, trying to make sense of it all, yet always filled with wonder (Poulos, 1999).[5] I eavesdropped on their ancient practice for nearly a year, but I still wonder if I ever "got" it. I always felt like an outsider. At least *that* was familiar.

In my dream, the *shvitzers* are going through their practiced ritual, soaping and rinsing, soaping and rinsing. I am sweating, hard. Then, as one of the *schmeissers*[6] dumps the bucket of water on the head of his friend, the scene shifts.

Now I am in my house again, and I hear the sound of water where it should not be. I venture around the corner, and discover a stairway down to a basement I did not know existed. There are many stairs leading down, down, down into the earth. Upon rounding the final turn in this winding staircase, I discover I am standing in a deep subterranean basement. The walls and floor are of what appears to be moist, gray clay. There is a light source, but it is not immediately clear what that source is.

As I look up, searching, I notice that the walls are seeping with a constant stream of grayish water. I look around, and discover that the whole room, which is a rectangle of about 1,500 square feet, is seeping: floor, walls, ceiling. And through the middle of the room flows a large stream, which may well be eating away at the foundation of my home. The water there is gray and murky, and appears to be filled with trash and foam and other signs of pollution. And anxiety, gray and murky as the water, starts to seep into my heart.

Looking around, I finally discover the source of light. The sun is peeking through a growing hole in my backyard, where the soil has caved in and fallen into the rushing stream.

I suddenly realize that the world is shifting around me, and it appears that everything is about to cave in. Fear grips me. As I turn to rush back upstairs to safety, the dark images of death and trauma and silence and secrecy and quiet, hidden pains that have haunted me all these years flood my consciousness. The bodies of my dead relatives float silently by. I am filled with dread, and worse. I open my mouth to scream, but no sounds escape.

And just as suddenly, the stream overflows its banks, and I am swept up into its current and carried into a long, dark tunnel. The stream is now a raging river, roiling and boiling. I struggle and sputter, but quickly find that I cannot fight the current. It is too powerful. I have no idea where I am going, but it is abundantly clear that I must go along for the ride. So I do the only thing I can do. I lean back and settle into the current and discover that the less I fight—the more I relax—the easier it is simply to follow the flow of the water. And suddenly I am thrown into broad daylight and the cold, clear, bracing water of a familiar mountain lake.[7]

As I come up for air, and slowly swim ashore, I realize that the sun is shining and the sky is bright and blue and clear. I stand on the shore, taking it all in. There is no sign of the home I inhabited for so long, which was clearly washed away in the flood. All around me are the familiar sights and sounds of the mountain forest I know so well. An osprey circles overhead, lazily searching for breakfast. A squirrel bounds up the trunk of a hemlock. A woodpecker thumps in the distance. A fish jumps somewhere behind me, and some unseen critter rustles in the underbrush off to my left. And a wave of peace like I have never known rolls over me.

And I know, for a certainty, that I am home.

And then I realize I am surrounded by all the people who have made my life meaningful—my loving family, my hilarious friends, my brilliant colleagues, my eager students. And everyone is talking and laughing and cutting up.

And I wake with a small smile and a new glint in my eye.

Flooding Consciousness, Flowing Writing

What to make of this little dream?

All ancient cultures have stories of great floods, symbolic of the sinful (separated) state of humanity, and of cleansing and renewal, of rebirth into a new, untainted world. Water, the life giving element, symbol of the deep unconscious and the cleansing power of *flow*, is ever-present in my dreams.

But this time, I find fresh meaning in its movement from the dark, murky underworld to the light of a fresh day.

Put simply, I see this dreamstory as a story of the birth of freedom—from the darkness, from the secrets, from the pain. Washed clean, I will no longer be hobbled by these burdens. I face this world, free at last. Here we are, simply, talking, laughing, enjoying life, and the wonder of nature, and the fine company of significant others.

So, of course, I do what I must: I sit down to write this chapter. And, as I write this accidental dream into dreamstory, I am drawn to the idea that, in fact, faith may save me yet. But, as the little known and less read member of Jesus' inner circle put it: "Faith without works is dead" (James 2:26).

Fortunately for me, the real work on this Earth is the work of writing accidental ethnography.

This dream of washing away the old and falling into the new is the story of mythic proportions I have needed all my life. A small, simple story, perhaps. But a very big story, too. It is a story of letting go of my old "home"—the dark, familiar damp place under the floorboards where all my secrets have been buried for so long—and of moving into a new one: the bright, open world of story-making.

It is my greatest hope that you, too, can come to inhabit this world. So, dear reader, as this book comes to a close, I dedicate this final chapter to you, to your journey through the dark basement tunnels of your life, to your own accidental writing process, to your emergence into the sunlight of the spirit that awaits you. I hope, in these final pages, to offer a gift that might, if not help you, at least urge you to let yourself be swept up in the stream.

I cannot promise or predict where this journey will take you.

But I can promise that it will be one helluva ride.

Here's what I have to offer, my parting shot at helping you through this thing, whatever it is.

Tonight, go to bed early.

Or late.

Either way, ask for a dream.

Who knows? You might get lucky.

Tomorrow morning, stumble into the kitchen, plug in the coffee, and settle in immediately, wherever you do your writing. Write whatever comes. Write like there's no tomorrow.

Maybe what comes will be your dream. Maybe, if you are lucky, some voice from your dream will tell you something you need to know. Maybe, if you're lucky, your dream will morph into a story.

Or maybe, as you search about your keyboard, you'll locate a small story from your deep past.

Maybe a secret will seep up from somewhere.

Or maybe a sound will trigger a memory.

Or maybe you'll find a little flash of inspiration born this very day.

Maybe you will write and write and write some more.

Maybe some of it will be worth keeping.

Or maybe you'll write a whole lot of nothing.

But write anyway. And keep writing as long as you can stand to, or at least as long as it takes for the coffee to brew.

Do this every day.

Who knows? You might get lucky.

After a time, you will feel the urge—or maybe the need—to venture out into your world. Do that. But as you go about your day, consider taking a moment to get lost in the forest. Consider attuning your senses—all of them, or at least all you can muster—to what is going on around you. Pay attention, or as the Buddhists put it, try to be *mindful* (Hanh, 1992, 1999, 2005).

You never know what you might find.

Who knows? You might get lucky.

And notice this: In every encounter there is a story, just waiting to be told. We just don't always know it.

As you encounter people in your world, consider searching for the story beneath the encounter.

And know this: There are secrets swirling all about us. But just because they *exist* as secrets doesn't mean they have to *remain* secrets.

Like I said, there is always a story waiting to be told.

Suppose, one day, that you are in conversation with someone. Perhaps it is someone in your family. As you fall into conversation, a hint of something beneath the words comes out—a shift of tone, a slip of emotion, a darkening of mood, a shard of a memory, a moment of possibility.

As you fall into accidental dialogue (Poulos, 2008a) you might well find something you were seeking all along.

What do you do?

Remember: They are notoriously slippery, those family secrets.

And yet they always seem to want, at some point, to come to the surface.

As Gadamer (1975) puts it, you'll want to "fall into" the moment. Follow the dialogue wherever it leads. Let go of agendas, and just *listen*.

Who knows? Maybe you'll get lucky.

Maybe—little by little, or all at once in a rush—a secret will become a story.

And then, one day, you might smell something pungent that triggers the trace of a memory.

Or perhaps you will hear a slight rustling sound that takes you deep into your memory.

Maybe you'll feel a rough texture that cries out to be remembered.

Or even see something that brings you up short, as a flood of images pours through you.

Maybe you'll take a bite of dinner and be transported to a time and place you had, until now, only dimly known existed somewhere in the recesses of your unconscious.

Writing Life

And then, there is the writing.

How to go about that?

What I can say is this: Writing is an act of faith.

Writing is the "works" that keeps faith alive.

When I get lucky, the writing just sweeps me away, like the stream in my dream, to a new home, to a whole new world of possibility.

So, as much as I can, I try to sit back, relax, stop fighting the current. Sometimes, I even enjoy the ride.

The first word is, of course, the most important one. A flood begins with a single raindrop. A story begins with a single word.

So, write the first word. And do your best to see what flows from it. Follow the flow. And all sorts of remarkable things may come to pass.

Write until you are spent. Then write some more.

Of course, there are times when I think I can write no more.

Sometimes, I feel like I'm in a drought. And then, one day, a raindrop falls. That first word shows up, and I just fall into it. If I am open to the flow, all sorts of things start to happen.

But when I am struggling to find the words, I often find myself seeking distractions, vaguely hoping that something will turn up. Sometimes, distractions are good. Sometimes, distractions give me time and space for the next storm to brew.

And when it gets really bad, I sit down, and try to write my anxiety into something. I focus all my attention on what is going on in my world, right here, right now.

Sometimes, I stumble into something I did not know was there.

Sometimes, I get lucky.

Mostly, I just stumble along, open to the accidental, making my way into the written word organically, following the lead of my fingers as they make their way across my keyboard.

Occasionally, I fall into a good story.

Sometimes, I just have to get up and take a walk.

Or a nap.

But usually, I stick with it. I write, and write, and write.

Generally, if I am persistent enough, something worth keeping turns up. And, when I must pause, I sit down immediately to read what I have written.

First, I read quickly, just absorbing the story for what it is.

Then I read again, pen in hand, looking to shift the words so that they can come to sing the tune on key. After all, we are looking for stories of mythic proportions, informed by the Muses, infused with memory and faith and keen insight.

Like musical performance, good writing takes practice and discipline and many small, fine adjustments. A good writer, like a good musician, is always tuning her or his instrument—and playing *with heart.*

After editing, I turn it face down on my desk and let it go.

Sometime later, usually the next day, I pick it up and read it again, edit it again, and sit down to rewrite it. Sometimes, I rewrite it several times before it's ready. The beauty of it all is that then I get to give it or send it to other people, who read it and respond, suggest, help me move it all to a new place.

Then there is more editing, tuning, developing.

And one day, the story just sings!

So I send it off to be published, and, after a long gestation, it shows up in my mailbox, published, ready to be read again.

And a funny thing happens, every time I read something I've published.

It all seems so *new* somehow.

Maybe *that's* how you know it's a good story.

Home

One morning in late August, I get up, decide to take my own advice. I stumble toward the kitchen, switch on the coffee pot, and make my way to my computer. I sit for awhile, staring at the blank screen. But nothing comes, so I seek distraction.

I walk outside to get the paper. It's still early, only six in the morning, but a thick gray mist has settled in.

We have been besieged these past few weeks by stultifying humidity and prodigious heat. Late summer in this part of the country is the reason someone invented air conditioning. Still, as I step onto my driveway, something seems different. I look up at the oak towering overhead. Have the leaves begun to turn, just a little?

Hope. There is always hope.

As this story comes to a close, I know there is hope for another.

I stand, lost in that thought for a moment. Then, I notice my shirt. It's already moist. I haven't even "worked up" a sweat here. It just came upon me. I find myself thinking, "Man, sometimes the air here is so wet, it might as well be raining." And, just like that, the first fat drop falls, splashing big across the left lens of my glasses, changing my vision, just a little. And, just as suddenly, I am caught in a downpour. By the time I make it back to my porch, I am soaking wet.

I smile and open the door, thinking of hope, and home, and all that is good.

Is hope born in that moment of cleansing that inevitably comes just when I need it?

And home. There is always home.

The place we call *home*: A warm, dry, cozy place, filled with love, joy, peace. As I sit down to write these last words, I know, in my heart, that I have come home.

Is home born in that moment when the heart takes over?

The Greeks called it *ethos*: the dwelling place.

Perhaps we will find that place—that dwelling place where all that is meaningful comes together.

That place where we find, in our hearts and in our lives, our ultimate concern.

That place where we can, in the end, find all that we seek in this world.

That place where we build what we need, and need what we build.

That place where together this strange collection of people I call my family might fall out of secret silence into dialogue, and, following the urgings of dialogic imagination and narrative conscience, build a new story of our lives.

That place where *ethos* (home) meets *pathos* (passion), and, via *logos* (the word), comes into dynamic play with *mythos* (story).

That place where we find the keys to the door of a new life, free at last of the dark, painful secret silence.

That place where, in the end, we can write our secret lives into stories of mythic proportions, stories that *matter*.

That place where we find the opening to a new life of life-writing.

Come home with me.

Write with me.

It is time.

Exercises

Writing Exercise 1: Writing Dialogue

As you go about your day, listen carefully and closely to the conversations around you. Tune your ear to the tones, the modulations, the pacings, and the rhythms of the voices around you. Carefully watch the language of gesture, space, and expression that people embody in their conversations. Listen for patterns of words, word choices, slang, style, and usage. If you have the opportunity, listen in on a conversation or two. Eavesdrop. What do people in your world say, and how do they say it?

Perhaps the most difficult writing to do is the writing of natural, smooth-flowing dialogue into your ethnographic stories. To prepare, I recommend reading the novels and stories of Michael Parker (Parker, 1993, 1994, 2001, 2004, 2005, 2007). He is a writer who is keenly attuned to the rhythm, the spirit, and the relational qualities of characters speaking into the air around them. There are other good models, of course, but in the end, you have to write the conversations that infuse your life in your own way, in your own voice and in the voices of your characters. Here it is important to be true to both the spirit and the content of the words as they were spoken, but also to the tone and tenor of your characters' conversations as they unfold.

All preparation and practice aside, of course, the words we have said about memory can offer comfort. We don't necessarily have to worry so much about getting it exactly right. There are times when we may have to seek just to catch the rhythm and the tone of a conversation as we recall it, without worrying too much about accuracy of re-presentation.

Certainly field notes are tremendously helpful. But you cannot always take notes; some of these conversations will involve you directly; many will require deep and careful attention and participation; and note taking can be a real distraction. Even though your memory can be fickle, it is also a powerful tool that can, with practice, be kept sharp. You will also want to sit down as soon as possible after a meaningful or important conversation and render it in writing as faithfully as you possibly can. Do this every day for a month. With some practice, you will become good at writing dialogue.

Writing Exercise 2: Futurestory

Sit down, relax, and close your eyes. Get calm. Center yourself quietly for a few moments. Try to clear your mind, then:

IMAGINE! The year is ten years in the future. Visualize your life as you wish it to be ten years from today. What will your life be like? Where will you live? What will your home be like? What will your family life be like? What will you do for work? How will you play? Imagine as much detail as you can. What are your hopes? Your dreams? Your aspirations? Write a story that carries you and some of the significant characters in your life out into your (obviously idealized) imagined future. Work to engage an intriguing plot, driving drama, vivid character development; focus on showing rather than telling, thick description, rich dialogue, dreams, and so on into a rich and fascinating tale.

Writing Exercise 3: Multiple "Takes"

To finely tune your writing, you simply must engage in *rewriting*. Try this: Read the novel *Big Fish*. Then, take one of the stories you have written—perhaps your favorite story, or your most gut-wrenching story—and, following the lead of Daniel Wallace, *rewrite* it in a series of "takes" that tell the story from a different perspective, or in a different key. Once you have accomplished this, place the stories side by side. Maybe you'll want to keep them all, weave them into a larger story of your life. Or maybe you'll just want to choose the best one, the one that sings in the right key for what you were trying to achieve.

Queries

1. What is the story of your life as a writer? How did you come to write ethnography? Where do you see this journey taking you?
2. Have you surrendered to the flow of your own life-writing stream? If not, why not?
3. What dreams have you had since you began reading this book? What do you make of your dreams?
4. How will you, from this moment on, live the life of an accidental ethnographer?

Notes

1. See Watzlawick, Bavelas, & Jackson, 1967, especially chapters 3 and 5.
2. The play *No Exit*, first performed at the Vieux-Colombier in Paris in May 1944, is probably Jean-Paul Sartre's most accessible attempt to get across his primary point about human existence: *As we live in an absurd universe, bounded by death, we humans are free choose the meanings and possibilities of life.* In this particular case, Sartre's character appears to be noting the problem of self-consciousness—the "hell" that is visited on us as we become aware of the gaze of the other.
3. I trust you have heard of Zeno of Elias, the Greek philosopher-mathematician who famously trafficked in paradoxes, the most memorable of which has to do with the infinite divisibility of space.
4. Read the Great American Novel, Steinbeck's *The Grapes of Wrath*. Read it, then watch the John Ford film, then read the book again. And somewhere in your journeys through this tale of unspeakable sadness, your hope will be restored.
5. The process of *shvitzing* is described in detail in my article, "Shvitzing/Kibitzing: Bodies, Communication, and 'Communion' in a Men's Locker Room," published in 1999. The process itself is relatively straightforward: Men sit in a sauna, heated by a special oven that brings the temperature to about 125 degrees Fahrenheit. Once a solid sweat is worked up, one of the *shvitzers*, known as the *schmeisser*, will grab a large piece of raffia, known as the "broom," dip it into a bucket of soapy water, and begin to deliver an elaborately orchestrated lathery massage to one of his cohorts. At the end of the massage (*schmeiss*), a bucket of cold water is dumped over the head of the recipient of the *schmeiss*.
6. The Yiddish word *schmeiss* (or *shmeiss*, depending on who you ask) is likely related to *schmeus* (to schmooze, or converse; to kibitz). *Schmeiss* is usually translated by *shvitz* practitioners as "rub" or "massage." Thus, the *schmeisser* is the one administering the rub or massage.
7. Flathead Lake, Montana, my spiritual home. Again.

Epilogue

Follow your bliss and the universe will open doors for you where there were only walls.

—Joseph Campbell, *Myths to Live By*

And there I have lived ever since, solitary and in wonder, wondering day and night, never a moment without wonder . . . not for five minutes will I be distracted from the wonder.

—Binx Bolling in Walker Percy's *The Moviegoer*

Aspen trees grow in the hard stone-carved and stone-filled soil of the Rocky Mountains, where few plants thrive. Conditions are harsh, winters are long, the air is dry and thin, the wind is fierce. But the rhizomes of aspens are tenacious. The little trees spread across the mountainside, pushing their way through the rocky soil, through a kind of fierce hardiness. And, yet, they appear almost delicate or fragile, wispy even. In the dark of night, the fragile but fierce beauty of the aspen fades quickly. But in the sunlight, they are a sight to behold!

Family secrets are, like the rhizomes of aspen trees, prolific, persistent, and strong. From one single secret, a grove of secrets that chokes out all other possibilities can take root and spread. Once secrecy takes hold in a family, it can be a very prolific, persistent, and powerful pattern. Engulfed in shadowy secrecy, the beauty of the family can fade. But in the sunlight of story, a family can be something wonderful to behold.

In the dark corners of the secret closets of our families lives the rhizome of a story.

In story, there is hope.

I find hope in the openings embraced in accidental ethnography.

I find hope in the thin hint, in the small clue, in the tiny noise, in the whispers and the flashes and the torrents.

I even find hope in dark interruptions, in frozen hearts, in deadly dis-ease.

I find hope in exposing the secrets to the light of story-making.

Perhaps, in our search for a little light to clarify the shadows of our world, we can find a small story—or, better, *a story of mythic proportions*—to salve our wounds, to heal our hearts, to release us into Hope.

I hope.

Today, we are gathered in my parents' living room. It is just an ordinary day, but we have decided to gather because we *can*, because actually, these days, we can be in each other's company and feel just fine. All of us are there: Mom and Dad; my brother Mike and his wife Katie, with their two-year-old daughter Namaste and Mike's older daughter Abby; my sister Mary; my younger sister Sarah and her two daughters, Ieva and Natalia; Susan and I and Eli and Noah. This is the family as it stands today.

And today, we are all laughing and talking and telling stories. But the stories have lost their edge. The arrows and the daggers are set aside, for now. We have called a truce. Instead of talking about our past, we speak of the children and how they keep us in our *present* lives. Sometimes, we even talk of hope for a bright future. Along the way, we notice that this new generation has awoken to the joys of music. And we all know music tells a story of the human spirit in a powerful, universal language. When she will, Abby plays piano and tuba, Eli is an accomplished guitarist, Noah is as good a rock'n roll drummer as I have ever heard, Ieva is learning to play violin. Natalia and Nama are dancers. The music—gift of the Muses—plays on.

And the silence is broken.

The silence is broken by the fine chords and melodies that come from deep within, somewhere in the soul.

The silence is broken by high squeals and deep laughter, the delight of children and the people enjoying their presence.

The silence is broken by the soft conversations we fall into, by genuine dialogue, by the stories, small and large, that we now tell freely.

I look over at my dad, who has been sad for so many years, and I see, as he watches the little girls dance, a bit of a twinkle returning to his eye. I look around at everyone else, and I see, as we watch the children laughing and dancing, that the weight has lifted a little.

Over at the edge of the room, the sunlight streams in through the window, brightens our corner of this world.

Perhaps we have lost our need for secrets.

Perhaps the light will banish the shadows of our dark past, once and for all.

Perhaps, in the simple act of enjoying the spontaneous joy of little children, we will find the opening we need.

Perhaps one day we will let go.

Perhaps one day we will all tell our stories, and laugh.

Here I find hope.

The next morning, I have an appointment with my therapist. We talk of life, of how good things are, of how I am writing this book, of how I feel I have emerged from a long, dark time. At the end of our session, he looks me in the eye, and says,

"Are we done?"

"Done?" I ask.

"Yes. You seem ready just to live your life. I mean, you can call me if you need me, but I think you are ready. Your depression has lifted. Your PTSD symptoms are fading. You are *living* again."

"Really?" I say. "Done?"

"I think you are ready." He smiles, stands, and hugs me goodbye.

I say, softly, "Thank you."

And I go home. As I arrive at my door, I hear the familiar sounds: dogs barking in the backyard, the rhythmic pounding of Noah's basketball on the driveway, Eli's guitar riffs curling out of his room, Sue rinsing dishes in the kitchen. And I know he is right. I am ready.

I am *home*.

References

Abram, D. (1996). *The spell of the sensuous: Perception and language in a more-than-human world*. New York: Vintage Books.

Afifi, T., Caughlin, J., & Afifi, W. (2007). The dark side (and light side) of avoidance and secrets. In B. Spitzberg & W. Cupach (Eds.), *The dark side of interpersonal communication*, 2nd ed. (pp. 61–92). Mahwah, NJ: Lawrence Erlbaum Associates.

Alexander, B. K. (2003). Fading, twisting, and weaving: An interpretive ethnography of the black barbershop as cultural space. *Qualitative Inquiry*, 9, 105–128.

Anderson, S. & Sabatelli, R. (2003). *Family interaction: A multigenerational developmental perspective*. Boston: Pearson.

Arnett, R. & Arneson, P. (1999). *Dialogic civility in a cynical age: Community, hope, and interpersonal relationships*. Albany: State University of New York Press.

Ashton, W. (2004). Tale of a sorcerer's apprentice. In W. Ashton & D. Denton (Eds.), *Spirituality, action and pedagogy: Teaching from the heart* (pp. 53–63). New York: Peter Lang.

Bakhtin, M. M. (1981). *The dialogic imagination* (C. Emerson & M. Holquist, Trans.). Austin: University of Texas Press.

———. (1993). *Toward a philosophy of the act* (V. Liapunov, Trans.). Austin: University of Texas Press.

Baxter, L. & Montgomery, B. (1996). *Relating: Dialogues and dialectics*. New York: The Guilford Press.

Biedermann, H. (1992). *Dictionary of symbolism: Cultural icons and the meanings behind them* (J. Hulbert, Trans.). New York: Facts on File.

Black, C. (1985). *Repeat after me*. Center City, MN: Hazelden.

———. (2002). *It will never happen to me: Growing up with addiction as youngsters, adolescents, adults*. Center City, MN: Hazelden.

Bochner, A. (1997). It's about time: Narrative and the divided self. *Qualitative Inquiry*, 3, 418–438.

———. (2000). Criteria against ourselves. *Qualitative Inquiry*, 6, 266–272.

———. (2001). Narrative's virtues. *Qualitative Inquiry*, 7, 131–157.

———. (2002). Love survives. *Qualitative Inquiry*, 8, 161–170.

Bochner, A. & Ellis, C. (1992). Personal narrative as a social approach to interpersonal communication, *Communication Theory*, 2, 65–72.

———. (1996). Talking over ethnography. In C. Ellis & A. Bochner (Eds.), *Composing ethnography: Alternative forms of qualitative writing*. Walnut Creek, CA: AltaMira.

———. (1999). Which way to turn? *Journal of Contemporary Ethnography*, 28, 485–499.

———. (Eds.). (2002). *Ethnographically speaking: Autoethnography, literature & aesthetics*. Walnut Creek, CA: AltaMira.

———. (2003). An introduction to the arts and narrative inquiry. *Qualitative Inquiry*, 9, 506–514.

Bradshaw, J. (1995). *Family secrets: The path to self-acceptance and reunion*. New York: Bantam Books.

Braithwaite, D. & Baxter, L. (Eds.). (2006). *Engaging theories in family communication*. Thousand Oaks, CA: Sage.

Braud, W. & Anderson, R. (1998). *Transpersonal research methods for the social sciences: Honoring human experience*. Thousand Oaks, CA: Sage.

Brown, N. O. (1947). *Hermes the thief: The evolution of a myth*. Great Barrington, MA: Lindisfarne Press.

Bruner, J. (1987). Life as narrative. *Social Research*, 54, 11–32.

Buber, M. (1970). *I and Thou* (W. Kaufmann, Trans.). New York: Touchstone/Simon & Schuster.

Campbell, J. (1948). *The hero with a thousand faces*. Princeton, NJ: Princeton University Press.

———. (1972). *Myths to live by*. New York: Bantam Books.

———. (1991). *The power of myth*. New York: Anchor.

Camus, A. (1955). *The myth of Sisyphus and other essays*. New York: Random House.

Chodron, P. (2000). *When things fall apart: Heart advice for difficult times*. Boston: Shambhala Publications.

Chopra, D. (2004). *The book of secrets: Unlocking the hidden dimensions of your life*. New York: Harmony Press.

Clair, R. (1998). *Organizing silence: A world of possibilities*. Albany: State University of New York Press.

———. (2003). *Expressions of ethnography: Novel approaches to qualitative methods*. Albany: State University of New York Press.

Coles, R. (1989). *The call of stories: Teaching and the moral imagination*. Boston: Houghton Mifflin Company.

Conquergood, D. (1993). *Homeboys and hoods: Gang communication and cultural space*. Evanston, IL: Center for Urban Affairs and Policy Research, Northwestern University.

Cupach, W. & Spitzberg, B. (Eds.). (1994). *The dark side of interpersonal communication*. Mahwah, NJ: Lawrence Erlbaum Associates.

———. (2004). *The dark side of relationship pursuit: From attraction to obsession and stalking*. Mahwah, NJ: Lawrence Erlbaum Associates.

de la Garza, S. A. (2004). *Maria speaks: Journeys into the mysteries of the mother in my life as a Chicana*. New York: Peter Lang.

Denton, D. (2004). The heart's geography: Compassion as practice. In W. Ashton & D. Denton (Eds.), *Spirituality, action and pedagogy: Teaching from the heart* (pp. 136–146). New York: Peter Lang.

———. (2006). *Re-imagining the wound: Of innocence, sacrifice, and gift*. In W. Ashton & D. Denton (Eds.), *Spirituality, ethnography, and teaching: Stories from within* (pp. 131–139). New York: Peter Lang.

Denzin, N. K. (1997). *Interpretive ethnography: Ethnographic practices for the 21st century*. Thousand Oaks, CA: Sage.

———. (2001). *Interpretive interactionism*. Thousand Oaks, CA: Sage.

Denzin, N. K. & Lincoln, Y. S. (2000). The discipline and practice of qualitative research. In N. K. Denzin & Y. S. Lincoln (Eds.). *Handbook of qualitative research*, 2nd ed. (pp. 1–28). Thousand Oaks, CA: Sage.

———. (Eds.). (2001). *The American tradition in qualitative research*. Thousand Oaks, CA: Sage.

———. (Eds.). (2005). *Handbook of qualitative research*, 2nd ed. Thousand Oaks, CA: Sage.

Eisenberg, E. (2001). Building a mystery: Toward a new theory of communication and identity. *Journal of Communication*, 51, 534–552.

Eliade, M. (1957). *The sacred and the profane: The nature of religion*. San Diego, CA: Harcourt Brace Jovanovich.

Ellis, C. (1995). *Final negotiations: A story of love, loss, and chronic illness*. Philadelphia: Temple University Press.

———. (1999). He(art)ful autoethnography. *Qualitative Health Research*, 9, 653–667.

———. (2001). With mother/with child: A true story. *Qualitative Inquiry*, 7, 598–616.

———. (2002a). Shattered lives: Making sense of September 11th and its aftermath. *Journal of Contemporary Ethnography*, 31(4), 375–410.

———. (2002b). Take no chances. *Qualitative Inquiry*, 8, 42–47.

———. (2004). *The ethnographic I: A methodological novel about autoethnography*. Walnut Creek, CA: AltaMira.

Ellis, C. (2007). Telling secrets, revealing lives: Relational ethics in research with intimate others. *Qualitative Inquiry*, 13, 3–29.

Ellis, C. & Bochner, A. (1991). Telling and performing personal stories: The constraints of choice in abortion. In C. Ellis & M. Flaherty (Eds.), *Investigating subjectivity: Research on lived experience* (pp. 79–101). Thousand Oaks, CA: Sage.

Fisher, W. (1987). *Human communication as narration: Toward a philosophy of reason, value, and action.* Columbia: University of South Carolina Press.

Floyd, K. & Morman, M. (2006). *Widening the family circle: New research on family communication.* Thousand Oaks, CA: Sage.

Fox, K. (1996). Silent voices: A subversive reading of child sexual abuse. In C. Ellis & A. Bochner (Eds.), *Composing ethnography: Alternative forms of qualitative writing* (pp. 330–356). Walnut Creek, CA: AltaMira.

Frankl, V. (2006). *Man's search for meaning.* Boston: Beacon Press.

Freeman, M. (1997). Death, narrative integrity, and the radical challenge of self-understanding: A reading of Tolstoy's Death of Ivan Ilych. *Ageing and Society*, 17, 373–398.

Freud, S. (1980). *The interpretation of dreams.* New York: Avon Books.

Gadamer, H. G. (1975). *Truth and method* (J. Weinsheimer & D. G. Marshall, Trans.). New York: Continuum Books.

Garfinkel, H. (1967). *Studies in ethnomethodology.* Cambridge, U.K.: Polity Press.

Geertz, C. (2005). Deep play: Notes on the Balinese cockfight. *Daedalus*, 134, 56–86.

Gergen, K. (2000). *The saturated self: Dilemmas of identity in contemporary life.* New York: Basic Books.

Giddens, A. (1984). *The constitution of society: Outline of the theory of structuration.* Berkeley: University of California Press.

———. (1991). *Modernity and self-identity: Self and society in the late modern age.* Stanford: Stanford University Press.

Glenn, C. (2004). *Unspoken: A rhetoric of silence.* Carbondale: Southern Illinois University Press.

Goffman, E. (1959). *The presentation of self in everyday life.* New York: Doubleday.

———. (1963). *Stigma: Notes on the management of spoiled identity.* New York: Simon & Schuster.

Gome, P. (1996). *The good book: Reading the Bible with mind and heart.* San Francisco: Harper.

Goodall, H. L., Jr. (1994). *Casing a promised land: The autobiography of an organizational detective as cultural ethnographer.* Carbondale: Southern Illinois University Press.

———. (1996). *Divine signs: Connecting spirit to community.* Carbondale: Southern Illinois University Press.

———. (2000). *Writing the new ethnography.* Walnut Creek, CA: AltaMira.

———. (2005). Narrative inheritance: A nuclear family with toxic secrets. *Qualitative Inquiry*, 11, 492–513.

———. (2006a). *A need to know: The clandestine history of a CIA family.* Walnut Creek, CA: Left Coast Press.

———. (2006b). Why we must win the war on terror: Communication, narrative, and the future of national security. *Qualitative Inquiry*, 12, 30–59.

Hanh, T. (1992). *Peace is every step: The path of mindfulness in everyday life.* New York: Bantam Books.

———. (1999). *The miracle of mindfulness.* Boston: Beacon Press.

———. (2005). *Being peace.* Berkeley, CA: Parallax Press.

Hauerwas, S. (1990). *Naming the silences: God, medicine, and the problem of suffering.* Grand Rapids, MI: Eerdmans.

———. (2005). *Cross-shattered Christ: Meditations on the last seven words.* Grand Rapids, MI: Brazos Press.

Hay, L. (1999). *You can heal your life.* Carlsbad, CA: Hay House, Inc.

Holman Jones, S. (1998). *Kaleidoscope notes: Writing women's music and organizational culture.* Walnut Creek, CA: AltaMira.

Hyde, M. J. (2001). *The call of conscience: Heidegger and Levinas, rhetoric and the euthanasia debate.* Columbia: University of South Carolina Press.

———. (2006). *The life-giving gift of acknowledgement.* Lafayette, IN: Purdue University Press.

Jameson, F. (1991). *Postmodernism, or the cultural logic of late capitalism.* Durham, NC: Duke University Press.

Johnson, R. (1991). *Owning your own shadow: Understanding the dark side of the psyche.* San Francisco: Harper.

Jung, C. G. (1959). *The archetypes and the collective unconscious.* London: Routledge.

———. (1964). *Man and his symbols.* London: Aldus Books.

———. (1989). *Memories, dreams, reflections.* New York: Vintage Books.

Jung, C. G. & Kerényi, K. (1949). *Essays on a science of mythology: The myth of the divine child and the mysteries of Eleusis.* Princeton, NJ: Princeton University Press.

Kalamaras, G. (1994). *Reclaiming the tacit dimension: Symbolic form in the rhetoric of silence.* Albany: State University of New York Press.

Kerényi, K. (1977). Mnemosyne—Lesmosyne: On the springs of "memory'"and "forgetting." *Spring: An Annual of Archetypal Psychology and Jungian Thought.* Zurich, Switzerland: Spring Publications.

Kierkegaard, S. (1976). The concept of dread. (W. Lowrie, Trans.). Princeton, NJ: Princeton University Press.

———. (1980). *The sickness unto death* (H. V. Hong & E. H. Hong, Trans.). Princeton, NJ: Princeton University Press.

Kuhn, A. (1995). *Family secrets: Acts of memory and imagination.* London: Verso.

Lamott, A. (1995). *Bird by bird: Some instructions on writing and life.* New York: Anchor Books.

Langellier, K. & Peterson, E. (1993). Family storytelling as a strategy of social control. In D. K. Mumby (Ed.), *Narrative and social control: Critical perspectives* (pp. 49–77). Newbury Park, CA: Sage.

LeClaire, A. (2001). *Entering normal.* New York: Ballantine Books.

Levinas, E. (1969). *Totality and infinity* (A. Lingis, Trans.). Pittsburgh: Duquesne University Press.

———. (1981). *Otherwise than being: Or beyond essence* (A. Lingis, Trans.). Pittsburgh: Duquesne University Press.

Lewis, C. S. (1998). *Grief.* Nashville: Thomas Nelson, Inc.

May, R. (1950). *The meaning of anxiety.* New York: Pocket Books.

———. (1972). *The courage to create.* New York: W.W. Norton & Co.

———. (1991). *The cry for myth.* New York: W.W. Norton & Co.

McGlashan, A. (1986). The translucence of memory. *Parabola: Myth and the quest for meaning,* 11, 4.

———. (1988). *The savage and beautiful country.* Einsiedeln, Switzerland: Daimon Verlag.

McLaren, P. (1988). The liminal servant and the ritual roots of critical pedagogy. *Language Arts,* 65, 164–179.

Mead, G. H. (1934). *Mind, self, and society: From the standpoint of a social behaviorist.* Chicago: University of Chicago Press.

Menchaca, D. (2004). Healing susto: Fragments of postcritical pedagogy. In W. Ashton & D. Denton (Eds.), *Spirituality, action and pedagogy: Teaching from the heart* (pp. 115–123). New York: Peter Lang.

Merleau-Ponty, M. (1962). *Phenomenology of perception.* London: Routledge & Kegan Paul.

Ong, W. (1982). *Orality and literacy: The technologizing of the word.* New York: Routledge.

Otto, R. (1923). *The idea of the holy: An inquiry into the non-rational factor in the idea of the divine and its relation to the rational.* London: Oxford University Press.

Parker, M. (1993). *Hello down there.* New York: Scribner's.

———. (1994). *The geographical cure.* New York: Scribner's.

———. (2001). *Towns without rivers.* New York: Harper Collins.

———. (2004). *Virginia lovers.* Encino, CA: Delphinium Books.

———. (2005). *If you want me to stay.* Chapel Hill, NC: Algonquin Books.

———. (2007). *Don't make me stop now.* Chapel Hill, NC: Algonquin Books.

Pelias, R. (2000). The critical life. *Communication Education, 49,* 220–228.

———. (2004). *A methodology of the heart: Evoking academic and daily life.* Walnut Creek, CA: AltaMira.

Percy, W. (1960). *The moviegoer.* New York: Alfred A. Knopf.

———. (1983). *Lost in the cosmos: The last self-help book.* New York: Picador.

Poulos, C. (1999). Shvitzing/kibitzing: Bodies, communication, and "communion" in a men's locker room. *Cultural Studies: A Research Volume, 4,* 193–215.

———. (2002). The death of ordinariness: Living, learning, and relating in the age of anxiety. *Qualitative Inquiry, 8,* 288–301.

———. (2003). Fire and ice: Flaming passion, reified structure, and the organizing body. *American Communication Journal 6.* Available online at http://www.acjournal.org/holdings/vol6/iss2/articles/poulos.htm (accessed August 28, 2007).

———. (2004a). Disruption, Silence, and Creation: The search for dialogic civility in the age of anxiety. *Qualitative Inquiry, 10,* 534–547.

———. (2004b). Spirited teaching: A pedagogy of courage. In W. Ashton & D. Denton (Eds.), *Spirituality, action and pedagogy: Teaching from the heart* (pp. 147–158). New York: Peter Lang.

———. (2006a). Dreaming, writing, teaching: Stories from within thin places. In W. Ashton & D. Denton (Eds.), *Spirituality, ethnography, and teaching: Stories from within* (pp. 167–181). New York: Peter Lang.

———. (2006b). The ties that bind us, the shadows that separate us: Life and death, shadow and (dream)story. *Qualitative Inquiry, 12,* 96–117.

———. (2008a). Accidental dialogue. *Communication Theory, 18,* 117–138.

———. (2008b). Narrative conscience and the autoethnographic adventure: Probing memories, secrets, shadows, and possibilities. *Qualitative Inquiry, 14,* 46–66.

Rehling, D. (2002). Stories that families tell: Narrative coherence, narrative interaction, and relationship beliefs. *Journal of Family Communication, 2,* 215–235.

Richardson, L. (2000). Evaluating ethnography. *Qualitative Inquiry, 6,* 253–255.

———. (2005). Sticks and stones: An exploration of the embodiment of social classism. *Qualitative Inquiry, 11,* 485–491.

Rogers, C. R. (1995). *On becoming a person: A therapist's view of psychotherapy.* New York: Mariner Books.

Ronai, C. R. (1996). My mother is mentally retarded. In C. Ellis & A. Bochner (Eds.), *Composing ethnography: Alternative forms of qualitative writing* (pp. 109–131). Walnut Creek, CA: AltaMira.

Salzberg, S. (1999). *A heart as wide as the world.* Boston: Shambhala Publications.

Sartre, J-P. (1958). *Being and nothingness* (H. E. Barnes, Trans.). New York: Philosophical Library.

Satir, V. (1967). *Conjoint family therapy: A guide to theory and technique.* Palo Alto, CA: Science and Behavior Books.

———. (1972). *Peoplemaking.* Palo Alto, CA: Science and Behavior Books.

Schrag, C. (1986). *Communicative praxis and the space of subjectivity.* Bloomington: Indiana University Press.

———. (1997). *The self after postmodernity.* New Haven, CT: Yale University Press.

———. (2002). *God as otherwise than being: Toward a semantics of the gift.* Evanston, IL: Northwestern University Press.

Shakespeare, W. (2003). *Hamlet.* New York: Washington Square Press.

Shotter, J. (1993). *Conversational realities: Constructing life through language.* Thousand Oaks, CA: Sage.

Siegel, B. (1990). *Love, medicine, and miracles: Lessons learned about self-healing from a surgeon's experience with exceptional patients*. New York: Harper.

Spitzberg, B. & Cupach, W. (1998). *The dark side of close relationships*. Mahwah, NJ: Lawrence Erlbaum Associates.

Steinbeck, J. (1939). *The grapes of wrath*. New York: Viking.

Sterk, H. M. & Sterk, K. J. (1993). Birthing: Women owning their stories. In C. Berryman-Fink, D. Ballard-Reisch, & L. H. Newman (Eds.), *Communication and sex-role socialization* (pp. 433–461). New York: Garland.

Stewart, J. (1995). *Language as articulate contact: Toward a post-semiotic philosophy of communication*. Albany: State University of New York Press.

Stone, E. (1988). *Black sheep and kissing cousins: How our family stories shape us*. New York: Penguin Books.

Taylor, D. (1996). *Tell me a story: The life-shaping power of our stories*. St. Paul, MN: Bog Walk Press.

Tillich, P. (1952). *The courage to be*. New Haven, CT: Yale University Press.

———. (1957). *Dynamics of faith*. New York: Harper and Row.

Tillmann-Healy, L. (1996). A secret life in a culture of thinness: Reflections on body, food, and bulimia. In C. Ellis & A. Bochner (Eds.), *Composing ethnography: Alternative forms of qualitative writing* (pp. 76–108). Walnut Creek, CA: AltaMira.

———. (2001). *Between gay and straight: Understanding friendship across sexual orientation*. Walnut Creek, CA: AltaMira.

Tolstoy, L. (2003). *The death of Ivan Ilych and other stories*. New York: Signet Books.

Towns, A. (2007). *Rosez 4 a gun: Da demonz of a young black male*. New York: iUniverse, Inc.

Trujillo, N. (2004). *In search of Naunny's grave: Age, class, gender and ethnicity in an American family*. Walnut Creek, CA: AltaMira.

Turner, L. H. & West, R. (2006a). *Perspectives on family communication*. Boston: McGraw-Hill.

———. (Eds.). (2006b). *The family communication sourcebook*. Thousand Oaks, CA: Sage.

Turner, V. (1969). *The ritual process: Structure and anti-structure*. Chicago: Aldine.

Turner, V. & Bruner, E. (Eds.). (1986). *The anthropology of experience*. Urbana: University of Illinois Press.

Van Maanen, J. (1988). *Tales of the field: On writing ethnography*. Chicago: University of Chicago Press.

Vangelisti, A. (Ed.). (2004). *Handbook of family communication*. Mahwah, NJ: Lawrence Erlbaum Associates.

Vangelisti, A. & Timmerman, L. (2001). *Criteria for revealing family secrets. Communication Monographs*, 68, 1–27.

Vonnegut, K. (2005). *A man without a country*. New York: Random House.

Wallace, D. (1998). *Big fish: A novel of mythic proportions*. Chapel Hill, NC: Algonquin Books.

Warren, J. & Fassett, D. (2004). Spiritually drained and sexually denied: Sketching an engaged pedagogy. In W. Ashton & D. Denton (Eds.), *Spirituality, action and pedagogy: Teaching from the heart* (pp. 21–30). New York: Peter Lang.

Watzlawick, P. Bavelas, J. B., & Jackson, D. J. (1967). *Pragmatics of human communication*. New York: W.W. Norton.

Weil, A. (2005). *Healthy aging: A lifelong guide to your physical and spiritual well-being*. New York: Alfred A. Knopf.

Yerby, J., Buerkel-Rothfuss, N., & Bochner, A. (1998). *Understanding family communication*, 2nd ed. Scottsdale, AZ: Gorsuch-Scarisbrick.

Zweig, C. & Abrams, J. (1991). *Meeting the shadow: The hidden power of the dark side of human nature*. Los Angeles: Jeremy P. Tarcher, Inc.

Index

About the Author

Christopher N. Poulos, Ph.D. is associate professor of Communication Studies at the University of North Carolina at Greensboro. An ethnographer and philosopher of communication with a keen interest in close personal relationships, he teaches courses in relational and family communication, ethnography, dialogue, rhetoric, and film studies. Recent publications include: "Accidental Dialogue: The Search for Dialogic Moments in Everyday Life" (*Communication Theory*, 18, 117–138); Narrative Conscience and the Autoethnographic Adventure: Probing Memories, Secrets, Shadows, and Possibilities" (*Qualitative Inquiry*, 14, 46–66); and "The ties that Bind Us, the Shadows that Separate Us: Life and Death, Shadow and (Dream) Story" (*Qualitative Inquiry*, 12, 96–117).

Printed in the United States
128771LV00004B/2/P

9 781598 741469